Brigid Brophy

# Brigid Brophy

Avant-Garde Writer, Critic, Activist

Edited by Richard Canning and
Gerri Kimber

EDINBURGH
University Press

Edinburgh University Press is one of the leading university presses in the UK. We publish academic books and journals in our selected subject areas across the humanities and social sciences, combining cutting-edge scholarship with high editorial and production values to produce academic works of lasting importance. For more information visit our website: edinburghuniversitypress.com

Edinburgh University Press Ltd
The Tun – Holyrood Road
12(2f) Jackson's Entry
Edinburgh EH8 8PJ

First published in hardback by Edinburgh University Press 2020

Typeset in 11/13 Adobe Sabon by
IDSUK (DataConnection) Ltd, and
printed and bound by CPI Group (UK) Ltd,
Croydon, CR0 4YY

A CIP record for this book is available from the British Library

ISBN 978 1 4744 6266 2 (hardback)
ISBN 978 1 4744 6267 9 (paperback)
ISBN 978 1 4744 6268 6 (webready PDF)
ISBN 978 1 4744 6269 3 (epub)

# Contents

# Illustrations

# Acknowledgements

This volume owes so much to the enormous generosity of Kate Levey, Brigid Brophy's daughter and literary executor, who facilitated all permissions for copyright material regarding her mother's estate, and who engaged personally with many contributors to this volume, as well as providing images and photographs from the Prop Art exhibition. On behalf of all the contributors, we offer Kate our most sincere and heartfelt thanks.

It has been a pleasure working with editorial staff as talented, responsive and enabling as those working for Edinburgh University Press: special thanks are due to Dr Jackie Jones, its Publisher of Literary Studies, Dr Ersev Ersoy, James Dale, Carla Hepburn, Rebecca Mackenzie, and, last but not least, our diligent copy-editor, Andrew Kirk. Ralph Kimber has compiled an outstanding index for this volume, and both Editors and all contributors are in his debt.

Sincerest thanks also go to Maureen Duffy for her generosity and oversight in enabling both the reproduction of images from the Prop Art exhibition and the excerpted text from its manifesto. Thanks are also due to Euan Duff, for generously allowing the reproduction of his Prop Art photographs, and to John Dixon and Rodney Hill, not only for finding and sending on 'The Librarian and the Novel' from the publication *Fiction Papers One*, but for coping stoically with the news of the latter succumbing to a fire in a co-editor's flat, and for subsequently ensuring the essay's accurate transcription. Further thanks are due to Dayna Miller at the Kingston University Archives and Special Collections for facilitating permission to reproduce the photographs of the edition of *Flesh* collaged by Brophy for Iris Murdoch. Thanks also to Sue Beesley for her photographs of Rodney Hill's Brophy library.

The Editors would like to give sincere thanks to the Iris Murdoch Society, Miles Leeson and Carole Sweeney in particular, as well as a number of other contributors, for contributions in support of providing the index for this volume.

Finally, Richard Canning wishes to thank his co-editor Gerri Kimber for her extraordinary editing skills, foresight and patience throughout. Without her there could have been no book.

# Introduction

*Richard Canning*

Brigid Brophy (1929–95) was a British – but, by descent, equally Anglo-Irish – novelist, short story writer, dramatist, essayist, critic, artist, poet, polemicist, activist and sometime celebrity. Many of her publications defy generic classification, and so the following summary of her output might be contested. She was the author of (probably) eleven works of fiction, including these eight (or seven?) novels: *Hackenfeller's Ape* (1953), which concerns the relationship between an ape in London Zoo and a professor observing the animal's mating rituals; *The King of a Rainy Country* (1956), portraying a set of bohemians in post-war London and Venice; *Flesh: a novel* (1962), which recounts the erotic tutelage of an inexperienced husband by his wife; *The Finishing Touch* (1963; rev. edn 1987), set in a girls' finishing school in France, which amounts to a fully-realised homage to Brophy's novelistic hero Ronald Firbank, while also containing a portrait of the art historian and Soviet spy Anthony Blunt in fictional and cross-gendering guise as the headmistress; *The Snow Ball* (1964), Brophy's Mozartian novel, whose characters attend a ball dressed as characters from *Don Giovanni*; *In Transit: An Heroi-Cyclic Novel* (1969), one of a tiny handful of novels in English to manage to conceal the anatomical sex of their chief protagonist entirely, with the further distinction of deploying that utterly contemporary dystopia the airport lounge as its chief locale; *The Adventures of God in his Search for the Black Girl: A Novel and Some Fables* (1973), puns on George Bernard Shaw's 1932 parables about religious faith in *The Adventures of the Black Girl in Her Search for God*; and lastly *Palace without Chairs: A Baroque Novel* (1978), a playful, Shavian dialogue questioning the nature of democracy, set in an imaginary Middle European kingdom called Evarchia. Brophy's writing career then dramatically and cruelly ended: she was diagnosed with multiple sclerosis in 1983, in her early fifties.

She also wrote shorter fiction: her career began with the story volume *The Crown Princess and Other Stories* (1953). Brophy's radio play *The Waste Disposal Unit* was broadcast and published in 1964. *The Burglar* (1967), her only published stage play, had a West End run starring Jim Dale and Sian Phillips, which was directed by Frank Dunlop. *Pussy Owl: Superbeast* (1976) was Brophy's only work of children's fiction, though she later wrote a work of non-fiction for children with illustrations from pictures by the nineteenth-century Russian artist Gregoire Gagarin, entitled *The Prince and the Wild Geese* (1982).

Brophy wrote several acclaimed and highly influential non-fictional works: *Black Ship to Hell* (1962), her first and perhaps strangest, investigates humankind's destructive and self-destructive instincts, by way of Freudian psychoanalytic thinking; *Mozart the Dramatist: A New View of Mozart, His Operas and His Age* (1964; rev. edn 1990), still in print, remains an oft-cited study of the composer's art; *Black and White: A Portrait of Aubrey Beardsley* (1968) was followed by a second immersion in the *fin de siècle*, *Beardsley and his World* (1976); *Prancing Novelist: Defence of Fiction in the Form of a Critical Biography in Praise of Ronald Firbank* (1973) is what the title proclaims – and much more. She penned a huge number of reviews, essays and comment pieces, many gathered in the three volumes *Don't Never Forget: Collected Views and Reviews* (1966), *Baroque-'n'-Roll and Other Essays* (1987) and *Reads: A Collection of Essays* (1989). As a critic she took no prisoners: these books describe in stark, always utterly informed and persuasive terms a social and cultural world view, as well as a series of literary and aesthetic judgements that could encompass classical music, the fine arts, dance, popular culture, the applied arts and the history of the world. Lastly, the iconoclastic and highly controversial *Fifty Works of English and American Literature We Could Do Without* (1967) saw Brophy collaborate with her husband, the art historian and director of London's National Gallery Michael Levey, and the Australian biographer and critic Charles Osborne.

Her legacy today, nevertheless, lies both within and far beyond literary or cultural contexts. Therefore, as the title of this volume – remarkably, the first book ever dedicated to her – makes plain, our aim is to celebrate Brophy in the round: as an avant-garde writer, critic and activist, and much else besides. Brophy was a vital driving force behind the establishment of the UK Public Lending Right in 1979. She was, moreover, a key player in the establishment of today's global animal rights movement, following her 1965 *Sunday Times* article, 'The Rights of Animals'. We can now clearly see, as Gary Francione's definitive account in this volume '"Il faut que je vive": Brigid Brophy and Animal Rights' argues, that she had formulated 'a nascent animal rights position twelve years before the publication of Tom Regan's *The Case for Animal Rights* (or eighteen years, if you measure it from her 1965 essay)' (p. 103). Not only this: as Francione reveals, Brophy's ideas had 'suggested elements of a truly radical animal *rights* position', even though the subsequent history of what Francione calls 'the Animal Movement' effectively became overshadowed by Peter Singer, a 'utilitarian who eschews moral rights', according to Francione. Singer's *Animal Liberation* (1975) and related advocacy may have had 'an arguably greater impact in terms of audience [than Brophy]' but it does not 'recognise any moral imperative not to use and kill animals' (p. 108). Brophy's ethically informed perspective, Francione indicates, was the harder road, and thus the one not taken by most animal activists. Had that not been the case, he polemically concludes, 'we would have an animal rights movement today rather than the "happy exploitation" movement that exists' (p. 113).

Francione's account is complemented in this volume by Kim Stall-wood's 'A Felicitous Day for Fish', part reminiscence, part evaluation of Brophy's contribution to animal rights. Stallwood's recollection of Brophy speaking at the RSPCA's Rights of Animals symposium at Trinity College, Cambridge in 1977 sees the character of Brophy – at least, as a public speaker – move centre stage: there was 'the dry humour, the deadpan delivery and the black nail varnish' (p. 211). In 1981, he recollects, she delivered an address, also entitled 'A Felicitous Day for Fish', at a meeting of the Council for the Prevention of Cruelty by Angling, where Brophy railed against:

> a fantasy to which our species is prone and which distorts our vision of the real world – the feudal, indeed the fascist, fantasy whereby we stamp around as the lords and bullies of everything and pretend that our most minor pleasures are so important in the scheme of things that they outweigh the entire life and outweigh the death agony of our fellow individual animals. (p. 214)

This polemical Brophy, characterised by what Stallwood calls her 'mordant humour and unrelenting analysis', could move effortlessly from one pointed observation or skewering to the next (p. 211). Thus, condescending to identify a trait within 'the British' which explains their proneness to confuse hunting and angling with notions of 'sport' or good sportsmanship, she opined that they are 'given to confusing the Royal Family with the Holy Family' (p. 214). Such iconoclastic moments, where Brophy's aloofness from British social or cultural mores was at its starkest, benefited obviously from her sense of her own Anglo-Irish heritage, inculcated by her author father John Brophy, and something which in turn captivated her fellow traveller, the novelist and philosopher Iris Murdoch, who, of course, had her own 'deep but twisted Irish roots'.[1]

Miles Leeson's 'Encoding Love: Hidden Correspondence in the Fiction of Iris Murdoch and Brigid Brophy' takes us further than anyone to date in considering the creative writings of both authors in an informed bio-critical light. The phrase 'deep but twisted' might even be co-opted to describe the complex, tortuous and highly intellectual approach the writers took 'to explore sexuality and gender in their work by importing their own relationship, laid out in letters and journals, on to the page' (p. 159). As Leeson concludes, '[f]or neither woman was this the most defining relationship of their lives, but it was certainly a formative, intense, near-decade lived out in London, in regular romantic short breaks, and on paper' (p. 159).

Brophy's embrace of Irish logic and lore was demonstrated by her love of Wildean paradox and inversion, best *shewn* in her study not of Wilde himself – too many vultures had sought out that prey – but of his Anglo-Irish modernist novelist disciple, Ronald Firbank. The 600-page monograph *Prancing Novelist* may have created a genre in itself: certainly, no book in literary criticism or biography remotely resembles it. Peter Parker's '*Prancing Novelist* and *Black and White*: Experiments in Biography' celebrates that title alongside Brophy's study of the English artist-illustrator Aubrey Beardsley, himself closely associated with Wilde and his circle. As Parker points out, nothing in Brophy's choice of subjects in her non-fiction, and, specifically, nothing about her implicit Pantheon or 'alternative Trinity' (p. 182) – of Firbank, Beardsley and Mozart – was casually arrived at or coincidental. Of *Prancing Novelist* and *Black and White*, Parker concludes: 'One mark of a good book is that it could not have been written by anyone else, and it is this that makes these two experiments in biography, characterised by the author's energy, wit, idiosyncrasy and combativeness, so exhilarating to read' (p. 191).

My own contribution, 'Penetrating (the) *Prancing Novelist*', seeks to harness that exhilaration which informs our reading of Brophy but which equally informed her own pursuit of the genius she identified in her three non-fiction subjects. I have focused on the largely neglected Firbank play *The Princess Zoubaroff* (1920), which offers a study in miniature of how far Brophy's own deeply developed Firbankian instincts could take flight, in respect of a work which other critics have ignored, but which Brophy's research quite correctly placed at the centre of Firbank's achievements, and at an essential turning point in his novelistic career too. My own reading of *Zoubaroff* develops out of Brophy's claims, on occasion taking them considerably further, and, on rarer occasion, adopting a Brophyan stubbornness in following a quite different interpretative path. It is remarkable, I argue, how Brophy could see in this male (if hardly masculine) author everything transgressive, winning and accomplished that she aimed for, and achieved, in her own fictions – including her tribute to the Firbankian, *The Finishing Touch*: 'Her Firbank, nonetheless, is a trailblazer, not only swapping genders, sexualities, ethnicities, nationalities and more, but effectively founding an impostor-canon of lesbian-themed works, penned by a queer man writing as the womanish "Ronald Firbank"' (p. 51).

On the way, Brophy's own readings in Firbank take in William Congreve, Oscar Wilde (reworking Congreve) and George Bernard Shaw. John Dixon's essay '"Shavian that she was"' offers a compelling, highly informed speculation as to what might have happened if Brophy had been approached by the Society of Authors to write Shaw's biography, rather than Michael Holroyd. Dixon notes from her writings on Mozart, Beardsley and Firbank what we might have expected in formal and structural terms, going on to trace Shavian elements throughout her fictional writings, from *Hackenfeller's Ape* to *Flesh*'s reworking of the Pygmalion myth, and from *The Adventures of God in his Search for the Black Girl*, the book of Brophy's most obviously indebted to Shaw, to *Palace without Chairs*. En route, Dixon takes in the entirety of Brophy's dramatic writings, with much to say about the scandalously overlooked *The Burglar*. In *The Adventures of God*, Dixon notes, 'God writes a reference for himself. A manifesto (a godifesto) is drawn up, with Shaw as shorthand scribe. It is not on the future of the black girl, but on God: "'I do not exist' signed with divine authority, God"' (p. 87). Jill Longmate's contribution, '"Heads and Boxes": A Prop Art Exhibition Collaboration by Brigid Brophy and Maureen Duffy', takes us to a different '[woman] ifesto'. The year 1969 saw the one-off Brophy–Duffy venture into the world of avant-garde art, as makers of sculpted poems. If the pun in 'Prop Art' suggested that the collaborators' work might have been whimsical in intent, the exhibition's co-authored '[woman]ifesto' –

extensively drawn on by Longmate – puts us right, as did Brophy in a contemporary interview:

> To be any kind of artist is a dangerous profession. There is a constant attempt to place limitations on the intellect and the imagination, and if someone comes up with something new – not newness of form which can become immediately fashionable, but newness of concept, people find this disturbing.
>
> So they say that what you have done is a joke, or that you are not equipped, or that you are deliberately trying to shock, or that you ought to stick to what you know. And in our case, there is always one objection to fall back on, the one which says: you are a woman. (p. 163)

Carole Sweeney's 'The Dissenting Feminist' tackles Brophy's complicated responses to feminist thought, revealing how her 'distinctively contrarian' approach to -isms or -ologies played out (p. 221). As Sweeney notes, in one review or article after another, Brophy displayed 'ambivalence towards the cultural politics of feminism' (p. 221) – nowhere more evidently than in a review of Germaine Greer's *The Obstacle Race: The Fortunes of Women Painters and their Work* (1979), in which Brophy declared that Greer had adopted a 'singularly squinting vision of our culture', whereby Greer's one 'shut eye excludes painters who were men, except where they impinge, as teachers, lovers or parents, on painters who were women' (p. 224).

In Brophy's own, previously unpublished contribution to this volume, 'The Librarian and the Novel' (1980), she argues by way of the female writers Patricia Highsmith, Jane Austen and Ruth Rendell, but also of Aristotle, Shakespeare, Mozart's letters and the art of Sandro Botticelli, that

> if we are to have a literature, if we are to have a literary culture, we need bad books as well as good books. This is partly because everyone *begins* on bad books, as Sartre pointed out in his autobiography; it is also a little because even readers of undeflectably highbrow tastes, including myself and including Jean-Paul Sartre, maintain into their adult lives a liking for books they would never judge good; but it is mainly because that is the way art works. (p. 48)

In his introduction to this lecture, John Dixon recalls her 'staggering in with a cup of black liquid. She was wearing a long velvety black dress' (p. 33). The talk was a hit – predictably, for Dixon, since Brophy knew what performance was, and even when scarcely audible, she showed that she 'had tailored the text to the audience'

(p. 33). Brophy never underestimated an audience, and never short-changed one either.

Little filmed evidence of this survives. She can be seen in just two television clips today: a 1965 BBC documentary entitled *A Woman's Place*, and a 1967 edition of Jonathan King's show *Good Evening*, where she memorably cites the then Poet Laureate Cecil Day-Lewis as her ideal husband, for his 'sheer sexiness'.[2] Her daughter Kate Levey's reminiscence in this volume, 'A Certain Detachment?', meanwhile, contrastingly emphasises Brophy and her husband's 'remarkably self-contained' existence: 'only intimate friends were truly welcome visitors' (p. 236). This moving account of her mother's latter years calmly adumbrates the shocking impact of multiple sclerosis on Brophy's character, where her previous 'almost pathological gentleness was ripped to shreds as illness incrementally stripped her of all that vital softness of consideration, of appreciation, of empathy, leaving in the end only a reduced, schematic persona, hostile towards my father particularly, and dissociated even from me' (p. 238).

Rodney Hill's inspiring memoir, 'Letter to Brigid', should be read alongside the above, since Hill recalls on finally meeting Brophy, 'reflecting on your gentleness and personal good manners. This seemed, on face value, to be in contrast to your sometimes barbed reviews. You could come across as aggressive in print and shy in life' (p. 142). Hill describes reading Brophy's non-fiction in *Don't Never Forget* as 'a revelation' (p. 138) – a discovery that led him to fantasise about the Leveys' domestic arrangements: 'Old Brompton Road began to get an almost mythic quality – "a beehive in Brompton"' (p. 140) as he puts it.

Phoebe Blatton's essay, 'Embodying the Fragments: A Reflection on the Reluctant Auto-Biography of Brigid Brophy', focuses on the account Brophy wrote of her early experiences of multiple sclerosis, 'A Case-Historical Fragment of Autobiography'. Blatton reflects on the seductive potential but also the challenges and risks in reading not just this, but Brophy's fictions too, and indeed her entire oeuvre, and, in so doing, constructing subjectively a 'Brigid Brophy' authorial persona, in all the ways Brophy herself knew readers did, and that she did too:

> What is it about, this imagining of Brophy as 'a real person'? Perhaps it is the sensation one has of reading her novels – and I think it specifically applies to novels for their immersive, long form – as a young person that seems so pointedly to have touched the core of what you feel before you have the words or experience to express it, and propels you on to a whole new plateau of experiencing the world. (p. 13)

Among Brophy's most celebrated opinions was her claim that the two most interesting things in the world were sex and the eighteenth century.[3] What, then, of the radicalism in her fictional portrayals of sex? Jonathan Gibbs's 'Brigid Brophy's Phenomenology of Sex in *Flesh* and *The Snow Ball*' winningly contextualises two key 1960s Brophy novels by way of comparison with Iris Murdoch, Kingsley Amis, but also the Marquis de Sade, D. H. Lawrence and Henry Miller. Like Murdoch, Gibbs argues persuasively, Brophy was 'interested in perverse, transgressive and anomalous sexual behaviour, and positively so', but unlike her peer, she was 'also interested in the erotics of sex in its more conventional forms' (p. 20). In the novels that Gibbs discusses, Brophy presents heterosexual coitus in utterly unfamiliar ways: '[i]n both cases she ignores the physical mechanics of the act, but concentrates entirely – and in detail – on the physiological and psychological experience: what sex feels like, and what goes through a person's mind when they are doing it' (p. 121). As ever, Brophy's radicalism was not just unmistakable, but also equally and simultaneously *sui generis*.

Michael Bronski's 'Brigid Brophy's Paradoxical World of Childhood' explores the subject of children and childhood across Brophy's fiction and non-fiction. He finds her interest in J. M. Barrie's *Peter Pan* unsurprising, 'since the narrative contains a matrix of many of the preoccupations foundational to her thinking' – including Oedipal conflict (Peter/Captain Hook) and literary metamorphosis (p. 23). Bronski's conclusion brilliantly identifies from this 'the theme that undergirds almost all of Brophy's work, which is the role of the joint powers of imagination and sexuality in the act of creation and re-creation. Peter's ability to fly – which he bestows on others through his wondrous fairy dust – is a form of aphrodisiac' (p. 23). Allan Pero's essay, '"Monster Cupid": Brophy, Camp and *The Snow Ball*', returns us to Brophy's Mozartian fictional esprit, taking in the myriad ways by which she harnessed her very particular sense of 'camp' style and literary stylistics towards often unexpectedly aphrodisiac ends. Pero returns us to Brophy's unholy Trinity – Mozart, Beardsley and Firbank – but takes in the widest range of theorists too, both expected (Sedgwick) and less so (Benjamin, Lacan). Above all, Pero reminds us that Brophy's embrace of her equally individualised sense of the baroque both abutted and contrasted with other twentieth-century flirtations with and reimaginings of that loosely defined form, disposition and/or personal style.

*The Snow Ball*'s protagonist Anna will find that, 'sex and Mozart having inevitably failed her', only 'her other faithless love' awaits her:

'death' (p. 207). A full quarter-century since Brophy's own death, the contemporary reader of her remarkable writings and, equally, the politically savvy activist of today, seeking inspiration and schooling in Brophy's bravery, intellectual confidence and rigour, can take comfort in the existence of this book. It should guide, instruct and hopefully sometimes perplex, by illustrating Brophy in – to borrow from Shakespeare's *Antony and Cleopatra* – her 'infinite variety'.

A last word on what follows: we editors struggled time and again to order these essays according to topic, emphasis, genre, and anything else. Ultimately, we naughtily determined to play a Brophyan trick, by presenting them in a none-too-strict alphabetical order. Brophy – the ghost at her own celebratory feast – appears in her due place, disrupting proceedings as well she might. This meant, however, that John Dixon's 'Introduction to "The Librarian and the Novel"' had to precede her talk, thus creating disorder. We also found it fitting, as surely will you, to leave the last word in this volume to Brophy's daughter and literary executor Kate Levey, who thus also appears out of alphabetical sequence. If any further instruction were needed, do read here as promiscuously, perversely and even prancingly as our subject might have herself. Then return to her books and celebrate with us.

## Notes

1. Peter J. Conradi, 'Iris Murdoch's Deep but Twisted Irish Roots', *The Irish Times*, 14 July 2019, <https://www.irishtimes.com/culture/books/iris-murdoch-s-deep-but-twisted-irish-roots-1.3950148> (accessed 31 August 2019).
2. *A Woman's Place*, <https://www.youtube.com/watch?v=Q2X3IDd1BuE>; *Good Evening*, <https://www.youtube.com/watch?v=BKMSP3nhJzM> (both accessed 31 August 2019).
3. See Jerome Weeks, 'Surprise! Casanova Wasn't Really . . . A Casanova', *Art + Seek*, 1 December 2017, <https://artandseek.org/2017/12/01/surprise-casanova-wasnt-really-a-casanova/#> (accessed 31 August 2019).

# Chapter 1

# Embodying the Fragments:
# A Reflection on the Reluctant
# Auto-Biography of Brigid Brophy

*Phoebe Blatton*

When talking about death, numbers matter immensely. Dates matter; the date illness was first recorded, dates marking the decline. The date of death. It will come around each year, reiterating the shock of death, whether it was expected or not. Age matters: *'too young'* or *'at least they had a good innings'*. The time of death, that point at which our mattering is blown apart, is recorded, to keep hold of things, to make things 'sensical'; this word, ironically, a back-formation of its older antonym 'nonsensical'. Language doesn't abide. It writhes against logic, through logic, creates its own. Language can describe death, but only from the outside. Numbers don't explain, but they delineate death, and they continue where we don't.

I had my first encounter with the novelist, playwright, critic and campaigner Brigid Brophy, aged 19, in a book of collected texts celebrating women's fiction from every year of the twentieth century. The collection featured an extract from Brophy's 1956 novel, *The King of a Rainy Country*, and a short biography, stating that she had died in 1995, five years prior to the compilation's publication. It is not remarkable to find out that a writer, though new to you and surely a source of further wonder, is dead. But it is saddening to know they might still have been alive and writing should they not have been, as people say, 'taken too soon'. Brigid Brophy died at only 66 years of age.

Excited by the extract, I bought a second-hand copy of *The King of a Rainy Country* on the internet, as it was out of print at that time. It has affected my life like no other novel, not only because of how I identified with the intangible school experience of the central character, Susan, as she falls in love with fellow pupil Cynthia, but because in Brophy's clear, yet ever-tantalising prose I detected a total revision of the concept of gender, deftly issued before such studies on the subject were established. For these reasons, I found myself astonished that it was out of print, angry at the howling omissions of writers such as Brophy from the predominantly white male canon of twentieth-century English literature, angry that writers like her were dismissed in her time as 'oddities' or merely 'fashionable', when in fact they were unashamedly progressive and 'other', thus writing to the experience of many. I realised that despite little experience, my friends and I might have to republish *The King of a Rainy Country* and reintroduce Brigid Brophy to a new audience. As a result of this endeavour, I find myself, in all humility, associated with her name. All because I had once so strongly associated with this 'cut-down version' of herself, as she once described Susan, in a rare concession to the autobiographical.

Brophy was staunchly 'un-autobiographical', as she touched upon in the essay 'Antonia' for the 1987 reissue of her novel, *The Finishing Touch*.[1] Therefore, an essay written one year earlier in 1986 was surely a concession of even greater rarity than the fictional offering made in *The King of a Rainy Country*. The essay, commissioned for the American Contemporary Authors Autobiography Series, and later published in Brophy's collection of non-fiction, *Baroque-'n'-Roll*, is written in twenty short sections, and called 'A Case-Historical Fragment of Autobiography'. The scrupulous detail and phrasing almost surpasses that which we might call 'typically Brophyan', telling of how Brophy had lived and worked for the past four years under the degenerative, humiliating and surreal effects of what was, for two years, a mysterious health condition. With each section, she systematically logs the progress of events and investigations that led to her diagnosis, in 1984, of multiple sclerosis.

Over the years I have collected books and ephemera that have passed through Brophy's own hands, often bearing her inscriptions. One of these items is a proof copy of Patricia Highsmith's psychological thriller *This Sweet Sickness* (1960), with Brophy's keen reviewer's notes in the margins. The book, as one would expect, is a no-frills paperback proof; musty smelling, with an age-spotted, blue-and-white striped cover that had not yet been assigned a final design. It is an exciting object because it represents a connection between two writers who fascinate me, and is tactile evidence that Brophy, like myself, was a great admirer of Highsmith's novels. Although I could conjecture this to an extent from the book, I have heard two accounts of meetings between the women that add further endorsement.

The first was from the writer and Brophy's long-time partner, Maureen Duffy. She told me about driving Brophy to Switzerland to meet 'Pat', to arrive at the reclusive writer's fortress of a house with Brophy cowering in the back seat in a rare show of nerves. Duffy conjured a vivid image of the formidable Highsmith sauntering towards the car, as though she might reach in through the half-open window, like a murderer from one of her novels, and strangle the naïve intruders. Nevertheless, Highsmith was famously awkward, which was often reflected in her physical carriage. Kate Levey, Brophy's daughter, told me that 'writers both, Brigid and Pat had in common a profound shyness about face-to-face meetings'.[2] In Andrew Wilson's biography of Highsmith, the writer's rigidity and discomfort in her own body is illustrated in an anecdote from Barbara Roett: 'I always remember that she was quite shocked when I once said, "I must go lie down in a bath." She'd never actually laid down in a bath.'[3]

Kate Levey provided the second story – a childhood memory of being off school sick, and for want of her mother finding a babysitter, being reluctantly taken to lunch at a Chinese restaurant in Earl's Court. Brophy had an unmissable date with Highsmith: 'That Pat had flown in from somewhere that morning struck me, in itself, as exciting and odd,' said Levey, 'but then the whole occasion was strange. Pat seemed large and rather severe.'[4] Highsmith, though clearly the subject of her mother's awe, unnerved the young Levey, especially when she opened the fold of her jacket to reveal a jar of live snails that she had smuggled into England from abroad (fables surround Highsmith and her pet snails, which she purportedly often transported in her bra). Some mild teasing ensued, with suggestions of the chefs getting hold of these snails for the menu: 'Pat's pet snails were not as troubling to me as the thought that she'd done something illegal, rigidly righteous child that I was.'[5] An air of illegality was surely part of what drew the two women to each other, both acutely non-heterosexual, attuned to perversity, and always worrying at the boundaries of conventional behaviour through their writing and their bodily experiences of the worlds in which they lived.

The proof copy of *This Sweet Sickness* is not something I look at often. I bought it during a period of time working at a second-hand bookshop on Charing Cross Road in London, where I witnessed the nerdy fetishism of rare book collecting. The majority of the collectors were male, mostly the sort that revel in a kind of 'out of society' existence that is maddeningly the privilege of men, and which expresses itself across a spectrum of behaviour from bad personal hygiene to blatant sexism, albeit of an often 'vintage' kind. Despite finding this association problematic, I too can be seduced by the seemingly magical, transmissive properties of first editions and signed copies of books by the authors I love. It was during this time that I picked up the proof, which as the stories above concur, is *proof* of another kind. There is a line that leads from the flecks of pencil in Brophy's own hand to an imagining of her body, hunched into the warm back seat of a well-travelled car, or to her pushing open the door of a busy Chinese restaurant holding her child's sweaty, reluctant hand, releasing it as she goes to embrace, with surely some excitement and trepidation, the daunting, unyielding body of Patricia Highsmith.

What is it about, this imagining of Brophy as 'a real person'? Perhaps it is the sensation one has of reading her novels – and I think it specifically applies to novels for their immersive, long form – as a young person that seems so pointedly to have touched the core of what you feel before you have the words or experience to express it, and propels you on to a whole new plateau of experiencing the world. It has made you think completely differently and broken your heart a little. The writer has helped you, in a profound way, to exist. It feels impossible that it is the work of a stranger.

A dedication from Brigid Brophy, in a first edition of *Baroque-'n'-Roll* that I own, reads 'This copy, belonging to Geoff Napthene, is inscribed with best wishes to him by Brigid Brophy. London, June 1987.' You could say that the opening essay of the volume – 'A Case-Historical Fragment of Autobiography' – about her life with multiple sclerosis has in fact begun in the dedication to Geoff, penned in blue ink. It's not that the dedication has any allusion to it, but rather that her stylish handwriting, lithe characters evoking the typographies of Art Nouveau, do not look quite as they appeared in the margins of my copy of *This Sweet Sickness*. Words take drunken dips and letters lurch away from each other – 'o's compress, and 'i's are stranded. Here is proof, of a less romantic kind this time. Proof that Brophy's body was in decline.

\*

Brigid Brophy and Iris Murdoch exchanged thousands of letters over their lifetimes. On strict orders from Brophy, every letter to Murdoch was burnt, so we shall only ever see the evidence of Murdoch's hand, and the nature of her responses (often surprisingly subordinate and deferential, as might befit the dynamic of a relationship that surpassed the platonic), to guess at the content of Brophy's letters. I wonder if those

letters, like my copy of *Baroque-'n'-Roll*, had become depressing visual
clues as to the state of Brophy's health. One can imagine her physical
decline showing on the page, while – cruel irony – the parallel decline of
her friend's mind into Alzheimer's disease might also have begun to show
in their meetings and exchanges. Murdoch features in 'A Case-Historical
Fragment', having met Brophy for lunch in the New Year of 1984 at a
restaurant that could only offer them a table up a flight of stairs: 'Iris
robustly put her hand beneath my elbow and hoisted me up it',[6] Brophy
simply notes, with no further elaboration on the famous writer, or their
old love affair, which was to become public knowledge years after their
deaths. In retrospect, that moment in which a hand held an elbow contains an elegy to something far greater, more physically and emotionally
entwined than one could guess.

A catalogue of relationships with women emerge in even a brief
consideration of Brophy's life. She was rarely without a passionate
attachment to another woman, despite her marriage to the art historian and director of the National Gallery, Michael Levey. She accepted
his proposal of marriage with the caution that, 'Until a year or so ago
I was at least 50% homosexual, and this was the half I acted upon.'[7]
Their marriage, however, was strong. It was a love absolute, but neither owned each other's hearts exclusively, nor seemingly wished to.
As a self-professed 'natural egalitarian', she wrote about the rights
of all sentient beings – fish included – which led to her veganism and
anti-vivisectionist stance. Indeed, she acknowledged that her illness
gave her 'a stake in the matter' of vivisection: 'What is the life of
this rat or the freedom from terror and agony of that monkey worth
to us?' was a question she thought not-to-the-point.[8] 'The pertinent
question', she replies, 'is what they are worth to that monkey or this
rat. His life is the only one that is open to him. His awareness, which
you can so easily suffuse with torment, is the only one he can experience.'[9] Shocked into bodily awareness and reckoning with mortality,
she continued to live according to logic, and would refuse any treatment that had benefited from the 'fascist atrocity' she regarded as
vivisection.

In 'A Case-Historical Fragment of Autobiography', it seems that
the surprise severing of a particularly important relationship might
be regarded as the 'catastrophic grief'[10] that triggered her illness.
Within the first paragraph we are offered a relay of psychological
'ambushes, trembles and tumbles'[11] by an unnamed 'assailant', who
resonates deep into the essay as they manifest in Brophy's flesh. In
true equivocal fashion, she simply orchestrates our feeling on the subject, by placing the event in the first section of the essay, of which, as

I have mentioned, there are twenty. According to her values, it is with the 'automated version of a formal logician'[12] (the computer) that she believes the causes of multiple sclerosis will – and should be – deciphered, with a catalogue of data that involves much questioning of the patients. Nevertheless, frequent mentions of the 'assailant' who maims her in her nightmares are indications of a fallible, angry Brophy, in a battle between reason and irrationality. In the end, there is a kind of amnesty of logic, and a vengeful suggestion that the 'assailant' has caused her illness. As though in surrender to the surreal nature of her condition, she leaves it until the seventeenth section to concede that 'the question of what does induce it [multiple sclerosis] may well drop out of the accumulated and sifted replies to a question as seemingly wayward as "Do you like blackcurrants?"'[13]

In line with her logical dismissal of mysterious forces, Brophy writes: 'If it is random bad luck to be struck down by the disease, it is random comparatively good luck to be struck down in a welfare state.'[14] It is a taut, deftly balanced sentence in which the devastation of being 'struck down' is immediately cloaked in a 'bigger issue'; a neater example of 'the personal is political' would be hard to find, and it clearly places Brophy politically on the left. It is arguably a sentence with even greater prescience today. But even within the welfare state, it is worth considering the privileges Brophy might have experienced as a sick woman of a particular class and ethnicity. Brophy mentions how her husband wrote to the head of the unit at the hospital in which she was being treated when there was a mix-up with her appointments. There's little doubt that a letter from the recently knighted director of the National Gallery would have carried some clout.

Perhaps it is tangential to cite here the case of the Afro-German poet, activist and educator May Ayim, who committed suicide in 1996 at the age of 36, but I believe it is in the spirit of Brophy to do so. Though very different writers, with very different lives, there are points of comparison between the women, notably their activism, and their contraction of multiple sclerosis. Ayim had been admitted to a psychiatric ward in Berlin in January 1996, shortly after a strenuous period organising Black History Month. The doctors eventually diagnosed her as having multiple sclerosis. They stopped the medication that had been prescribed to her for severe depression, and discharged her in April. Following a subsequent readmission and release from the hospital, on 9 August 1996 she jumped from the thirteenth floor of a Berlin building. In the case of any suicide, the question of whether it could have been prevented is always difficult to answer, but on hearing this story I was struck by the apparent failure of care surrounding Ayim's depression and multiple sclerosis – illnesses that were almost certainly related.

I doubt that Ayim would have come across Brophy's essay in the few months between her diagnosis and death, but if she had, would she have recognised the 'obsessive and fearful state of mind' that Brophy experienced before her diagnosis, interpreted as 'intimations from my body [that] were alerting my mind to facts it did not know'?[15] It would require another essay to assess the various issues surrounding the death of Ayim, which surely points to an intrinsically racist system, but I think that both writers would want us to consider how two people from First World countries, with the same disease, might well have received different 'treatment' according to the bodies they inhabited.

*

Where it could seem quite odd, in an essay that is ostensibly about Brophy's reckoning with a slow, surreal illness, to encounter one section given over to the details of the Public Lending Right (the campaign that Brophy and Duffy spearheaded to ensure that writers were paid for their inclusion in public libraries), in Brophy's hands this diversion into a relatively unexciting though significant enterprise is integral to the emotional head-spin that is experienced by the end of the essay. It is because she enjoyed the 'mechanical and relaxed delight' of logic, 'which served me as, I imagine, knitting serves some of my friends',[16] that she came to embrace and enjoy her immersion into the rules of British copyright.

Brophy's essay is sometimes infuriating, because it is so controlled, so seemingly sat bolt-upright in a bath full of murky water. Brophy writes with a kind of pedantry that can read like the reporting of a ponderous detective story. But in this sense, she is talking us through the *intellectual knitting* she could so enjoyably lose herself in when presented with puzzles in the minutiae. The disease that had so ravaged her was, of course, a puzzle that she knew she couldn't solve. The essay often reads like an attempt to exercise control, the twenty sections resembling 'steps', like the literal steps she has to take with extreme effort. Before the illness was diagnosed, we hear of how Brophy would scale the six steps of the minor portico that led to the communal front door of her building. After heaving herself up via the railings, 'I crawled on all fours through the communal hall, wondering whether the occupant of some other flat would at that moment come down the staircase or, having begun to do so, would retreat thinking "There's that eccentric Lady Levey crawling across the hall."'[17] Never does she let the tragedy of her illness fully erase the humour and sense of the surreal that so colours and defines her writing. In the twentieth section of the essay, Brophy concludes with a typically equivocal segue into a memory of standing on the 'wind-racked grass at the top of the site of Troy. To one side were the quasi-terraces cut by the excavation to disclose the layers of the successive cities.'[18] She is there with two companions, one of whom we might assume to be her husband, and the other, perhaps, Maureen Duffy, though she does not say. The important thing is that they are three, and are approached by three local children, 'seriously beautiful, and without a touch of the urchin, seriously serious',[19] bearing long-stalked, vermilion poppies. The scene ripples with an earthy, magical atmosphere that one might associate with the film director Federico Fellini. Indeed, it is as though the whole scene might suddenly melt like celluloid and disappear into its own oblivion.

At the very last, she reveals a kind of writing that conveys the surrealism of her condition. It choruses that experience of a 'strange, unnatural numbness', lying in bed at night and not being able to 'tell whether I have crossed one ankle over the other unless I look to see'.[20] Brophy does not write about flowers without knowledge of their symbolism; in the myths of ancient Greece, as she was fully aware, poppies were used as offerings to the dead. Recognising this courtesy as an act of 'high Homeric custom',[21] Brophy searches for something to offer the children in response. In her pockets she has a handful of boiled sweets that she describes as 'big cellophane-swathed ovals in the deep, not quite transparent colours of jewels'.[22] Having created this upward arc of poetic description, in the next moment we are adroitly brought over the peak and into the decline with a knowing, yet poignant admission of the absurd: 'I am the ancient Greek ghost, sent down in the ultimate sense, who on meeting Charon proffered a boiled sweet as the price of the ferry passage.'[23]

The children did not accept the sweets, a sign perhaps that at that moment she had not been deemed 'unfit' enough to make the passage. Yet writing in 1986, she knows that 'all that has happened to me is that I have in part died in advance of the total event'.[24] Brophy expresses her losses physically, through the body. The knowledge that she will never see Italy again is described as 'an unbearable medallion that bends my neck'.[25] She describes the past as, 'except through memory and imagination, irrecoverable in any case, whether or not your legs are strong enough to sprint after it'.[26] Perhaps the recollection of the children of Troy is her way of saying that the future, her present, was ever thus, and she will attempt to accept it.

The coincidence of numbers strikes me again. 'A Case-Historical Fragment of Autobiography' is in fact a summation of everything you need to know about Brophy, though she will challenge you, like the excavators of Troy, to 'disclose the layers'.[27] In 2015, on the twentieth anniversary of her death, the University of Northampton arranged a conference to celebrate her life, to which I was invited to talk about publishing *The King of a Rainy Country*. When I talk about the novel, I celebrate how it achieves nothing so ill-conceived or presumptuously linear as a point of enlightenment, but rather illustrates what it is to merely glean a shimmer of that which is intangible. We speak of losing someone as 'an intangible loss', meaning that the grief caused by their absence is too great to quantify. The intangible loss I feel for Brophy is rather more literal, because of course, though having grown close to those who knew her, in particular her daughter Kate Levey, I never met Brigid.

Could it be that an 'intangible loss' is as intangible as the love that prefigured it?

At the end of *The King of a Rainy Country*, Susan learns of the death of Helena, a friend (though that word falters in its reach) whom she has only just made. I have since been told that Helena might have been named after a girl called Helen, who Brophy knew at Oxford (from which she was 'sent down' for 'unspecified offences').[28] Helen had apparently been killed. Brophy writes as someone who completely understands the way in which trauma does not necessarily erupt immediately, but quakes from the inside, over time. Perhaps this especially applies to the experience of those who have had to live and love as 'other' and, more often than not, with shame. When Susan learns of the death of her friend, there is no obvious response. Instead, she is gripped by the sudden, inexplicable urge to call her dentist:

> I asked if I could have an appointment at once.
> 'Is it urgent? Are you in actual pain?'
> 'No. That's the trouble.'
> 'I don't quite see what you mean.'[29]

Brophy wrote *The King of a Rainy Country* at the age of 27. Until her diagnosis with multiple sclerosis she had only experienced exceptionally good health. Nevertheless, these lines of Brophy's, delivered in the voice of her semi-autobiographical, 19-year-old self, reveal a woman who had always faced the intangible, proffering her sweets: 'I haven't been for some time', Susan tells the receptionist, a kind of Charon of the dentist's chair. 'There's bound to be something that needs doing, isn't there?'[30]

## Notes

1. Brigid Brophy, *The Finishing Touch* (London: Gay Men's Press, 1987).
2. Kate Levey, private correspondence with the author, May 2012.
3. Andrew Wilson, *Beautiful Shadow: A Life of Patricia Highsmith* (London: Bloomsbury, 2003), p. 4.
4. Kate Levey, private correspondence with the author, May 2012.
5. Ibid.
6. Brigid Brophy, 'A Case-Historical Fragment of Autobiography', in *Baroque-'n'-Roll and Other Essays* (London: Hamish Hamilton, 1987), pp. 1–27 (p. 14).
7. Kate Levey, 'Mr and Mrs Michael Levey', *Contemporary Women's Writing*, 12.2 ( 2018), pp. 142–51 (p. 150).
8. Brophy, 'A Case-Historical Fragment', p. 21.
9. Ibid., p. 21.
10. Ibid., p. 1.
11. Ibid., p. 1.
12. Ibid., p. 21.
13. Ibid., p. 22.
14. Ibid., p. 23.
15. Ibid., p. 23.
16. Ibid., p. 10.
17. Ibid., p. 17.
18. Ibid., p. 26.
19. Ibid., p. 26.
20. Ibid., p. 25.
21. Ibid., p. 27.
22. Ibid., p. 27.
23. Ibid., p. 27.
24. Ibid., p. 26.
25. Ibid., p. 26.
26. Ibid., p. 26.
27. Ibid., p. 26.
28. Kate Levey, private correspondence with the author, October 2015.
29. Brigid Brophy, *The King of a Rainy Country* (London: Coelacanth Press, 2012), p. 263.
30. Ibid., p. 263.

# Chapter 2

# Brigid Brophy's Paradoxical World of Childhood

*Michael Bronski*

The brilliance of Brigid Brophy lies in her ability cautiously, but unnervingly, to unveil and reveal the layers of consciousness – and unconsciousness – that construct our humanity through dreams, language, actions and moral decisions. Using Freudian theory, literature, myth, visual arts and music, her fiction and critical work is a glittering, often paradoxical, fun house of perception and invention. Yet curiously, for all her reliance on Freud and her deep concerns about human development, children and childhood are often not overtly present in her work. Sometimes, almost phantom-like, they linger in the background of the texts. As opposed to the larger genre of queer novels about childhood – James Courage's *The Young Have Secrets* (1954), L. P. Hartley's *The Go-Between* (1955), Maureen Duffy's *Love Child* (1971) – young children sometimes flit through Brophy's novels as minor characters or memories, but she is not very interested in them. Frequently she has more interest in older children – adolescents and young adults – but almost always in the context of their relationships with parents or parental figures.

At the same time, however, children – and more importantly, the psychological and moral state of childhood – haunt her work. Woven through a great deal of Brophy's analytic imagination is the paradoxical – even queer – idea of childhood as being both idyllic and horrific: a place of both innocence and dangerous, potentially deadly knowledge. There has been important new work on the concept of queer childhood, such as Karin Lesnik-Oberstein and Stephen Thomson's important essay 'What is Queer Theory Doing with the Child' (2002), and Kathryn Bond Stockton's *The Queer Child, or Growing Sideways in the Twentieth Century* (2009),[1] which mostly address the liminal spaces that childhood occupies in traditional concepts of social development. These concerns are not particularly pertinent to Brophy's world view. Brigid Brophy being Brigid Brophy – and Sigmund Freud being Sigmund Freud – the connections between children/childhood and liberating and dangerous knowledge are primarily to do with sex. A pithy, epigrammatic interrogative story – or 'fable' as the collection's subtitle indicates – entitled 'Sources', from the collection *The Adventures of God in His Search for the Black Girl*, is indicative of Brophy's orientation:

> 'Those bawdy songs Ophelia sings: where did she learn them?'
> 'In childhood – indeed at a children's party: from Juliet's nurse.'[2]

This charming, ironic brace of question and answer is resonant of – or perhaps a gloss on – the 'Nurse's Song' in William Blake's *Songs of Innocence and of Experience*. Tinged with the juxtaposition of the excitement of sexual desire and children's parties, and coloured by the shadow of Ophelia's fate, the reader can hear the dissonance between 'The little ones leapèd, and shoutèd, and laugh'd/ And all the hills echoèd', and 'Your spring and your day are wasted in play,/ And your winter and night in disguise'. Brophy's view of the human condition – and by extension childhood – is suspended between rue and revelation.

Again and again in Brophy's work the question of how knowledge originates is central. This, of course, is pivotal to Freudian thought and the formation of consciousness (and, in far more complicated ways, the unconscious) in the infant and its development. That is why it is surprising that Brophy rarely addresses childhood per se, though the concerns appear throughout her work. In a 1964 review of Jean-Paul Sartre's autobiography *The Words* she writes:

> He has a *talent* for *naïveté*. If he is ignorant of one or two things which everyone else knows, he says several which everyone knows but no one else has pointed out. 'I was a fake child,' he writes – 'J'étais un faux enfant.' Only now that he says it about his own childhood does he recognise that of course all children are fakes; indeed to be a child is to be in a false position. *The Words* performs a tremendous feat. It exposes the pretentiousness of childhood.[3]

Of course Brophy, in true Firbankian fervour, adores exaggerations, ostentations and falseness, and would find childhood pretentious because she understands it, simultaneously, as both a social construction as well as a scam perpetrated on children by adults to facilitate and impose a veneer of pseudo-innocence. This imposed *affect* of *innocence* is, most often, foisted on children to deflect from adults their own, often sad and devastating, reality of *experience*. Brophy's use of 'pretentious' is significant, since she uses it – as she does many words – idiosyncratically, to mean both the exaggerated state of pretence or falsehood, as well as the delicious, if imposed, element of pretending.

The idea of childhood being constructed, for Brophy, is both in tune with and contradictory to her psychoanalytic theories that childhood is a site of mythological and psycho-sexual conflict between children and adults. This is a major theme in her book *Black Ship to Hell* (1962), and Brophy has no problem finding Oedipal tensions throughout Western thought and literature. In an analysis of the sorcerer's apprentice (which she traces from Lucian through the Goethe ballad, to Disney's popularisation of Paul Dukas's programme music), she argues that to give life to an inanimate object is the 'oldest form of magic', and is, in essence, the usurping of the father's power by the son (surprisingly, she does not mention Jesus' raising Lazarus from the dead here as an example):

> The power is, of course, quintessentially the father's: it was by exercising it he *became* a father: and the story sees to it that the son, who, who by sexual rebellion is trying to put himself in the father's place, is really putting himself in the way of becoming a father himself, is punished by the magical power turning against him.[4]

Brophy complicates this psychoanalytic theory of succession in her discussions of Mozart's relationship with his father, Leopold. She notes that many artists' biographies begin with 'his father intended him for law/church/medicine/commerce', and then the son defies the father to be an artist. The situation is different, as Brophy notes, in Mozart's case: 'both were artists' in the same medium:

> Leopold was both the real father and the master of the apprentice. There was no question of his being displeased by his son's choice of profession: it was his own choice, both for himself, and more important, for his son. Art by psychogenesis, a rebellion against paternal forces in society and the artist's own psyche. For Mozart, however, art could not wholly express rebellion against his father in person, because Leopold as artist, was likewise a rebel. Mozart had no occasion to usurp Leopold's place: Leopold had destined him to occupy it – including the place of breadwinner – from the start.[5]

Brophy's meditation on Mozart and his father provides an alternative – and in her world view, highly idiosyncratic, or at least unusual – exception to the father/son conflict: not quite polar opposites, but close. (Brophy did not write about this complex personal/professional dynamic with her own father, the noted novelist John Brophy.) As brilliant as her analysis of the relationship between Mozart and his father is, she writes far more compellingly on the structural and performative aspects of this dynamic, and especially the effect it has on childhood. Nowhere is this more apparent than in her discussions of James M. Barrie's *Peter Pan* (1904).

Brophy discussed *Peter Pan or The Boy Who Wouldn't Grow Up* – the play, not the subsequent prose fictions that Barrie wrote about the character in 1906 and 1911 – at least three times: in *Black Ship to Hell* (1962), in a 1964 essay on Louisa May Alcott included in *Don't Never Forget* (1966), and in a critique of it – presumably by her, as the language and concerns are strikingly similar – in *Fifty Works of English and American Literature We Could Do Without* (1966). Brophy's preoccupation with *Peter Pan* is not surprising since the narrative contains a matrix of many of the ideas that are foundational to her thinking. The Oedipal conflict between Peter and Captain Hook (through double casting, the evil alter-ego of Mr Darling, and, no doubt to Brophy's delight, an Etonian) is central to this, as well as the literary metamorphosis of the mythical, amoral, sexual Pan to Barrie's relentlessly youthful anti-hero. These, in many ways, are subsumed under the theme that undergirds almost all of Brophy's work, which is the role of the joint powers of imagination and sexuality in the act of creation and re-creation. Peter's ability to fly – which he bestows on others through his wondrous fairy dust – is a form of aphrodisiac. As Brophy comments in a footnote quoting Freud's *The Interpretation of Dreams*, in discussing the sorcerer's apprentice's animated broom:

> Dr. Paul Federn (Vienna) has propounded the fascinating theory that a great many flying dreams are erection dreams, since the remarkable phenomenon of erection, which constantly occupies the human phantasy, cannot fail to be impressive as an apparent suspension of the laws of gravity (cf. the winged phalli of the ancients).[6]

This image reappears in *Black Ship to Hell* in her discussions of the winged Cupid (Eros) who is sentimentalised in both high and popular culture.[7]

It is telling, however, that with such rich psychoanalytic material, almost all of Brophy's discussions of *Peter Pan* centre on Barrie's interactive plot device of having children clap if they believe in fairies, and thus save Tinkerbell's life after she has drunk the medicine that Wendy has left for Peter, but which has been poisoned by Hook. In *Black Ship to Hell* Brophy quotes Peter – from earlier in the play – saying 'Children know such a lot now. Soon they don't believe in fairies, and every time a child says "I don't believe in fairies" there is a fairy somewhere that falls down dead';[8] she uses this as a metaphor for the struggle between belief in God and the knowledge produced by science.[9] In 'Sentimentality and Louisa May Alcott' – which is an acknowledgement of the power of sentimentality and a critique of its use in art – Brophy attacks Barrie for betraying children by obliging them – essentially by emotionally blackmailing them – to applaud in order to keep Tinkerbell alive.[10] A few years later Brophy discusses *Peter Pan* more fully, if briefly in a few pages, and after comparing the genius of Barrie to the genius of Freud (high praise from her), she accuses the author of *Peter Pan* of immorality for not only betraying children but betraying art.[11] As she states in 'Sentimentality and Louisa May Alcott', 'sentimentality does one thing that neither morality nor art can stand for – it is hypocritical'.[12]

At the beginning of 'Sentimentality and Louisa May Alcott' Brophy admits to being afraid of Alcott's writing 'in a quite straightforward way – because she makes me cry. Being an unsentimental writer, I am not a bit afraid of her example, which doesn't tempt me. It is not as a writer, but as a reader I fear her.'[13] Brophy is so frightened by sentimentality – presumably because it is a rejection of her rationalism and her dedication to the empirical – that she is compulsively drawn to it in Alcott's novel. This tension fuels many of her attitudes about children, and is, to a large degree, the key to Brophy on children and childhood: she is afraid of sentimentality, and it is nearly impossible – since the late nineteenth century, or rather, since Victorian literature – to write about children without sentimentality. As she notes in her essay on Alcott:

> I think Oscar Wilde said that no man of feeling could read the death of Little Nell without laughing. But the unwitty and much more terrible truth is that no one can read it without crying. Dickens has made the illegitimate appeal to real life and, no matter what ludicrous nonsense he makes of the death of Little Nell, the death of children *is* sad.[14]

This astute observation tells us a great deal about Brophy – and, incidentally is a telling comment on Wilde's disinclination to empathy, or at least his valuing of the insightful ironic *over* empathy – and informs how children appear, if briefly, in much of her writing. It isn't that Brophy is contradicting Wilde here, *exactly* – she most probably knew that his tales for children were criticised, on publication, for being too sophisticated and adult in intention and content – but rather is pushing against his use of flippant irony, self-defensively, to claim emotional space of her own. Yet how do you write about children and childhood without the hypocrisy of sentimentality?

Brophy's novel *Palace without Chairs* (1978) concerns a quintet of grown-up children – Heather, the youngest, is 16 – of the royal family of Evarchia, a medieval-esque monarchy that resides in the late twentieth century and is grappling with a communist party fighting for power, labour unions, an increasingly dysfunctional bureaucracy and electronic surveillance. All of the adult children have a complicated relationship both with their parents and with the idea of monarchy, but for a good deal of the novel they are more concerned about the shocking and inexplicable lack of chairs in the palace. Whenever Balthasar, the second oldest, attempts to order new chairs he is stymied by the overwrought requisitioning system run by committees and the Royal Comptroller, and waylaid by philosophical discussions of the very nature of chairs:

> 'The definition of a chair,' the High Chamberlain said, 'may appear to be a matter of common sense. But the moment you begin to think about it, common sense lets you down. For example, not everything that people sit on is a chair. One can, for example, sit on a wall. Yet a wall is not a chair [. . .]' 'I suppose,' the Comptroller said, indicating that he was weaving a very thin speculation [. . .] 'it might be argued that a wall *is* a chair when someone is sitting on it. It becomes so to speak, an *acting* chair.'[15]

It quickly becomes clear through Brophy's baroque narration and syntax that the chairs – which were present in their youth – are a metaphor for the lost childhood of the royal siblings. A series of missing chair images is beautifully crowned by a scene in which Heather and Ulrich, attempting to have a conversation about (literally) life and death, are faced with the lack of chairs in the former royal day nursery. Heather flings herself on to an old wooden rocking horse, which breaks a leg under her weight: 'Ulrich stared at the rocking horse's leg. One splintered section of the shaft was now overlapping the other, painfully suggestive of bone. He felt Heather had broken his childhood. "And now there's absolutely nowhere to sit in here," Heather said.'[16]

Just as their childhood can never be regained – or requisitioned by committee – Brophy makes it clear that it is inextricably bound up with power. Ulrich is betrothed to the Countess Clara Claribond, but 'in a precise and technical sense the love of Ulrich's his life' was Tom, the royal groom. Fleeing from his father's harsh schooling, Ulrich took shelter in Tom: 'The love Ulrich bestowed on Tom, who must have been then, though Ulrich didn't notice it at the time, a fairly young man, was complete and, Ulrich intended, irrevocable. Sexless in act, it was thoroughly sexual – indeed, specifically homosexual – in content.'[17]

Ulrich and Tom – both essentially children – had horses (actual horses, not rocking horses) as their bond: 'It was in the smell of Tom's occupation and Tom's physical being that Ulrich had lost his dread of horses.'[18] In *Palace without Chairs* – and elsewhere in Brophy's work – childhood exists as a flight from parents, as well as being highly, even idealistically, sexualised. The sexual impulse here is often homosexual in nature: Heather, the youngest of the five royal children, has seduced each of her six successive female tutors, in large part because the power dynamic intrinsic in institutionalised heterosexuality is inimical to the potentially egalitarian world of childhood.

When childhood, or adolescence, appears in Brophy's writing, it is almost always about, or inflected by, power: the Oedipal conflicts that shape and structure *Black Ship to Hell*, the two-way power negotiations between Mozart and his father, the psycho-sexual dynamic of *Peter Pan*, the lesbian students and their teachers in *The Finishing Touch*, the playful physical struggles between Eros and his younger brother Anteros, and the Freudian family romance in *Palace without Chairs*. It is also not coincidental that aspects of royalty and monarchy also play a part in so much of her writing – they occur in the fiction, but also as themes in the reviews and the theoretical work. Like the biological family, monarchical royalty is structured on power relationships that shape human relationships, particularly with regard to age and sexuality.

This is abundantly apparent in *Palace without Chairs* which brings together, under the canopy of fiction, many of the themes of *Black Ship to Hell*. The father and son themes of conflict – which are, in essence, conflicts between children and adults and meditations on the nature of childhood – are rife in the novel, but Brophy begins to provide us with some resolutions. Ulrich, the oldest, decides to relinquish his claim to the throne, to the dismay of the king:

> He came into the little room, spread his arms and said in a quiet deep voice: 'My son.'
>
> Ulrich had never received that form of address from him before and was embarrassed by it.
>
> He was embarrassed again, perhaps even less rationally, when he was last able to withdraw from the sorrowful slow embrace of the wide arms [. . .][19]

When the king professes to having received a 'painful wound' from Ulrich's relinquished claim, the son states that he cannot imagine why:

> The king sighed. 'Can't you imagine what it feels like? To have labored to preserve and pass on a heritage – to have tried to share with you its problems and educate you in the expertise needed to deal with them – an expertise no one else could teach you – to bring you up in a knowledge of all of the richness and subtlety of certain cherished traditions and then to find that you reject them all.'
>
> 'Papa, I reject nothing.'
>
> 'Except,' the king said, his voice suddenly as brisk as a trumpet, 'your duty.'[20]

*Palace without Chairs* is Brophy's retelling of the Freudian family drama – now tinged with sadness and, at times, empathetic understanding – that haunts much of her work. Ulrich's rejection of duty, his legacy and burden, is essentially a break-up scene between him and his father, replete with sexual embarrassment, emotional misunderstandings and recriminations. In the novel, Ulrich's refusal to play the family script as a loyal, dutiful son is the beginning of a series of tragedies – including the deaths of several other royal heirs, as well as his mother, the queen. The family – whose hierarchical structure mimics that of monarchy and royalty – cannot sustain itself with the acceptance and enactment of traditional dynastic transitions.

As opposed to Brophy's myriad other examples of father-and-son struggles – Don Giovanni and Il Commendatore in Mozart and Da Ponte's opera *Don Giovanni,* Jesus and God in the Christian gospels, Rodion Romanovich Raskolnikov and Porfiry Petrovich in Dostoyevsky's *Crime and Punishment* – she correctly understands Ulrich's refusal of the crown as a moral decision to end the cycle of power sharing through transference. In the universe of *Palace without Chairs* – and perhaps Brophy's Freudian universe as well – this refusal, and the ensuing deaths, are the logical outcome when the boundaries, expectations and presumed duties of childhood are broken.

While the royal family are enacting their own drama, the Royal Astean Opera – the national theatre company – must postpone its new production of Verdi's *I Normani* (a Brophy-imagined sequel to *I Vespri Siciliani*), in part due to creative conflicts and in part to the assassination of Archduke Sempronius, the third of the royal children. *I Vespri Siciliani*, with its themes of father-and-son conflict and duty versus love, is the perfect backdrop (we can only imagine what Brophy imagined the sequel would be like) for the drama in the royal family. *I Normani* was to be 'set in the medieval period, in modern dress'.[21]

Brophy's emotional focus in the novel – which indeed is in modern dress and essentially set in the medieval period – foregrounds childhood, and the refusal of those who are trapped in it to remain so. Her conclusions, however, are daunting. Playing and replaying the assigned roles of children and parents is at best a cultural repetition compulsion, and refusing to engage breaks the cycle, but can lead to wide-scale disruption.

Reflecting on this, the overriding theme of *Black Ship to Hell* is that cycles of human activity, culture and social change (which are essentially various degrees of stagnation) have led us to the brink of catastrophe. In the post-Second World War climate in which the book was written, Brophy was most probably thinking of nuclear war; today we have a larger menu of cataclysms from which to choose. Being an anti-religious, anti-sentimental rationalist, she believes that humans can make decisions that will move culture closer to Eros than to Thanatos. It is these moral decisions – and acts – that humans must make every day that will guide culture.

Brophy is also concerned, in the opening chapters of *Black Ship to Hell*, with the idea of the *acte gratuit* – an impulsive act lacking motive – and yet as a Freudian she knows that an *acte gratuit* is a cultural illusion to explain away what is not obvious or what we do not want to consider: all acts have motives, causes and antecedents. When she does write about children and childhood in her work there is always an understanding that these motives and causes begin in childhood. The condition of childhood, treacherous as it may be, is – for now – an inescapable reality of being human. On some level, for Brophy, the *acte gratuit* is simply the act of *being*.

In her 1965 essay 'Detective Fiction: A Modern Myth of Violence', Brophy suggests that the enormous popularity of the twentieth-century detective story – the 'whodunit' – is really a quest by readers to see who didn't do it; a quest to reaffirm their own innocence as the ending reveals that they *didn't* do it.[22] In many ways Brophy's avoidance of childhood, or her writing around the issue, is a repetitious denial that the nightmare of childhood – its power struggles, its constant reiteration of false ideals of innocence, its sentimentality, and especially its limiting the freedom of children *as* humans – is as powerful as it is. Ulrich has the moral character to reject the expectations and implications of his childhood – a decision that Brophy applauds. It is not, however, without consequences. In *Black Ship to Hell* Brophy rather grandly states: 'Well, then: if we are to save civilisation, we must re-form our attitude towards it.'[23] This could easily be applied to how Brophy views childhood as it exists today. Her construction of childhood now is as a psychoanalytic labyrinth in which humans are faced with myriad, consequential decisions that they have little chance of actually getting right; but if the right decisions are made, there is a chance of – albeit complicated and sometimes painful – survival.

## Notes

1. Kathryn Bond Stockton, *The Queer Child, or Growing Sideways in the Twentieth Century* (Chapel Hill, NC: Duke University Press, 2009); Karín Lesnik-Oberstein and Stephen Thomson, 'What is Queer Theory Doing with the Child?', *Parallax*, 8.1 (2002), pp. 35–46.
2. Brigid Brophy, *The Adventures of God in His Search for the Black Girl* (Boston, MA: Little, Brown, 1973), p. 26.
3. Brigid Brophy, 'The Words', in *Don't Never Forget: Collected Views and Reviews* (New York: Holt, Rinehart and Winston, 1966), p. 290.
4. Brigid Brophy, *Black Ship to Hell* (New York: Harcourt, Brace and World, 1962), p. 350.
5. Brigid Brophy, *Mozart the Dramatist: A New View of Mozart, His Operas and His Age* (New York: Harcourt, Brace and World, 1964), p. 259.
6. Brophy, *Black Ship to Hell*, p. 350, n. 1. The Freud text is taken from the 1913 A. A. Brill translation of *The Interpretation of Dreams* (London: Allen and Unwin, 1945).
7. Brophy, *Black Ship to Hell*, p. 469.
8. Ibid., p. 194.
9. Ibid., p. 195.

10. Brigid Brophy, 'Sentimentality and Louisa May Alcott', in *Don't Never Forget*, p. 116.
11. Brigid Brophy, 'Peter Pan', in *Fifty Works of English and American Literature We Could Do Without* (New York: Stein and Day, 1967), p. 112.
12. Brophy, 'Sentimentality', p. 115.
13. Ibid., p. 116.
14. Ibid., p. 115.
15. Brigid Brophy, *Palace without Chairs* (New York: Atheneum, 1978), p. 55.
16. Ibid., p. 127.
17. Ibid., p. 59.
18. Ibid., p. 58
19. Ibid., p. 191.
20. Ibid., p. 192.
21. Ibid., p. 151.
22. Brigid Brophy, 'Detective Fiction: A Modern Myth of Violence', in *Don't Never Forget*, p. 121.
23. Brophy, *Black Ship to Hell*, p. 131.

# Chapter 3

# Introduction to 'The Librarian and the Novel'

*John Dixon*

Working in the public library system during the late 1970s and early 1980s was not a particularly rewarding experience. It was at best – to quote from *The Pilgrim's Progress*, one of the fifty works of English literature that Brigid Brophy felt the world could do without – a 'slough of despond'. The Minister for Local Government had said 'the party's over'. There were to be cuts in spending, and libraries, always the Cinderella service, were a prime target. Many libraries were threatened with reduced opening hours or even closure. There was talk of charging for library use, for the loan of fiction; charges for museum and gallery entrance had already been introduced.

In 1975 I joined the library service of the London Borough of Tower Hamlets. The authority had not really come to terms with the Amalgamation of London Boroughs Act of ten years before. Three East End authorities – Stepney, Bethnal Green and Limehouse – were amalgamated to become the London Borough of Tower Hamlets. They were not really hamlets, nor were they in the shadow of the Tower; and there was little evidence of cooperation. Much resentment lingered, with rivalry and personality clashes between older members of staff still wedded to their former boroughs. However, these same staff would temporarily unite against incoming staff, especially newcomers who had gained a professional library qualification.

The older staff claimed they knew from years of experience and from being local exactly what the readers wanted. 'Libraries as supermarkets' was the ideal. Detailed and informed discussion at book selection meetings was taken to be a farce, and the only promotion of book stock thought necessary was the prominent siting of the returned books trolley on the basis that readers just wanted to read what other readers had read. New staff took a different perspective. The borough was changing and the readership with it. The old attitude of 'give them what they want' was passive, not pro-active. The bulk of the issues were fiction: genre fiction, bought by the yard, and spine-labelled Romance, Crime, Western, Sci-Fi. New fiction was not encouraged, rarely bought and never promoted or circulated between libraries.

Many attempts were made to correct this situation. A series of book lists was produced, for the most part just typed and duplicated. This was viewed by the hierarchy at most as 'inspired time-wasting'. One list, however, because it dealt with the history of the local area, did get sufficient approval to warrant a professional printing. This was *The East End in Fiction*, a list with annotations of fiction by writers who had lived or worked in the East End or whose novels were set wholly or partially in the East End. This was acceptable to the hierarchy, in the same way that historical fiction was acceptable; it tended to the condition of non-fiction.

Only a limited amount could be done within the borough, and the experience of other librarians and library authorities needed to be drawn upon. I was at that time a member of the Association of Assistant Librarians (a branch of the Library Association). It held regular meetings, discussions and the occasional one-day course. It also ran a quarterly magazine, *The Assistant Librarian*. The editor was always keen for new material.

Early in 1980 I submitted a satirical article on 'Book Selection'. It was accepted and published in the June 1980 issue.[1] It was written as fiction, illustrated, and concerned a novice librarian at a book selection meeting faced with the dilemma of selecting for purchase a copy of her best friend's first novel. In the next issue, September 1980, several letters were published, some in agreement, some deploring the levity of tone. (It was deemed appropriate to write *about* fiction, but not *in* fiction!) The editor billed the correspondence as the 'The Great Fiction Debate' and it simmered for several issues. I floated the idea of a day-course on Fiction Provision in Libraries. This was approved, and involved drawing up a detailed proposal, aims-&-objectives, likely audience etc., and, of course, the names of speakers. We would need a representative from a major fiction publisher; perhaps someone in the academic field researching reading habits; possibly someone dealing with other formats of fiction, such as talking books or large print. But most definitely we would need an author.

There were many talented authors around in the late 1970s, but were they also competent public speakers? Were they committed to promoting fiction and the rights of the reader and writer? The name that stood out was Brigid Brophy, greatly respected in the literary world for her novels, stories and essays, but also for her work with the Writers' Action Group, and the campaign for Public Lending Right, in which she and Maureen Duffy had earned grudging admiration in their attempts to convince an intransigent arts minister, a government and the Library Association (to say nothing of some of my more traditional work colleagues) of the rightness and modesty of the PLR proposals.

I had previously contacted Brophy by post with regard to my article on book selection. I had asked if the final paragraph, a quote in praise of fiction, could be improved, or if she could come up with, or even write, anything better, assuring her that not all librarians were against authors; some had become authors. She commended the article, reassured us that she was far from being against librarians and certainly not against libraries, and said the quotation was fitting. I later contacted her about giving a talk at the proposed course. In her writings she had made clear that she was reticent about public appearances. As she wrote in 'The Rights of Animals' (1966): 'I was attacked by stage-fright on the many occasions I took part in discussions or debates on television, when I regularly feared (often, I suspect, correctly) that my facial fixity and my lack of fluency would harm rather than promote the cause I was trying to present.'[2] However, she accepted, and the publicity went out for an event – 'Fiction in Libraries' – to be held on 1 October 1980, organised by the Association of Assistant Librarians. The venue was Holborn Library in central London, the cost £5.50 (£4 to students), lunch not supplied. We contacted some of the more progressive small publishers. The tickets sold well. The day before, we put up an exhibition of Brophy dust jackets.

On the day itself, the first three speakers all arrived on time to deliver their talks. Brophy was the last speaker, and there was some trepidation about who should be around to greet her and lead her up the lecture hall. I happened to be keeping a diary at that time and the day's entry reads: 'She hadn't arrived by the afternoon tea-break and we were getting a little worried when I turned round and saw her staggering in with a cup of black liquid. She was wearing a long velvety black dress.'[3]

Brophy read from her text and to begin with was not always audible. But she held attention because she had tailored the text to the audience:

> Fiction is immensely valuable but, precisely, useless [. . .] Fiction
> may have incidental and accidental consequences that are socially
> useful. For example, as everyone here well knows, Britain has the

largest public library service in the western world, and roughly 70 per cent of adult borrowing from public libraries is borrowing of fiction. In this country, therefore, fiction clearly has an admirable spin-off effect, in that it provides a livelihood for quite large numbers of public librarians. [*Much laughter.*]

Brophy also dealt with the similarities that both the librarian and the fiction reviewer, such as herself, shared in cataloguing or classifying serious fiction:

> John Dixon has written amusingly and ironically about the sheer absence in fiction for the cataloguer's teeth to bite on. [. . .] The addicts of category novels will make their own way to the western or crime shelves. There is nothing a librarian can do for a borrower who simply wants a good read. (It's hard to imagine one who wants a bad read – or should I perhaps amend, who knowingly wants a bad read.) Indeed, general fiction is infuriating in the impossibility of classifying or (I speak now as a reviewer) sensibly describing it [. . .]
>
> Novelists and librarians alike must resign themselves to the truth that fiction is useless for all direct practical, social or moral purposes – that is every inch as useless as, say, string quartets and symphonies. In other words, the stuff can be defended only on the grounds that it is an art form. And defended it still has to be.

In her defence of fiction, she took particular issue with dating the first novels to the 1740s, and went back via key works to mythology – 'which is only old fiction of anonymous authorship'. She touched on other lines of defence that she had used in several previous works. Brophy rounded off with the publishing crisis that had particularly hit the novel, and the balance between hardback and paperback, and also the range of titles: 'In this situation, the future of creative literature in English may well lie in the lap of public libraries – a lap that is itself being squeezed for funds, indeed, corseted.' There were a few questions after she had finished her talk, and then the other three speakers came back for a general discussion. Brophy made telling points and showed that not just in the presentation of a paper, but in the cut and thrust of debate, she was a formidable performer.

At the end of the conference we went to get a taxi for her. It took an inordinate amount of time to arrive, during which she smoked a couple of cigarettes. She was all courtesy and gratitude, and later sent a card of thanks. Her agent, Giles Gordon, wrote in his obituary of Brophy: 'She raised the level of the thank-you letter to a minor art form.'[4] Our card read: 'Congratulations on yesterday's success for fiction. May I ask you to tell my taxi-procurer, whose address I don't know, how touched I was on reaching home to find that he had pre-paid for my journey?'[5] The texts of the conference speeches were collected and printed by the Association of Assistant Librarians in a publication called *Fiction Papers One*.[6] It included a few reviews and replies that we had received from a questionnaire sent to current and previous arts ministers about their readings habits. In fact, though we collected further material, a *Fiction Papers Two* never materialised.

It did, however, spawn another course, this time more geared to local and demographic circumstances. In Tower Hamlets there was a large elderly population, who relied on large print books. We circulated titles and took them to old people's home, including the largest, which was evocatively known as Mount Everest. The range of titles was very limited: out-of-copyright standard light fiction authors of yesteryear, romances, westerns, costume historical and a couple of non-fiction titles. There was a distinct need to spur the publishers. Other publishers at that time – Virago, Women's Press, Gay Men's Press – had begun to issue women's/gay classics. (Gay Men's Press, in 1987, would reissue a revised edition of Brophy's 1963 novel *The Finishing Touch*.) There seemed no reason why Large Print publishers should not search out older titles, and negotiate new ones. The one-day conference was held in March 1984 at Holborn Library and led to several radio interviews, including one on the LBC programme *Sight and Sound*, for the partially sighted and hard of hearing.

In the wake of the publicity and the final acceptance of PLR (for which Brophy wrote the standard handbook), I was commissioned by the Library Association (not just the *Assistant Librarian* now!) to edit a book on fiction in their series Handbooks on Library Practice. This was completed in 1986 and was well reviewed. For a time, with a greater awareness among librarians about the importance of fiction, and the imaginative reissue of titles from smaller, independent publishers, it did seem that there was cause for some optimism. And though forty years later the situation in libraries, publishing and the ability of authors to get published may have hit a new low, the reissue of Brophy's talk to a wider audience is not untimely. It may not add a great deal to what she had already written over a string of works, but it is a good introduction to her thoughts on fiction and the world of books.

## Notes

1. John Dixon, 'Book Selection', *Assistant Librarian*, 73.6 (1980), pp. 82–7.
2. Brigid Brophy, 'The Rights of Animals', in *Reads* (London: Sphere, 1989), pp. 123–34 (p. 131).
3. John Dixon, unpublished diaries, 1 October 1980.
4. Giles Gordon, 'Obituary: Brigid Brophy', *Independent*, 8 August 1995.
5. Postcard from Brophy in the possession of Rodney Hill.
6. Brophy's talk first appeared in 'A Writer's View', in *Fiction Papers One: The Librarian and the Novel* (AALSED, 1981), compiled and with an introduction by John Dixon, based on papers given at an AALSED day school on 1 October 1980, at Holborn Library.

Chapter 4

# The Librarian and the Novel: A Writer's View

*Brigid Brophy*

*A transcript of a talk given by Brigid Brophy at a day school organised by the Association of Assistant Librarians on 1 October 1980.*

I read last summer in a magazine a review of a volume of stories by Patricia Highsmith. It's a volume (*The Animal-Lover's Book of Beastly Murder*) that I think an absolute marvel. So, as a matter of fact, did the review. Yet I finished reading it with a sense that I and the review were at cross purposes. It rounded off its many paragraphs of praise with a sentence it obviously thought to be the ultimate in laudation: 'This', it declared, 'is the first fiction book I've read for years that isn't useless.'

On and off I've been wondering ever since what 'use' the reviewer found in that volume of fiction and had hoped but failed to find in other volumes of fiction. My own view is that fiction is immensely valuable but, precisely, useless – even when it's fiction by Patricia Highsmith. That is not to deny, of course, that fiction may have incidental and accidental consequences that are socially useful. As everyone here well knows, Britain has the largest public library service in the western world, and roughly 70 per cent of adult borrowing from public libraries is borrowing of fiction. In this country, therefore, fiction clearly has an admirable spin-off effect, in that it provides a livelihood for quite large numbers of public librarians. Alas, it is only in very few and very exceptional cases that it does as much for the writers of the fiction.

I fear, however, that neither librarians nor novelists can flatter themselves that theirs are among the obviously useful professions such as medicine or street-sweeping. Librarians may sometimes be able to make the claim about the 30 per cent of adult borrowing that concerns non-fiction, especially of course when the librarian acts as a computer dating service in bringing the borrower and the right non-fiction book together. If you direct a reader to the map he needs in his researches, you have done an intellectual equivalent of the kindness you do when you give a stranger directions in the street. If you direct a reader to a DIY book on building rabbit hutches, you have probably been instrumental in performing a kindness to animals. It is of course true that Colonel Smithers may be researching into local history only in order to write the dullest conceivable account of the totally undistinguished Smithers family; and Mrs Smithers may be consulting all those books on ancient Egypt only in order to lend colour to her patently bogus claim that in an earlier incarnation she was a pharaoh's concubine. However, the rather smugly named caring professions are rightly not held responsible for ultimate results. It is my doctor's duty to help me recuperate after 'flu, even if I then use my newly recruited strength to beat up my husband.

It would not surprise me if librarians feel that the fiction books under their wing rather deprive them of their sense of doing a public service. John Dixon has written amusingly and ironically in the *Assistant Librarian* about the sheer absence in fiction of anything for the cataloguer's teeth to bite on; and I think the teeth of the caring professions must find the stuff equally mishmashy. The addict of category novels will make his own way to the western or the crime shelves; and there is nothing a librarian can do for a borrower who simply wants a good read. (It's hard to imagine one who wants a *bad* read – or, I should perhaps amend, who knowingly wants a bad read.) Indeed, general fiction is infuriating in the impossibility of classifying it or even (I speak now as a reviewer) sensibly describing it. 'Do you like novels about broken marriages?' is strictly a meaningless question, which can elicit only the strictly non-significant answer 'Well, I like *some* novels about broken marriages.' The same is true of 'Do you like novels written in short sentences?' Neither content nor style offers enough opportunity for precision to serve even subjectively as a classification. Often, it seems, the only way a reader can get any sort of order into the appalling generality of general fiction is to fall back on using the author as a brand name. And that, I suppose, is why so many of the writers most honoured (CBE and upwards) in contemporary Britain are those with the knack of producing, once a year, over decades, a rewrite of their first novel. It's like plonk that's sold under a brand name. It saves you bothering with districts and vintages. You can be sure of getting the same flavour each time you buy a bottle – even if it isn't, as a matter of fact, a flavour you much liked in the first place.

Alas, I don't think that librarians or novelists can compensate themselves for this specific awkwardness in the nature of fiction by the argument that, in providing the citizenry with fiction at large, they are providing people with something that does them good. Much energy has been spent on claims that one specialised category of fiction, pornography, tends to deprave and corrupt its readers without anyone's managing to produce an irrefutable instance of an obviously depraved and corrupt person who would demonstrably not have been any such thing had he never read a word of pornography. The related proposition, that reading great literature has an 'ennobling effect' on the reader, has had a shorter run in vogue. It was last put forward (in, I think, 1970) by President Nixon, and I suppose a shadow that later fell over the ennobling effect on his own character may have deterred the theorists. I can't believe, however, they would have had any better success at producing ennobled characters than the deprave-and-corrupt school have had at producing corrupted ones. I have been intimate with two or three addicts of great literature (all of whom are, incidentally, also addicts of lesser literature). Their addiction has certainly made their conversation more interesting than it would otherwise have been – at least to my ears, but then I'm an addict, too. But I cannot detect any ennobling effect either in their character or in my own – apart, that is, from any nobility that might have been there in any case.

I am afraid that novelists and librarians alike must resign themselves to the truth that fiction is useless for all direct practical, social or moral purposes – that it is every inch as useless as, say, string quartets and symphonies. In other words, the stuff can be defended only on the grounds that it's an art form. And defended the stuff still has to be. I say 'still' because 162 years have passed since the (posthumous) first publication of the novel in which Jane Austen defended novels in one of the great virtuoso passages of English prose and tore satirically into the hypocrisy of the reader who devours a novel but, when asked what she is reading, replies 'Oh! it is only a novel' and lays it down 'with affected indifference or momentary shame'.

The shame of being caught – or indeed catching oneself – enjoying a novel is still a commonplace of British intellectual life, though most people are perfectly content to be caught enjoying a violin concerto. When you surrender to a novel, you are entertaining a series of what look like truthful factual statements which, however, you know not to be true and which the author is not trying to deceive you into supposing true. To the literal minded or to puritans it is as though you deliberately let yourself be gulled by a lie or set yourself to be lulled by a daydream. As a matter of fact, a sequence such as treble A F C F (new bar) A G F G C is not *true* either. But music has the advantage that, though you can't say it's true, neither can you say it's false – whereas the very word 'fiction' is cognate with 'figment' and 'to feign'.

Although music has had a rough ride from the puritans at various times in Western history, and is still having one in some sections of Islam (I learned from a recent article in *The Guardian* that the present regime in Iran is trying to reinstate the old ban on secular music), the general modern Western attitude to music is that listening to it is a rather laudable activity – provided, of course, that it is 'serious' music, a purely technical term that means, except in the case of Anton Webern, that it goes on for longer in one piece than non-serious music. Indeed, there is more than a touch of reverence in our official establishment attitude to music, a suggestion that music is somehow slightly *more* than an art – which is of course the most philistine suggestion that can be made.

Modern respect for serious music owes not everything but much to the invention of radio and the need to fill long stretches of air time. I have always suspected that the sanctification of music was bestowed on it personally by Lord Reith. Of course, now that television has become dominant, some desanctification is to be expected. Perhaps the BBC was beginning to let the halo round music go crinkly at the edges when it began to disband orchestras, which it wasn't wholly stopped doing by the Musicians' Union strike. But it is interesting and symptomatic that, during the high noon of radio, it was a musical education and musical opportunities that the BBC splendidly gave to the population of this country. I'm ever so glad it did. But the interesting fact remains that it never gave us anything comparable in relation to the art of fiction. True, it did and does bits. It developed radio drama – against the grain of radio, where you have to resort to technical ingenuity merely to indicate that a character has entered the room, whereas the voice of a reader on radio could, if it were used in an intimate instead of declamatory style, come close to impersonating the voice in one's head as one reads a work of fiction. That potentiality, however, was never developed. We have, we still (thank goodness) have, a radio channel on which we can listen almost continuously to serious music. We have no continuous, serious fiction channel. My own theory is that someone once put the idea to Lord Reith who, with the words 'Oh! you mean only a novel!', put the suggestion aside with affected indifference or momentary shame.

The belittlement implied by 'only a novel!' takes, as philistinism usually does, diverse forms. Indeed, I've come to realise that almost any fiction will be believed on the subject of fiction. Many people proclaim that, in this stressful and rushed modern world (they must be people who never have occasion to travel on the Southern Region) they haven't time to read fiction – which is very odd of them, because they must be implying that their reading speed is significantly lower for fiction than non-fiction.

This curious implication is, however, a nothing compared to the blatant but very common nonsense embodied in these two quotations: quote number one: – 'the more than 200 year history of the novel'; quote number two: – 'the advent of the novel in roughly 1740'. The first quote is from Susan Sontag, from an essay she published in 1961; if she was then thinking that 'the novel' was 'more than 200 years old' she was probably placing its inception at the same time, namely 'roughly 1740', as my second quotation, which is from Ruth Rendell.

My immediate thought, on reading that novels began in roughly 1740, was that the first part of *Don Quixote* was published in 1604, and if *Don Quixote* is not a novel nothing is a novel and the form doesn't exist. Moreover, it's a novel of that highly sophisticated and literary kind that reviewers often disparage as incestuous – that is, it is a work of fiction about the effects of being addicted to reading fiction. And indeed there were novels aplenty for the character Don Quixote to read well before Cervantes published the novel *Don Quixote* in 1604. Thomas Nashe's *Unfortunate Traveller* dates from 1594; Thomas Lodge's *Rosalynde*, to my taste a better novel, from 1590. I think one could legitimately claim Malory's *Morte d'Arthur* as a novel. Caxton printed it in 1485. True, Malory didn't make up the story, but neither did T. H. White, who used the same story in *The Once and Future King*, which Collins and Fontana classify as fiction. I confess I can't read Japanese, but on the strength of the two translations I've read I don't believe anyone could deny that Murasaki's *Tale of Genji* is a novel. It was written at an unknown date before 1015.

And indeed one can go further back still. Here is my third blatant poppycock quotation (source: – the main article on the arts page of *Tribune*, during January 1980): 'the novel – the one newly invented literary form since ancient times'. Simple rubbish. That very charming novel in very elegant Greek *Daphnis and Chloe* was written in the second or third century AD. It is a novel sophisticated enough to pretend to be naif. Indeed, it is a polished example of a form that was accepted and fairly common in ancient Greek literature; and if you consult the Loeb edition (which my Greek is now so rusty that I have to do), you find a scholarly appendix called 'Appendix on the Greek novel'.

At the very least, then, novels – prose fictions that admit they are fictions – are 1600 years old. How the hell do people get away with saying they are 200 years old and began in 1740? If I tried to state in print that gravitation was discovered and formulated during the later stages of the Roman Empire, which is a historical blunder of comparable size, the heavens, starting with the editor or publisher's editor to whom I sent my typescript, would fall on me. But you can get away with murder about novels, because they're not a serious subject, being of course 'only novels' and if you untruthfully make them out to be a recent and upstart form so much the better, because that gives hope that they will turn out to be only a temporary fad and will soon go away.

In the belittlement of novels, novelists, I am sad to say, have thrown in their contribution. Indeed, that is the launching pad for Jane Austen's flight of satire. The progress of the friendship in *Northanger Abbey* between Catherine Morland and Isabella Thorpe is recorded in terms of their reading novels together. It is from this that Jane Austen takes off into her denunciation of the 'ungenerous and impolitic' custom among novelists of scarcely allowing their heroines to glance at a novel ('Alas! if the heroine of one novel be not patronised by the heroine of another, from whom can she expect protection and regard?') and from that she proceeds to her injunction to her fellow novelists: 'Let us not desert one another; we are an injured body' – a virtuoso passage indeed, both in the rhetorical architecture that carries it to its crescendo and in its bursting out of the naturalistic convention, its admission that, for all its verisimilitude of manner, this novel which you are reading *is* a novel, with a novelist in control – a technical device, a distancing or alienation of the reader who suddenly has to look at the novel in perspective, of a kind that contemporary academic critics are in the habit of supposing unique to the literature of the twentieth century.

Alas, novelists of our own time have disregarded her injunction almost as often as critics of our own time have failed to notice her technique. I have not yet done with the quotation in which Ruth Rendell placed the 'advent of the novel' in the 1700s when she should have put it in the 300s and with a query even then. I am sorry to seem to ill-requite a novelist whose thrillers have given me much pleasure. But then it is precisely because I am a devotee of her oeuvre that

I have had occasion to notice that there is another mistaken idea about fiction which she puts, in various guises, into many of her works; she seems in the process of making it a trademark like Hitchcock's appearances in his own films. In the book that came first to my hand as I prepared this talk, *Make Death Love Me*, the idea I am talking about is embodied in a fictitious non-fiction book which the hero leafs through. Ruth Rendell at least permits herself and the reader some ambivalence of response, since her hero's comment is to think longingly of the many novels he has yet to read. First, however, he reads this bit of (supposedly) non-fiction:

> The real has been discarded by mankind as ugly and untenable, to be shunned and scorned in favour of a shadow land of fantasy [. . .] How has this come about? The cause is not hard to find. Society was not always sick, not always chasing mirages and creating chimeras. Before the advent of the novel, in roughly 1740, when vicarious living was first presented to man as a way of life, and fiction took the lid from the Pandora's box of fantasy, man had come to terms with reality, lived it and loved it.

The idea that vicarious living was first presented to man in 1740 is one of those that no one would entertain for an instant were they not to the detriment of fiction. If it were true, there would have been no audience for the Elizabethan theatre or indeed for the ancient Greek theatre. It is not humanly possible to sit through *Hamlet* without simultaneously living vicariously as Hamlet and suffering your mind to be temporarily taken over and occupied by Shakespeare's mind. Indeed, it is not possible to read *The Iliad* without living vicariously as Achilles and Helen and Hector and without seeing the world under the ironic and tragic construction Homer put on it, and the fact that he did so in hexameters rather than prose makes not a shred of difference to the psychological essence of what the reader does. For the matter of that, you were no doubt living vicariously when, as an ancient Greek peasant, you listened to the village storyteller recounting the myths. And indeed the Ruth Rendell passage refutes itself with its references to chimeras and Pandora's box. People have been living vicariously for millennia through the story of how Glaukos was sent to kill the monster that was one third each lion, goat and dragon, and through the story of Zeus having Pandora made out of clay and despatched to plague Epimetheus. Mythology is only old fiction of anonymous authorship.

Fantasy is the raw material of all creative literary arts, including drama and poetry – which of course *are* fiction, a fact that shouldn't be obscured by our habit of giving them separate names, which is a matter of convenience justified by the fact that they use conspicuously different technical means. It is possible that if we habitually mentioned the fact that *Paradise Lost* is fiction too, people would find it less easy to disparage novels – though on second thoughts, no; people who can be intellectually condescending to Thackeray and Henry James could condescend to anything.

As a matter of fact, if I give myself up to following certain rhythms and melodic lines and let my consciousness be taken over by Mozart's designs and structures, I am not for the time being living in my own person and facing the realities of my own situation. But unless it is a Mozart opera I have dived into, which is a literary as well as a musical experience, you can't quite accuse me of living vicariously. Musical inventions are fantasies; they don't mirror or report anything previously existing in reality; but they are not fantasies whose content consists of the feelings, thoughts, words and deeds of people. All the arts provoke the puritans, because they give and often openly profess to give pleasure, though it is usually pleasure of that paradoxical kind that Aristotle diagnosed in the case of tragedy, whereby one seeks in art the things one tries hardest to avoid in one's own real life, such as having one's heart broken or suffering that stab of total betrayal that you feel when a writer puts the knife in and delivers a stroke of consummate irony. But the literary arts provoke the puritans in a particular way because they have dramatis personae about whom they present a continuous texture of episodes. The source of the shame people feel when they are caught reading a novel is, I think, that a novel has a strong textural resemblance to those shaming things we have all had, though we may not admit to having had one since the age of six, namely daydreams, whether of the erotic variety or the even more shaming vainglorious kind.

The formal resemblance to a daydream is shared by novels, plays and poems. However, a poem has to seem more clever than a novel; it has to manipulate repetitive rhythm and perhaps also rhyme, and so it has an element of intellectual puzzle that holds the reader at an admiring distance. A poem can't even *seem*, as a novel can, to flow as effortlessly and self-indulgently as a daydream. With a play (except, perhaps, when it's on television) or a film, at least there are other people present in the audience. But a novel – apart from the nineteenth-century habit of family reading aloud, which had less to do with the nature of novels or even families than with the cost of providing artificial light for more than one person to read by in the evenings – a novel excludes sociability and is designed for you to shut yourself up with it alone in your reading head, and is thus instantly identifiable by puritans as a form of solitary vice.

In fact, reading a novel or indeed writing one is an infinitely more complex act than having a daydream in which you, the author and the audience, are always the hero and get lots of sex or glory or both. The most perfunctory novel needs more intellectual structure than a daydream and has to be more careful about plausibility; and the fantasy comes from a much deeper level of the novelist's mind. Indeed, many novels are less like daydreams than like real dreams, the involuntary kind we have during sleep, in that they present unconscious fantasy fairly naked in an atmosphere of pure surrealism. I am thinking not only of supposedly esoteric and avant-garde novels of the last few decades but also of a very pop surreal novel, *Alice in Wonderland*. To some extent every novel pits the fantasy content against the requirements of the design, and I suppose the very best novels, those of Jane Austen for instance, are the ones where the most irrepressible invention is matched against the utmost intellectual severity of the structure.

I have, you will notice, let fall a value judgement. When I say Jane Austen's are the best novels, the statement is, needless to say, qualified by 'in my opinion'. And I would like to speak about opinions in the context of fantasy. Fantasy is the raw material not only of the creative arts but of all creative thought. A theory or a hypothesis is simply a fantasy. If I observe the iron filings lying inert in the test tube and I am a creative scientist, my mind will come up with dozens of fantasy hypotheses about why this might be: the filings have been a mere catalyst in another chemical reaction; they have accidentally been bombarded by zeta-eta-theta rays, etc., etc., in very much the same fertile and frequently frivolous way that the novelist comes up with ideas for ending the novel that he's taken as far as the last-but-one chapter. The difference lies in the way you test the two sorts of fantasy. The scientist tests whether his will work in the real world. He weighs the iron filings; actually, they weigh less now than they did at the start of the operation: discard hypothesis A, devise (again calling on fantasy) a method of testing hypotheses B, C, D, etc. The novelist can't test against reality. He can only test whether the thing works in the structure of the novel he is writing. If I have my character Peter run over by a bus half way through Part Three, have I introduced this evidence of a random and rather nasty universe too soon for it to continue to echo into the last chapter or is Part Three going at such a pace that I can afford to put it in a third of the way through, but if I do will it fail to make a symmetry with Peter's thoughts on the subject of buses half way through Part One?

In judging where Peter's accident will work best, most economically, most towards unifying the whole book, I have nothing to rely on except my own opinion. When writers remark on what a lonely job writing is, I think they really mean that they are constantly having to take decisions about which no external criterion can help them. And then of course the reader has nothing to rely on except *his* judgement, and he is quite likely to say to the writer 'I went along with you all the way until you had Peter killed by that bus. I thought that was a real cop-out as a method of getting rid of a character.'

As between scientific hypothesis A and scientific hypothesis B, decision is possible and provable. In practice, I may not be able to follow the subtlety of the scientist's logic, or his logic may be wrong, but he and I agree that there is a correct answer. Even if hypothesis A, B, C, D, etc. all fall to the ground, one day someone's fantasy will come up with a hypothesis that will be correct and proved correct. But between my judgement and my reader's judgement of what works in my novel there's no arbitrating. Naturally everyone believes in his secret heart that he has absolute taste and an unerring artistic eye, though when I notice how some of my error-proof artistic judgements have altered over the years I experience a little doubt about my infallibility; at least, I can't have been infallible over the whole course of my aesthetic existence, but if two aesthetic beings are to continue on speaking terms with each other they must from time to time beg each other to remember that either or both might be mistaken.

And that, I think, we must all do doubly in the present crisis of publishing. As you know, fiction, although it is such a popular category with library borrowers, has been particularly stringently squeezed in the crisis. Its economics have been distorted, even though British publishers traditionally keep the hardback price of fiction down to just below two-thirds of the average hardback price. I have never known quite how to interpret this tradition: is it that publishers think fiction so popular that it can be sold on a massive scale or is it that they think public librarians despise it so utterly that they won't buy it at all unless tempted by getting it cheap? Either way, the result from the writer's point of view is the same: since your royalty is a percentage of the published price, fiction writers who don't sell massively, which is of course the huge majority, are even worse off than non-fiction writers who to the same extent don't sell massively – always supposing, that is, that the fiction writer's work is published at all, the chances of which get smaller and smaller month by month as the crisis darkens.

People with a feel for a coming crisis knew there was a disturbance about ten years ago when novels that previously would have gone into paperback without hesitation suddenly stopped doing so, and the paperback publishers began ordaining larger and larger numbers of thousands as the sale they must be able to count on before taking on a title. Thus the range of fiction titles, the sheer variety of types of novel, was narrowed in paperback, which presently caused it to be narrowed in hardback too; and now, of course, the narrowing of types available is threatening to reach bootlace proportions.

Where fiction is concerned, and I am not sure that this is true of non-fiction, it is, if I may exert my faculty for value judgements again, the better novels that are squeezed out first if they haven't an established brand name author to protect them. Five years ago publishers were still boasting that there were no literary masterpieces floating the rounds unable to find a publisher. It was only just true then. It was true only in the sense that some very good novels floated around and ended up with perfectly honourable publishers whom, however, no one, including booksellers, had ever heard of, who paid the author an advance of £100 and never sold enough copies to show royalties. Now the boast isn't true even to that extent. Even with my limited, one-person field of vision I know of one masterly typescript, by an already established and much-praised writer, that has been for some months seeking a publisher in vain. I know established novelists who are realistically, not paranoidly, anxious about their publishing future, let alone their chances of living off their work if it is published; and I suspect I know some who, being versatile enough to have choice in the matter, are practising self-censorship and writing less well but more saleably than they could.

In this situation, the future of creative literature in English may well lie in the lap of public libraries – a lap that is itself being squeezed for funds, indeed corseted. You will not be surprised that I want to plead for public librarians to go on buying fiction and, in particular, to go on buying over the whole range, narrowed though it has already been, that publishers make available. During the PLR campaign an MP remarked to me that he was wholly in favour of PLR, he agreed with me that it should be paid on fiction and non-fiction alike, but he also thought it should be paid only on good books in both categories; as he talked on, it slowly became clear to me that he really and seriously thought that telling a good book from a bad book was as simple as telling a green binding from an orange one.

Librarians and even reviewers are not so unsophisticated. But there are two relevancies of which we all need reminding. One is that, if we are to have a literature, if we are to have a literary culture, we need bad books as well as good books. This is partly because everyone *begins* on bad books, as Sartre pointed out in his autobiography; it is also a little because even readers of undeflectably highbrow tastes, including myself and including Jean-Paul Sartre, maintain into their adult lives a liking for books they would never judge good; but it is mainly because that is the way art works. You don't get the plays of Shakespeare suddenly springing up pure and virgin out of nothing. You get a crowded Elizabethan theatre with dozens of quite appalling, sensational, blood-and-thunder revenge plays and dozens of tedious chronicle plays – huge numbers of which Shakespeare had evidently swallowed whole and large chunks of which, by way of plot or language or theatrical device, he pinched for his own work.

Again, Mozart's letters demonstrate that whenever he got the chance he went to the opera night after night, lapping up work after work by composers contemporary with him whose very names are now obscure. His own operas are the pinnacle on a solid mass of eighteenth-century operatic work, much of which entertained him, much of which he thought dross, much or more of which we should probably think dross nowadays – or we might not; we are not given the opportunity to see and hear them staged. And that is my second point. Each of us probably has the self-knowledge to recognise that his taste is not truly infallible – or at least he knows it can't be proved infallible. But I think we need to remember that the consensus of informed opinion is not infallible either. It is not necessarily true that the only novels worth reading in Britain today are those judged worthy of review by the editor of the *TLS* or – I will go further – even by the editor of the *London Review of Books*. There is one true moral fable that should be taken to heart and made a talisman by everyone who has professionally to choose between one work of art and another and by everyone who consults or helps to form the consensus of artistic opinion. There was once a Florentine painter whose work nobody bothered to look at seriously for 300 years because the consensus of informed opinion, of those most knowledgeable about and most sensitive to the art, agreed that his work was not worth looking at. His name is Botticelli.

# Chapter 5

# Penetrating (the) *Prancing Novelist*

## *Richard Canning*

This critical pursuit of the queer modernist Ronald Firbank (1886–1926) focuses on the neglected play *The Princess Zoubaroff* (1920), but is equally a reflective account of writing on Firbank in the wake of Brigid Brophy's achievements.[1] Almost exclusively among his critics, Brophy not only recognised this play's significance in relation to Firbank's wider importance, but she traced it through many inspired close readings and often provocative biographical and contextual references. In her unique approach to biographical-critical literary studies, *Prancing Novelist: A Defence of Fiction in the Form of a Critical Biography in Praise of Ronald Firbank* (1973; hereafter *PN*), Brophy deftly pursued her subject, exposing his creative instincts, formal methods and literary resourcefulness.[2] She equally – often acidly – reacted to the very different perspectives of her predecessor Miriam Benkovitz's *Ronald Firbank: A Biography* (1969).[3]

The digital age offers the twenty-first-century literary critical biographer almost limitless opportunity to review Brophy's critical judgements, and to revisit both these and the 'Brophyan method' – sometimes extending these further; sometimes subjecting them to critique or restraint. This essay strongly defends Brophy's radical, ingenious 'defence of fiction in the form of a critical biography' of Firbank, celebrating her approach while simultaneously complementing her findings and – occasionally – querying them. New findings, however, are always secured on the back of Brophy's industry, and by way of my co-option of distinctly 'Brophyan' methods.

'Pursuing' Firbank and 'penetrating' his works necessitates scrutiny of *PN* – unquestionably Brophy's greatest non-fictional publication, as celebrated in Peter Parker's 1995 essay '"Aggressive, Witty and Unrelenting": Brigid Brophy and Ronald Firbank'.[4] For the critic and biographer of Firbank, the pursuit is akin to riding in a sidecar, with Brophy in the saddle. Overwhelmingly the speed and forceful directedness of Brophy as critic-biographer motorcyclist proves invigorating. On rarer occasions it can frustrate, as false leads are pursued, the occasional wrong turn is taken, and a few vital pathways are neglected. The near-limitless purview afforded today by the internet was unavailable to Brophy and offers near-infinite opportunity – and some hazard, too – for the twenty-first-century critical biographer of Firbank, who perforce writes in the shadow of Brigid Brophy.

This opportunity-cum-hazard is yet more pronounced concerning *The Princess Zoubaroff* (hereafter *TPZ*), a work about which almost nothing perceptive has ever been written except by Brophy. She alone perceived *TPZ*'s importance not only to our understanding of Firbank's oeuvre, but to much else besides, including the legacies of William Congreve, Oscar Wilde and George Bernard Shaw. 'Penetrating' *TPZ* – and, by proxy, its implied author – was something that Brophy's intelligence and insight left her uniquely capable of attempting. Paradoxically it was something that her forceful personality also made very slightly impossible. Like all biographers, Brophy shaped her subject to taste. Nonetheless, nobody has got nearer to Firbank's design or intention. This essay proceeds from Brophy's strengths, pursuing them still further. Just rarely, it imitates a Brophyan stubbornness, insisting on a different pursuit of Firbank's cryptic legacy. I 'penetrate' *TPZ* to comparable ends, then, and only occasionally through different means. This essay's findings stand firmly on the shoulders of Brophy, unquestioningly an undervalued literary-critical biographical giant.

Those pursuing Firbank or Brophy must take acute methodological risks. Brophy was brilliantly prepared to do so in her genre-begetting *PN*. When its own reviewers failed to understand that work's achievements, she experienced herself Firbank's crucifying sense of being neglected.[5] For *PN* is a book quite unlike any other author's, and its dazzling originality is just what its subject might savour. In it, Brophy comes across as brilliant, driven and obsessive – the very qualities she most identified in Firbank. Her deepest admiration for this neglected queer modernist had already generated one ripe fruit: Brophy's 'novel in a superficially Firbankian idiom', *The Finishing Touch* (1962/1987), which, in initial and revised forms, preceded *and* succeeded *PN*.[6] *The Finishing Touch* relates the travails of an English princess attending a French finishing school managed by a lesbian couple; it was as evidently spun from Firbank's oeuvre as his own books were from one another. Each Firbank fruit involved him 'restaging' or 'remounting' several preceding ones. Analogies to both the theatre and the visual arts are apt, since arguably both Firbank and Brophy took as much from dramatists and painters as from other prose writers. Firbank's creative method not only glanced at theatrical modes of writing and visual modes of representation but co-opted them loosely to his chosen form: the novel, but more precisely the *Firbankian novel*. Brophy traces this process of recasting and rethinking across *PN*'s near six hundred pages.

The fact that her revised version of *The Finishing Touch* appeared in the Gay Men's Press list – alongside that other classic *In Transit* (1969) – saw her own career channelling Firbank's.[7] His pursuit of Sapphic themes and same-sex inclinations was, and remains, an unequalled act of creative, cross-gendered, Anglophone writing. Brophy's two novels, meanwhile, strayed on to a gay male fiction list; something Firbank's obviously could never have achieved. Her Firbank, nonetheless, is a trailblazer, not only swapping genders, sexualities, ethnicities, nationalities and more, but effectively founding an impostor-canon of lesbian-themed works, penned by a queer man writing as the womanish 'Ronald Firbank'. (To his mother and sister alone he remained 'Artie', the diminutive of Arthur.)

*TPZ*'s plot will hardly be familiar.[8] A newly married couple, Eric and Enid Tresilian, visit another young married couple, Adrian and Nadine Sheil-Meyer, at their villa outside Florence. Enid, remarkably disappointed in marriage, encourages her husband to visit the Swiss Engadine valley with school chum Adrian. Nadine suddenly admits that she is pregnant; she gives birth offstage. Act II sees both women recruited by the Russian Princess Zoubaroff – whose first name Zena is concealed in the *Dramatis personae* – to retreat to a Sapphic-sounding convent (her villa). Adrian and Nadine's baby boy is left in their Scottish nurse's care. The men stay away longer than envisaged; rumours reach their wives that their husbands may have been killed mountaineering. They seem indifferent. Act III has the men unexpectedly return – finding, with relief, that their wives are preparing to join Zoubaroff's convent community. The nurse resigns, leaving the baby with his father, who does not even know his son's name. Adrian nonetheless reflects on which school to send him to, taking advice from Lord Henry Orkish, a shady figure, haunting proceedings alongside his younger consort Reggie Quintus. Other *personae* include Lady Rocktower and the author Mrs Blanche Negress (Firbank's veiled self-portrait).

This dazzling, scarcely penetrable work is brilliantly analysed by Brophy.[9] Its fundamental intent she fully grasped: to push still farther than Firbank's four mature novels had towards openly proclaiming same-sex relations as more congenial and enduring than heterosexual ones. Brophy sees a 'transvestism of the imagination' turning him into a queer author*ess* in the wake of Wilde's downfall.[10] By describing love between women, Firbank and his *personae* at a pen-stroke reach a place of greater safety than that afforded to British men, since same-sex affairs between women were scandalous rather than illegal.

Why turn from the 'dialogic novel' which constituted Firbank's mature style in *Vainglory* (1915), *Inclinations* (1916), *Caprice* (1917) and *Valmouth* (1919)? Brophy argues winningly that Firbank never stopped writing plays: these novels, with their innovations in dialogue, (anti-)plot structuration and spectacle, remained, in part, unstaged, unstageable dramas.[11] By turning what were play-like things full of poetry into novels – though they were symphony-like too, containing secret messages in a previously unheard polyphony – Firbank destabilised generic boundaries. He did to his own writing what Ezra Pound would do to T. S. Eliot's *The Waste Land* in 1921–22, or what W. B. Yeats would do – in his *Oxford Book of Modern Verse, 1892–1935* (1936) – to Walter Pater's study of Leonardo's *La Gioconda* in *The Renaissance* (1873). In this anthology, Yeats described how the 'free verse' version of Pater's words he created through line breaks alerted us to the 'revolutionary importance' of Pater's message, which risked being ignored as prose.[12] This is helpful, even if, frustratingly, Brophy makes only passing mention of Pater and ignores Yeats entirely in her study – though Firbank was steeped in both writers' works.

For Brophy, Firbank's choice of the theatrical genre for *TPZ* was not business-as-usual either. It enabled him, for the first and only time, to write polemically:

> In *The Princess Zoubaroff* alone, Firbank is openly socially prescriptive, though his prescription for society has to be read only in the play's design, not in its speeches. The design is for happy homosexuality. Two married couples part and take up homosexuality. The play even answers, quite in non-fiction terms, the social question of what homosexual people should do about parenthood.[13]

She argues persuasively that Firbank's haunting by Wilde's downfall led him to pose a simple (childish?) question: might the Irishman's tragedy have been avoided, had he been female? She then suggests a literal embodiment of the imaginary, 'non-Wilde' author*ess*: the lesbian poet Renée Vivien.[14] Little discussed in Anglophone contexts in the 1970s, Vivien secures a passing but very trenchant mention in *PN*. Nowadays, I argue, her relevance to Firbank's play is much clearer.[15] But Brophy provided the critical link. The British-American Pauline Mary Tarn (later Renée Vivien), born in 1877, was raised in both England and France. She was groomed to become a genteel English lady in 1893 in Chislehurst – just down the road from young 'Artie' Firbank, then seven, whose family lived at The Coopers.[16] This childhood home's extensive garden was always the model for the Eden out of which Firbank's fictional *personae* are cast.

Vivien subsequently rebelled, running away to Paris aged 21 on inheriting her father's fortune. By this time Wilde, in stark contrast, was in Italy in exiled decline, also self-reinvented – as 'Sebastian Melmoth' – but miserably destitute. Vivien's escape and self-reinvention caused family scandal, reverberating in Chislehurst itself, but nothing criminal had occurred. Reinvented as a French expert on and translator of Sappho, she became the sometime lover of the notorious American heiress Natalie Clifford Barney. Barney and Vivien pursued their Greek predecessor, travelling to Lesbos in 1904, where they fantasised over establishing a community of young Sapphic devotees. This is a partial inspiration, I argue, for *TPZ*, even if the play had – superficially – to describe its own women's devotions more spiritually. In Mytilene Vivien translated Sappho, while Barney read aloud her own Sapphic verse which advocated open sexual relations. Barney practised the free love she preached – to Vivien's despair. One phrase from her volume *Éparpillements* (*Scatterings*, 1910) especially resonates in terms of *TPZ*'s plot: 'To be married is to be neither alone nor together.'[17] Firbank's wives and husbands experience the literal and dramatic truth of this.

Both Vivien and Barney wrote a play about Sappho. Barney's, *Equivoque* (*Ambiguity*), revised the usual account of its subject's death, making her suicidal leap the result of thwarted same-sex passion. Performed in her garden in Neuilly in 1909 and published shortly afterwards, it caused a local scandal, forcing Barney to move home. It is very probable – though dependent on how much Firbank heard of Paris's Sapphists when he lived there in 1911; whether through the queer actor Edouard De Max, or De Max's acolyte Jean Cocteau – that this precedent inspired *TPZ*, another play entirely garden-bound in which lesbian passions hold sway. Barney's exodus from Neuilly to central Paris, meanwhile, seemingly suggested to Firbank his own 'casting out' from The Coopers in 1907 – the result of his father running out of money. The Firbanks moved to a series of modest flats in central London.[18]

Other congruities between Firbank and Barney/Vivien may be coincidental but are striking. All three travelled widely – in Egypt particularly, and across Mediterranean Europe – in the same years. Vivien was obsessed with the colour and flower violet, the name of an unrequited childhood crush. Firbank's novels are crammed with violets. Barney's salon included the author Colette, with whom she had an affair, and Gertrude Stein, with whom she had a great rivalry. Stein later promoted Firbank to anyone who would listen – including Ernest Hemingway. Barney also knew Marcel Proust and James Joyce – peers of Firbank whom he may neither have met or read, but about whom he was well informed. As a child, Barney had even met Wilde; Firbank's pursuit of anyone 'Wilde-related' is legendary, though as an author he is entirely misunderstood when classified as himself backward-looking, recherché or 'Wildean'. Firbank was firmly modernist, as Brophy's *PN* illustrates throughout. His Wilde obsession involved wanting to impress the dead author, wanting to become him (but better) and wanting to outdo him as a queer author (no contest). Firbank, a generous acolyte, paid tribute to the nearness with which Wilde had come to becoming a queer writer. But if Wilde was a failed dandy – reverting invariably to dandyism's opposites, aestheticism, sensualism and consumerism – Firbank was the reconstructed Wilde as dandy supreme: more chaste, reclusive, remote and quieter than the Irishman, Firbank was, critically, queer in mind alone, and thus unruffled by societal stigma or legal sanction.

Brophy's *PN* understands the strength of Firbank's pursuit of Wilde but does not always stress strongly enough just *how* post-Wildean Firbank was. In childhood, his Anglo-Irish mother – 'Baba' – almost certainly read him Wilde's fairy stories; Firbank certainly knew all Wilde's mother's writings too. In adolescence, Wilde would have loomed as the oppressed/oppressive queer martyr, destroyed through the English courts which Firbank's father, Thomas, as a Tory MP, indirectly represented. At Cambridge, Firbank studied alongside and immediately befriended Wilde's son, Vyvyan Holland. After the misfired work of juvenilia *Odette* (1905), Firbank repeatedly wrote of both Wilde and Wildean themes and *personae*. However, just as his most revered artists Paul Cézanne and Henri Matisse were made possible by the Impressionists, but transcended their example, so too Firbank's mature style challenged Wilde's symbolist and aestheticist tenets, or 'made them new'. Where Wilde's prose eddied and meandered, Firbank's was endlessly slashed, reduced, compressed. The same process befell *TPZ*. Consequently 'Firbankian stylistics' were truly first seen in Firbank – though co-opted (or copied) by others, including Stein, Hemingway, Aldous Huxley, P. G. Wodehouse, Henry Green, Anthony Powell and Evelyn Waugh. Few acknowledged the debt. Ultimately, it took two post-war Firbankians – Joe Orton and Brigid Brophy, both novelists-turned-playwrights too – to pay full and apt tribute.

*TPZ* is not about Sappho. Firbank glanced at others' writings but – like both Orton and Brophy – never 'borrowed' wholesale. *Vainglory* and *Inclinations* had given full vent to Sapphic pursuit anyway: literarily in the first novel, where a new line of Sappho is celebrated in London; figuratively in the second, in which Geraldine and Mabel's elopement to Greece conspicuously resembles that of Barney and Vivien. Indeed, Firbank surely did have in mind the twinned lives of Barney/Vivien, alongside the miserably contrasting ones of Wilde and his lover, Lord Alfred Douglas. For *TPZ* is not just an 'extension' of Wilde's greatest comedy *The Importance of Being Earnest* (1895), but also its re-envisioning, whereby queer desire is not indirectly suggested by subtext, but forces itself centre-stage. *TPZ* is Firbank's partial inversion of *Earnest*, but also its part-sequel. Brophy fully appreciated the play's part re-enactment of the Wilde–Douglas tragedy, but does not see quite its earnest – or Uranist – yet frivolous return to *Earnest*.[19]

*TPZ*, then, took the passion of the two Sapphists' efforts, joining it to Wilde's critical intelligence and wit. Wilde's wit obviously had its own antecedents, especially in William Congreve. Brophy argues that, in rewriting the Congrevan comedy of manners, Firbank arguably outperformed Wilde himself.[20] Congreve's *The Way of the World* (1700) is nominally invoked, since *TPZ* dramatises two lifestyles: the 'way of the world' inferentially and 'the Way of the Cross' literally; this phrase is precisely how Lord Orkish describes the women's retreat.[21] Firbank's next fiction, *Santal* (1921), equally dramatises a choice between worldly and spiritual pursuit, in an Islamic context. Again, Brophy alone has been equal to its achievement.

Regarding *TPZ*, Brophy mentions Shaw, whose *Heartbreak House* (1919) was first staged in November 1920.[22] For her, Shaw's play not only inspired Firbank to publish *TPZ* before a production (an ill-conceived move in Firbank's case) but informed the ethnicity of its titular hero, since *Heartbreak House* is 'A Fantasia in the Russian Manner on English Themes'. Here she comes unstuck, however: her desire to see another Shaw in Firbank looms over *Prancing Novelist*, making frequent but unconvincing intrusion. Princess Zena Zoubaroff's Russianness might reflect how steeped Firbank had been in Russian culture – seeing Anna Pavlova perform; attending a Gogol play. More obviously, it glances at the glinting influence of Firbank's adored *Ballets russes*, which he saw in London, Paris and beyond – or one of its semi-detached – and Sapphic – performers, the expatriate Ida Rubinstein. Rubinstein had starred in the doomed D'Annunzio–Debussy–Bakst–Fokine collaboration *Le Martyre de Saint Sébastien*, which glittered briefly in Paris in 1911 and which *Vainglory* shows Firbank had seen, as had the young T. S. Eliot.[23] From 1911 to 1914, Rubinstein was the lover of the American painter Romaine Brooks. When Brooks tired of Rubinstein, she moved on to Natalie Clifford Barney: a long-term, stable(ish), three-way relationship with Duchess Elisabeth de Gramont, writer and close friend of Proust, ensued.[24]

The precise source of Zoubaroff's ethnicity and surname, however, hides in plain sight. Remarkably Brophy missed it. 'Zena' is kin to Wilde's heroine in his tragic flop *Vera, or the Nihilists* (1880); Vera Sabouroff dies, saving Mother Russia. Perhaps we should aver that Zena is the *true* Vera: not just reanimated and rendered comic rather than tragic but destined for a happier ending than Wilde offered. Brophy only interprets 'Zoubaroff' charmingly as a faux-Russian rendering of 'exuberant'.[25] She is on safer ground with 'Zena', identifying the name with the ancient Athenian stoic Zeno; though this princess pays lip service to 'austerities' and 'Rules', she cannot stop herself straying quickly into very non-stoic behaviour.[26] This 'Zeno', however, is not the only fitting referent. Brophy fully understood Firbank's ability to superimpose multiple references on to a single *persona*, but she underestimated how far this went. For a stronger claim might be made for Verona's patron saint, San Zeno: Firbank had loitered in the wonderful Romanesque basilica he found there in 1912 (he sent a postcard to Baba); the crypt was allegedly where Romeo and Juliet married. *Caprice* had already retold that Shakespearean tragedy in queer, comic form.

The Veronese San Zeno was an African Christian, significantly, whose surviving *Sermons* feature extensive wordplay and neologism, two things Firbank loved and endlessly deployed.[27] Zeno advised on how adult baptism should take place (complete immersion only): a conspicuous connection to Wilde's *Earnest*. He is also the patron saint of newborn babies and toddlers. The sudden arrival of a baby is what propels *TPZ* into a second Act. Moreover, according to legend, Zeno was stolen at birth and replaced briefly by a changeling. We must hold the thought of disputed parentage just yet, but it will return.

First, another Saint Zeno, accompanied by a male Saint Zena. These are both Catholic and Orthodox saints; Firbank's habitual cross-gendering makes this Saint Zena the strongest 'begetter' of his own Zena Zoubaroff. Saint Zena (or Zenas) of Philadelphia was the inseparable companion of the martyr-saint Zeno. Formerly Zeno's slave, he chose, once released, to remain as Zeno's servant. Both saints were killed under Diocletian (whose name 'contains' Firbank's 'Enid', and almost 'Nadine' – more soon), when they proselytised their shared Christian faith.[28] Firbank's Princess Zena has extensive wealth – like this Saint Zeno (with his Zena) – which she shares with many others through the convent, as Zeno did with his many former slaves, including Zena. Like Saint Zeno, Firbank's Zena reflects both Christian devotion and a not-incompatible desire not to be separated from her beloveds.

But what if Firbank's Zena nodded back instead to his last novel *Valmouth*'s implicit Cornish setting? Firbank's 'Valmouth' is and is not Falmouth; whether he visited the county or not, his awareness of it was very extensive. It was most likely indebted to the Revd Sabine Baring-Gould's 1910 guidebook in the *Cambridge County Geographies* series, which would have alerted Firbank to the eighteenth- and nineteenth-century packet-ships which plied between the port and the West Indies.[29] The packet-ship history thus partly explains the presence of apparently West Indian *personae* in Valmouth.

Baring-Gould's guide also explains the geography of the county and mentions the church in the village of Zennor. Had Firbank heard of D. H. and Frieda Lawrence's stay in Zennor during the war? Frieda's German ethnicity made it essential they make themselves scarce, or go into retreat, like Firbank's women. Almost certainly he had. Firbank had been in Oxford, equally reclusive and seemingly never invited to Lady Ottoline Morrell's own Arcadia outside that city, Garsington Manor (unlike the Lawrences later). He was nonetheless pursued by Morrell's favourites, including Siegfried Sassoon, his lover Gabriel Atkin, Osbert and Sacheverell Sitwell, the poets Frank 'Toronto' Prewitt and Thomas Earp, and Vivian de Sola Pinto, who had fought alongside Sassoon in the trenches and developed an academic career specialising in Lawrence.[30] All these figures attended Firbank's only known reading of his work at Oxford's Golden Cross restaurant in February 1919: he read from the work-in-progress *Valmouth*.

Zennor's church, St Senara, meanwhile, is dedicated to the Cornish saint who miraculously and Firbankianly changed sex.[31] The first reference to 'Sanctus Sinar' in 1170 records a male saint. By 1235, and then onwards, 'Sancta Sinara' is female. From 'Sinar' – where we might also hear 'sinner' – is derived Zennor – pronounced locally as 'Zena'. In Firbank's allusions, the pronounced sound of a word is always a surer guide to its referent than spelling, not only because Firbank spelled poorly, but often because he made changes to disguise the 'signifieds' to his 'signifiers'. He was never obvious.

To illustrate the sustained connection between *TPZ* and Wilde's last comedy *Earnest*, rather than his first failure *Vera*, Firbank made a series of specific references which Brophy sadly missed. Its two married couples are reinventions of Wilde's Algernon/Cecily and Jack/Gwendolen, as they might become after *Earnest*, but all given new names and a new location, Florence. The theme of the disputed name which delays *Earnest*'s resolution is replicated in *TPZ*'s closing moments, but now involves Adrian's son. Wilde is partly present throughout, somewhat disguised as Lord Henry Orkish, who has, however, many other sources. Brophy does see that Orkish is a half-portrait of the Irishman as he might have been in (safe) Florence – as if he had neither been sentenced nor died; as if he had fled London as his friends urged before his arrest.[32] Although his Reggie Quintus bears the name of Reginald Turner (1869–1938) – Turner was the loyal friend who watched Wilde die, and still lived in Florence – he is a triple portrait, at least. In part, he is an embellished, very well-preserved representation of the *young* Lord Alfred Douglas (as opposed to the jowly and cantankerous 1920s Douglas), thus described in a stage direction as '*Incredibly young. Incredibly good-looking.*'[33] Brophy also sees Reggie Quintus as an informal version of 'Rex [Carolus] Quint[us]', since Charles V was not only Emperor but King of Spain.[34] This sends her winningly back to Firbank's only work of art criticism, 'An Early Flemish Painter' (1903), which concerned (supposedly) Jan Gossaert's portrait of – in Firbank's own words – 'Charles Quint'.[35]

But Reggie Quintus cannot suggest the Holy Roman Emperor himself, Brophy argues, but rather the author of the essay, 'Arthur Firbank', posing in his own invention (as he always did, somewhere or other) as a very young sometime art dealer and critic. Firbank's sole contribution for the journal *The Academy*, 'An Early Flemish Painter' was written especially for its then editor: none other than Lord Alfred Douglas. Later, it led to a scandal at Cambridge, which almost embroiled the young Firbank. In *TPZ*, this is cleverly broached. Reggie is said to have '*figured as hero already in at least one* cause célèbre', a reference, Brophy persuasively explains, first to Wilde's downfall, and then to the one concerning Douglas, *The Academy*, Robert Ross and (nearly) Firbank too.[36] The consequence of this near-miss was Firbank's reading of Douglas as mentally unstable, treacherous or both; he dissociated himself from Wilde's erstwhile partner, uniquely removing him from his large collection of Wilde familiars.[37] This means for Brophy that Reggie is both a version of Douglas and a partial, disguised self-portrait. Thus, Reggie is Douglas, translator of Wilde's *Salomé*, when he offers a painting of '*Iaokannan*' to the Princess for her convent.[38] Brophy even finds a rhythmic echo in 'Reggie Quintus' and 'Bosie Douglas', noting helpfully that Robert Hichens had already reinvented Douglas in his satirical novel *The Green Carnation* (1894) as 'Reggie Hastings', a wry naming indeed.[39] But at other times, Brophy argues, Reggie represents Firbank – devotee of Wilde, and for Brophy his more ideal husband.[40]

Still more complex is Wilde's presence in Firbank's play. Lord Orkish is only referred to by first name, slyly, once: but he *is* Lord Henry Orkish. Though the name Lord Henry suggests Wilde's own fictional semi-self-portrait, Lord Henry Wotton in *Dorian Gray*, that name was intended by Wilde to invoke several historical figures whom Brophy does not refer to. Foremost is the Jacobean ambassador to Venice, Sir Henry Wotton, who famously quipped that 'an Ambassador is an honest man sent to lie abroad for the good of his country'.[41] This patron of the arts and intimate of John Donne was recast by Wilde as *Dorian Gray*'s own worldly art lover, unduly influencing the young. His (queer) biographer Logan Pearsall Smith published his life of Wotton in 1907, a book that Firbank probably devoured. But Wilde's Wotton was also based on a real-life Florentine expatriate, Lord Henry Richard Charles Somerset, 'Wotton' loosely referring to Somerset, which includes a town called Wootton. With patience, we can reveal the significance of Somerset's life, as Brophy did not. First it is helpful to note that Logan Pearsall Smith himself was related to the Somersets' scandal, if loosely, as a photograph of him with Lady Henry Somerset from 1904 confirms.[42]

The Somersets' son was born in 1874, but Lord Henry Somerset's marriage to Lady Isabella Caroline Somers-Cocks collapsed soon afterwards because of her husband's infatuation with a 17-year-old youth, Henry Smith. This led him to flee for Italy; his wife was ostracised in London society, for divulging the circumstances behind the separation and suing for custody. Firbank makes certain – though hardly explicit – the link to this Somerset by having Lord Orkish pronounce Adrian's son's name as 'Charles Augustus Frederic Humphrey Percy Sydney' – though Adrian insists that he prefers 'Gervase'. Somerset's own son was called Henry Charles Somers Augustus.[43] Firbank removed 'Somers', just as Wilde did with his 'Wotton' invention, but adds four other names, each one significant. Still more confusingly, this was not the only boy-loving Somerset. Henry's younger brother, Lord Henry Arthur George Somerset, had been caught in the Cleveland Street scandal which preceded Wilde's own, visiting a male brothel repeatedly as 'Mr Brown'. This Somerset too had fled to Bad Homburg vor der Höhe in 1889, but returned quickly to England, only to find charges pending. He fled once more, travelling around Europe but finally settling in France.[44]

*TPZ*'s storyline more closely follows the story of the elder Somerset. He had known his boy-lover since the latter was seven; this is reworked by Firbank in the Eric/Adrian schoolboy inseparability, but not in the apparent tendencies of Lord Orkish towards the young, since Orkish's 'play' with Adrian's baby reflects putative parentage (see below). A personal connection for Firbank accompanied this Lord Somerset's life-in-exile: in 1902 Somerset foolishly persuaded himself that he could return to England for the coronation of Edward VII. He would have shared the event with Firbank's parents, who were thrilled to have been invited. However, Somerset was pursued immediately by a private detective, with his estranged wife's mother urging his arrest – a very precise echo of the Marquess of Queensberry's pursuit of his son's partner Wilde. Somerset retreated to Florence without being charged, but, like his brother, dared not set foot in England again; he died in 1932. Firbank used this very-living Somerset to magically reimagine Oscar Wilde's life as if the downfall had never happened. He ensured that his own partial Wilde, Lord Orkish, did not get stuck with a wholly Douglas-ish Reggie, but made Reggie partly reflect himself.

As Brophy notes, the surname that Firbank supplies – 'Orkish' – suggests 'Orchid-ish' and thus the 'cult of the purple orchid' which, in 1904, his tutor Rollo St Clair Talboys had warned Artie of: the 'insidious & exotic poison all of it like the rank odour of dead men's sins'.[45] It also suggests audibly the one quality in Wilde that Firbank did not like: his *mawkishness*.[46] Certainly, *The Picture of Dorian Gray* (1891) has Wilde's Lord Henry Wotton cutting an orchid for his buttonhole; he describes the flower in chapter 17 as a 'marvellous spotted thing, as effective as the seven deadly sins'.[47] Wilde recycled this in *A Woman of No Importance* (1893) when – in Act I – Mrs Allonby seeks out Lord Illingworth's 'orchid [. . .] as beautiful as the seven deadly sins', though more significant in that play is the early revelation that Illingworth had abandoned Mrs Arbuthnot and their child, refusing thus to grant the latter a name.[48]

But Firbank's Orkish is a deliberate misspelling of 'Orc-ish', not only because this is 'orchid-ish' or 'orchidaceous', as Brophy claimed, but because Wilde himself had embedded a reference to Masonic Rosicrucianism in his orchids. What Wotton plucks alludes, diabolically cleverly, to the Order of the Rose and Croix (ORC) or Rosicrucians, whose members and tenets must remain 'HID[den]': hence, ORC-HID. In a wonderful accident that Wilde the Greek scholar understood and that Brophy notes too, 'orchis' is also the testicle.[49] In Greek mythology, a father was said to be able to beget a son if he ate a plant with large tuberous roots. If the mother ate an orchid with small tubers, the offspring would be female. Firbank's Orkish is affiliated to Rosicrucianism, but not quite of it; he is of the 'Order of the Rose and Croix' [ORC], more or less [ISH]. He arrives telling of the mysterious Alpmuriels, who, though separating, are also trying to have a child by 'unmysteriously eating' [orchids].[50]

Lord Orkish's Catholic devotions are openly declared, if in sacrilegious form, as he 'regal[es] us with a whole rosary of piquant anecdotes', in Nadine's words.[51] As Brophy states, Firbank was perennially found with orchids, including in a portrait by Alvaro Guevara from late 1919; the author later recalled being 'huddled up in a black suit by a jar of Orchids, in a decor suggestive of Opium – or (even) worse!'[52] This portrait does not have black orchids – though, since black is rare in natural flora, the black orchid itself symbolises the dark, diabolical-leaning Rosicrucianism practised by Aleister Crowley, with whom Firbank's would-be consort Evan Morgan, Viscount Tredegar, had flirted. Wilde himself had invented a similarly 'in-joke' flower for young homosexuals, the artificially dyed green carnation. In fact, Firbank's play contains many hidden allusions to Crowley's life – from his mountaineering expertise and co-option of the achievements of Wilde and John Dee to his allegedly monstrous bisexuality – and it may be that Firbank sought above all to capture the scandalous Satanist – himself a failed non-graduate of Trinity College, Cambridge – in his net.[53] To be 'ORC-ISH' might also be to be CRO-wley-ISH, with the usual nominal inversion adopted.

Other *TPZ* names signify in similarly polyvalent manner – with much, understandably, not caught by Brophy. The 'Tresilians' nod to George Macaulay Trevelyan, who was the history don at Trinity until 1903, and then the most influential Edwardian historian. He had also been a member of the Apostles, like the music scholar Edward Dent and poet Rupert Brooke, both of whom Firbank had befriended; he would, then, have heard much about this prominent

college figure.[54] Trevelyan had written up the history of Italian uni-
fication in three books about Garibaldi (1907–11) which touched
on a vital political issue for Florence's English colony, who were
utterly pro-unification, and in proactive ways.[55] Among Trevelyan's
oft-recalled quotations was 'a little man often cast a long shadow';
in *TPZ*, Lady Rocktower mentions a 'young Italian lieutenant' for
whom her daughter Glyda has fallen – 'though I thank God on my
knees, dear Zena, she has scarcely caught a glimpse of his shadow'.[56]
This, equally, refers to the derailing of the Sapphic romance between
Gerald[ine] and Mabel in Firbank's *Inclinations* – undone by the
sinister heterosexual lothario Count Pastorelli; in many ways, *TPZ*
rewrites that novel.[57] *Inclinations* has a tragic diptych structure: in
part one the Sapphic Gerald[ine]/Mabel relationship takes flight;
part two has Mabel jump ship and fall for the Count. *TPZ* rewrites
the queer elopement by *not* allowing the shadow of heterosexuality
to enter at all, as Brophy understands.[58]

Firbank's mild adjustment – Trevelyan/Tresilian – makes a joke
either of Trevelyan's reputational 'resilien-ts' at the time – no critique
could touch him – and/or the absence of 'resilience' in the couple's
week-long, failed marriage. As Brophy was aware, Lady Rocktower,
meanwhile, remodels Congreve's 'Lady Wishfort', the tower of rock
representing the '-fort' which is wished for.[59] (Her role as the aunt
who declines to give her blessing to Mirabell and Millamant in turn
inspired Wilde's Lady Bracknell in *Earnest*.) Firbank, like Wilde, imi-
tated Congreve in playing with lovers' names to suggest their suit-
ability – but to bolder ends; his plot thus fully 'queers' that of *The
Way of the World*.

Eric and Enid, first, are so named because of *Érec et Énide*, a
twelfth-century romance by Chrétien de Troyes, as Brophy states.[60]
From this point on, however, she has little sense of how or why
other *TPZ* names follow. Firbank's Enid and Nadine are meant to be
together not only since 'Nadine' contains 'an Enid', but because the
phrase 'Enid and Nadine' is palindromic. This trumps the imperfect
echo between the first names of the married Sheil-Meyers, Nadine
and Adrian; the latter also suggesting both the queer Emperor
Hadrian of Antinous renown, and his namesake, the titular hero
of Frederick Rolfe's *Hadrian the Seventh* (1904), a very important
novel for Firbank. For Nadine, who effectively leaves him holding
the baby, Adrian becomes 'a nadir'. The choice of the young men's
destination, meanwhile, the Engadine, 'contains' both wives' names –
as well as 'Enid' backwards. It is anagrammatically 'e.g. Nadine'.
This suggests that these women cannot be escaped – or perhaps that

staying married heterosexually is less realistic or enjoyable than climbing a Swiss mountain. This said, Aleister Crowley pursued his gay sexual relations, improbably, through the Alpine Club, and hero-worshipped one Oscar Eckenstein, with whom he climbed; thus, the Engadine also echoes 'Eckenstein'. Perhaps coincidentally, Firbank's two male leads, Eric and Adrian, are, respectively, also 'found' within the names of *Earnest*'s two heroines: Eric in 'Cecily Cardew'; Adrian within 'Gwendolen Fairfax'.

Brophy has an ingenious derivation for the Sheil-Meyers, since 'Casa Meyer' sounds like a badly-pronounced 'Casa mia'; *TPZ*'s setting is indeed meant to evoke Firbank's childhood home The Coopers and the idea of the 'artificial pastoral' – the perfect, if unnatural world – which informed everything Firbank had written.[61] *TPZ* was also spun from Firbank's abandoned novel 'Salomé', which was ultimately renamed *The Artificial Princess*; that novel's garden too becomes a theatre, as Brophy notes.[62] But we can push still farther here. If the house were referred to not as 'C/Meyer' but 'C/Sheil', we find anagrammatically precisely half of The Coopers' location: the town that Firbank considered Paradise, *Chisle*-hurst. About the poorly rendered Italian throughout *TPZ* Brophy mis-stepped, concluding that Firbank failed to thrive when taught Italian at Cambridge; consequently, in *TPZ* it 'ran rather to gibberish than to glibness'.[63] But surely, this being a play about an expatriate 'colony' that he strongly disliked, Firbank wickedly embedded a series of routine linguistic distortions – inflicted inflections by the real-life counterparts to his play's *personae*. The dramatist consistently replicated the level of (Anglo-)Italian he knew first-hand that figures such as Somerset, Reggie Turner, Violet Paget *et al.* had (not) 'mastered'.

Another extensive allusion in *TPZ* has never come to light, but further explains Evan Morgan's anger on seeing the play's dedication to him. The missing link is John Dee, astronomer, astrologer, occult philosopher, mathematician and advisor to Queen Elizabeth I, with whom Morgan – like his close friend Crowley – was obsessed and whose pursuits in the occult he followed. Firbank's play was discreet, but Morgan had shared his Rosicrucian and Satanic habits with him – ultimately to Firbank's apparent disgust. Thus, *TPZ*'s dedication to Morgan was an act of dark revenge on the author's part. He and Morgan had probably both learned most about Dee's life either from Crowley directly, or else – given its date of publication – from the first Dee biography, written by Charlotte Fell Smith (1909).[64] Dee was of Welsh stock, like Morgan; his surname came from the Welsh word 'du', meaning black. His father Ro[w]land had married one

Jane Wild, whose name almost precisely anticipates that of Oscar Wilde's mother, Jane, Lady Wilde. The congruity between Dee's life story and Wilde's *A Woman of No Importance* plot further suggests an awareness of, and probably a sense of affinity towards, Dee on the superstitious Irishman's part. If we consider John Dee as the fruit of their marriage, he combines both parents' origins, and is thus the first 'Wild-Dee' progeny. In Firbank's immediate world, meanwhile, the first son of the Wildes with whom he was most obsessed – Oscar and Constance – was Cyril, his friend Vyvyan Holland's brother, who was killed on 9 May 1915 fighting Germany, in the war Firbank despised. As well as captivating Morgan and Crowley, Dee had a further significance as a founding don at Trinity College. The stage effects he produced for an Aristophanes play there led directly to Dee's magical renown.[65] Firbank desperately wanted such magic to ensure his own play's good fortune, after his five published fictions to date had been so ignored.

Subsequently Dee travelled around Europe, meeting with eminent thinkers, including the Italian mathematician Federico Commandino. 'Commandino' helps us: his first name explains the selection of 'Frederic' among *TPZ*'s baby's given names. His surname explains the reference to the 'Italian lieutenant' cryptically ('commandino' = small soldier; hence also the importance of Trevelyan's quip concerning little men casting long shadows). Moreover, among the manuscripts in Dee's unrivalled library was an incredibly rare Latin magic treatise entitled *The Book of Soyga*, a copy of which Morgan is said to have procured in Glasgow in 1916 – an unlikely claim, but one he apparently made.[66] The book – Dee's own long-lost copy now recovered, and providing the evidence – is full of (Hebrew-inspired) backwards-writing, further supporting Firbank's 'hidden messaging' throughout *TPZ*, including through palindromes and anagrams.[67]

Dee's other acquaintances included the MP, adventurer, explorer and pioneer of the Irish plantations (and co-begetter of the long legacy of Anglo-Irish Protestantism which Firbank's mother had inherited) Sir Humphrey Gilbert, who provides another of the *TPZ* child's names. The next, 'Percy', refers to Henry Percy, 9th Earl of Northumberland, known as the 'Wizard Earl' for his alchemical success; he was Dee's friend and neighbour. There is a further direct connection to the Firbanks too: the Percys' ancestral seat, Petworth House, begat the town in which Thomas Firbank retained a property (when disposing of The Coopers). Dee tutored the young poet Philip Sidney, whose *Arcadia* (1580) plays a further vital role untraced by Brophy: that poet's surname provides the last of the baby's given names, 'Sydney' (the 'i' to 'y' change is both/either classic Firbankian irreverence and/or equally a reflection of Elizabethan spelling instability). Sidney referred to Dee in a letter to a friend as 'our unknown God' – literally, *ignotum deum nostrum*, meaning Dee was actually 'Areopagus', the figure who inspired Sidney's literary circle.[68] Sidney wrote this in code, the sound of *deum* punning on Dee's name; his Welsh origins too are mentioned, as well as a reference to Dee's 'hieroglyph monad'.[69] 'Charles Augustus Frederic Humphrey Percy Sydney': thus, all elements of Lord Orkish's proposed name are accounted for. Firbank was never casual or accidental in his allusions, camp and improvised as they may have seemed; Brophy is the one critic who has understood his seriousness.

*TPZ* offers a strikingly non-heterosexual Arcadia. It both renews and revises the paradise offered by Sidney. Startlingly, Firbank was aware of an author in Sidney's outer circle, who had clung to his peer's coat tails to secure his own fame by both borrowing from and extending the *Arcadia* (which Sidney himself had left unfinished, and which was itself a rewrite of the first 'Old Arcadia'), just as Firbank here jokingly suggests that he might be seen as borrowing from Wilde (and Congreve in turn), rather than transcending them. That poet was Gervase Markham: forgotten today, but not only a soldier in the terrible Irish campaigns of the Earl of Essex, but author of *The English Arcadia* (1607). Markham had sought to befriend Sidney's peers, including Henry Wriothesley, 3rd Earl of Southampton, the young patron of Shakespeare and – since 1817 – taken to be the 'fair youth' of his *Sonnets* – although Wilde's 'The Portrait of Mr W.H.' (1889) had notably and effectively disagreed. *The English Arcadia*'s preface compares Markham's efforts to 'extend' Sidney's masterpiece, with what one present-day critic calls 'breathtaking hubris', to Virgil's reimagining of Homer, and Spenser's of Chaucer.[70] Firbank was not – I don't think – expressing true concern at his own abilities in publishing a reimagined *Earnest*; this is, rather, a comical allusion to a very different case, whereby a very minor author shamed himself by inviting comparison to a far greater.

In *TPZ*, Gervase is the otherwise unlikely name that father Adrian insists on the baby being given – overruling the many given (and implicitly queer) names that combine those of Dee's intimate friends, and that are (almost) bestowed by Lord Orkish.[71] Eric suggests 'Gerry' as a derivative, but Adrian counters, insisting on Gervase precisely, and thus: '*Exeunt, Gerrying and Gervaseing one another to house.*'[72] Assuming that we accept the Gervase

Markham 'extension to *Arcadia*' correlation, the inference may yet feel uncertain. Will the young Gervase inherit the queer, Arcadian world promised by *TPZ* and the tendencies of its many non-heterosexual *personae*, including both parents? That is the '. . .' of *TPZ*. Firbank never planned a sequel (and in any event, *TPZ* to his mind was the legitimate queer half-sister of or sequel to *Earnest*). Given his play's utter failure even to be produced in his lifetime, he had even less encouragement to continue to write dramas, as opposed to novels. Brophy would experience something similar with *The Burglar* (1967/68), only ever a mildly noted contribution to the stage, despite its West End run. (Concerning Arcadias, perhaps coincidentally, yet another historic 'Zeno' may have inspired Firbank's princess's name: Zeno the Isaurian, the fifth-century Byzantine emperor, married an 'Arcadia' – though San Zeno of Verona wrote a panegyric towards the male Saint Arcadius, who was martyred by amputation, too.)[73]

*TPZ* not only perpetuates the storylines of the four Wildean protagonists from *Earnest*, while finding room in Lady Rocktower for a rewritten quasi-Lady Bracknell, and also, in Orkish and Quintus, new versions of Wilde, Douglas and Firbank. It also sustains its inversion of sexual norms by drawing on the remarkable relationship between John Dee and the young forger and self-declared alchemist Edward Kelley, who used a pseudonym to hide a criminal past. The pair were intimate – with no suggested homoerotic tenor – and drew the attention of members of the Hermetic Order of the Golden Dawn in the 1890s, including W. B. Yeats, Maud Gonne and Bram Stoker – as well as the Welsh mystic Arthur Machen and the English Anglo-Catholic author Evelyn Underwood, author of the best-selling *Mysticism* (1911), a title that Firbank and Morgan may well have known of.[74] Wilde's widow Constance was a member alongside Arthur Conan Doyle – as was Evan Morgan's tutor in the mystic arts, Aleister Crowley, until he was kicked out in 1900.

Crowley fell under Dee's spell totally; by October 1909, he was 'buried in Kelly right now', according to a letter he wrote to J. F. C. 'John' Fuller, an early devotee.[75] Crowley came to consider himself a reincarnated Edward Kell[e]y, signing off by that name. Subsequently Crowley took a lover, Victor Neuburg, to Algiers (where Firbank followed immediately after completing *TPZ*), allowing Neuburg to impersonate the scribe Dee, while he embodied Kelley to whom angels spoke. Though Crowley treated Neuburg sadistically, shaving his head and walking him around like a dog, he allowed the young man to take the active role in penetrative anal sex, considered by Crowley as 'magickal sex'. The relationship continued until 1914 in Paris, when Neuburg broke off relations, only to be cursed by Crowley in terms that caused him an immediate breakdown. The clincher in terms of relevance to *TPZ* is that Crowley argued that their 'magickal sex' (sodomy) could beget a 'magical child': not a baby perhaps, but an idea or issue. Symbolically, though, he represented it as a baby, which Firbank literalised in *TPZ*, mocking Crowley's sexual delusions through the Orkish/Quintus relationship even as it also echoed that of Wilde/Douglas and (platonically) Dee/Kelley, echoes that Crowley had himself embraced.

According to Ellic Howe, the Order sought to rediscover how Dee and Kelley had conducted spiritual conferences with angels who spoke in the so-called 'Enochian language', dictating whole books to Dee, only ever through Kelley, the essential intermediary. Dee's Kelley used a 'scryer', or crystal ball, in turn. This ball passed into the collection of Horace Walpole (at least as Walpole declared), ending up in the British Museum, where it is known today as the 'Seal of God'.[76] Surely Morgan and Firbank saw it? In *TPZ*, Reggie Quintus, channelling Firbank, but also Kelley, the young man in the intimate alchemical affair, foretells a black future that may not be dark at all. He consults a crystal ball and finds: 'A nigger!' Lord Orkish, the Crowley to Reggie's Victor, or the Dee to Reggie's Kelley, or the Wilde to Reggie's Douglas, leans over '*enthralled*' and asks: 'Only *one*?'[77]

This comment in turn predicts Firbank's future fictions – the non-white story *Santal* he already planned, but also the West Indies novel gestating inside, the book which came to have two titles (not that even this most prescient author could predict that): *Sorrow in Sunlight* or *Prancing Nigger* (1924), a book entirely populated by non-whites whom, as Brophy perfectly understood, Firbank never sought to objectify but rather to idealise. Brophy fully gets the significance of the crystal-ball-contained negro – 'nigger' being no term of offence, incidentally, for Firbank or for the jazz-loving subculture he frequented – but entirely misses the significance of Crowley (though she does get his importance to *The Artificial Princess* and to relations with Morgan), or of Dee and his crystal ball.[78]

Dee preferred to describe the Enochian language simply as 'the language of Angels'. Hence, the servant in Firbank's *TPZ* is called Angelo, '*a boy of sixteen, fair, sleek, languishing, a "Benozzo Gozzoli"*'; Brophy traces this figure from the brush of Gozzoli to the *Artificial Princess*'s 'page in a Benozzo Gozzoli [. . . who] was paid a large wage to look wilful'.[79] True: but Gozzoli appealed to Firbank too not simply on aesthetic grounds, but for his bold anachronism. Gozzoli's daring update of the story of the Magi in 1459–61 accommodated various members of the contemporary Medici family, dressed in sumptuous fashion, in the frescoed interior of Florence's chapel of the Palazzo Medici Riccardi.[80] For 'magick' lovers, too, the Magi were crucial in the Christian story. Firbank dragged the deeply historical figures of Dee, Kelley and the circle of the Earl of Essex, Spenser and beyond into his contemporary world, by way of Wilde and Crowley, and always richly disguised – just as Gozzoli had invested the Magi with the appearance and apparel of his Medici commissioners.

If the Dee/Kelley relationship has no erotic tint, to Firbank the intimacy between mage and spokesman-for-the-Angels might have seemed still closer – just as, in *TPZ*, the self-appointed convent mother Zena gathers her women for a spiritual communion which nevertheless feels sensual and permissive. But there was also the more carnal 'remake' of it by Crowley (with Neuman) in mind. The most remarkable echo of the Dee–Kelley affair, however, lies in the fact that the alchemical pair met when Dee was married to his third wife, Jane, who was the same age as Kelley. The men fell out sensationally when, in 1587, Kelley informed Dee that the Archangel Uriel had instructed them to share everything – including their wives. Dee complied unhappily, but, upset and jealous, soon cut off relations forever. It was argued even at the time that his next son, the unexpected Theodore, may have been Kelley's: the boy appeared less than nine months before they parted.[81] Crowley perverted this into his notion of the 'magical child' created through gay sodomy – something Firbank's former consort but soon-to-be dispatched friend Morgan apparently admired, but which Firbank himself chose to ridicule. In *TPZ*, this is retold brilliantly in Nadine's unexpected pregnancy, and her suddenly giving birth to a boy deprived of a name (a circumstance that is worked into Wilde's *A Woman of No Importance* too, by accident or design), but who Lord Orkish plays with and hovers over, finally seeking to force a name of his own invention on the boy by deceiving the presumably cuckolded (by Orkish) Adrian.

The two Renaissance alchemists had, much earlier, abandoned their wives for an unexpectedly long period, as they travelled Europe with a Polish aristocrat. Their journeying took six years – just as Eric and Adrian abandon their wives, and the play *TPZ* itself, until their unexpected latter return. They did not mountaineer; this fetish was Crowley's queer one, grafted by Firbank on to the Dee/Kelley story.

The real Jane Dee died in 1604, five years before her husband, succumbing to the plague. Firbank fits this into *TPZ*, too, since after Nadine's 'dreadful' pregnancy is announced, she gives birth offstage, which, to Firbank's Enid, 'sounds almost as though she were sickening for the Plague'.[82] John Dee's late decline in reputation and poverty foreshadowed Wilde's in intriguing ways: when he returned home to Mortlake from European travels, he found his remarkable library – then the largest in England – ransacked and looted, just as the Irish author forfeited his own book collection during the trials, selling titles off for pennies.[83]

*TPZ* develops much further the approach of Wilde's *Earnest*, displaying the abject failure of heterosexual romance on stage, while effectively announcing – where Wilde could only hint – the viability of optimal same-sex relationships, which come into being directly as a consequence of that failure. In Firbank's lifetime, nobody saw the genius behind the play – except, ironically, Evan Morgan, who could only react with fury, and insisted on the dedication being removed before *TPZ*'s publication; he would have feared Crowley's anger or curse, as many did, but, carefully, suggested only that it would displease his father. This neglect of *TPZ* continued after Firbank's death. Evelyn Waugh, in an early, generous estimation, understood that Firbank's humour had a 'peculiar temper' quite unlike Wilde's: the latter was 'at heart radically sentimental' and his wit was 'ornamental', whereas Firbank's was 'structural'.[84] This is perceptive; it is just a shame that Waugh would later reverse such a positive judgement. He went on to quote one of *Zoubaroff*'s exchanges:

> NADINE [*introducing*]: My husband.
> BLANCHE [*genially*]: I think we've slept together once?
> ADRIAN: I don't remember.
> BLANCHE: At the opera. During *Bérénice*![85]

It is a fine joke, but it also a Firbankian double-blind, since the real story in *TPZ* is not this casually announced adultery-that-actually-is-not, but the effective adultery apparently perpetrated between Nadine and Orkish, and the more widespread betrayal of heterosexual partners by *personae* who simply, as Brophy fully recognised, preferred their own sex.

Waugh outgrew his fondness for Firbank as his own Catholic faith intensified, and he is one of many Firbank acolytes whom Brophy chastises. Travelling with her through *TPZ* brings us far beyond the gestural appreciation of even the young Waugh; with

Brophy, we are in the company of someone of temperamental and intellectual affinity with Firbank. *Prancing Novelist* is the only book without which no serious Firbank scholarship may be undertaken. It affords so many vital bits of evidence needed for further, still more allusive critical readings of Firbank's books – which remain acutely needed. Ultimately the Anglo-Irish queer modernist and his Irish-born, unclassifiable successor were perfectly aligned. Brophy shared her subject's ingenuity and referential resourcefulness. Her instincts proved almost always correct. Brophy's intuitive sense of Firbank's achievement was fully formed and convincing.

Furthering her pursuit of Firbank may lead today to a somewhat deeper penetration – with the wind in the right direction, and the benefit of online resources. But penetrating works of such complexity and ingenuity is a challenge which, without the brilliant example of Brophy's *Prancing Novelist*, would never be possible.

## Notes

1. Ronald Firbank, *The Princess Zoubaroff: A Comedy* (London: Grant Richards, 1920); the edition cited here is 'The Princess Zoubaroff: A Comedy', in Ronald Firbank, *The Complete Firbank*, with an introduction by Anthony Powell (London: Duckworth, 1973), pp. 699–765.
2. Brigid Brophy, *Prancing Novelist: A Defence of Fiction in the Form of a Critical Biography in Praise of Ronald Firbank* (London: Macmillan, 1973).
3. Miriam J. Benkovitz, *Ronald Firbank: A Biography* (New York: Alfred Knopf, 1969).
4. Peter Parker, '"Aggressive, Witty and Unrelenting": Brigid Brophy and Ronald Firbank', *Review of Contemporary Fiction*, 15.3 (1995), pp. 68–78.
5. Steven Moore, *Ronald Firbank: An Annotated Bibliography of Secondary Materials, 1905–1995* (Normal, IL: Dalkey Archive Press, 1996), pp. 45–8.
6. See Brophy, *PN*, p. 49; Brigid Brophy, *The Finishing Touch* (London: Secker and Warburg, 1963; rev. edn London: Gay Men's Press, 1987).
7. Brigid Brophy, *In Transit: An Heroi-Cyclic Novel* (London: The Book Service, 1969; 2nd edn, London: Gay Men's Press, 1989).
8. In addition to the printed versions, there is a full audio recording of *TPZ* at <https://archive.org/details/princesszoubaroff_1706_librivox> (accessed 12 October 2017).
9. See especially Brophy, *PN*, pp. 326–44, 486–502.
10. Ibid., p. 367.
11. Ibid., pp. 486–91.

12. See Neil Corcoran, 'Modern Irish Poetry and The Visual Arts: Yeats to Heaney', in Fran Brearton and Adrian Gillis (eds), *The Oxford Handbook of Modern Irish Poetry* (Oxford: Oxford University Press, 2012), pp. 251–65.

13. Brophy, *PN*, p. 367.

14. Ibid., p. 366.

15. Brophy drew on Jeanette H. Foster's *Sex Variant Women in Literature* (London: Frederick Muller, 1958) for her Vivien. I have also drawn on Karla Jay, *The Amazon and the Page: Natalie Clifford Barney and Renée Vivien* (Bloomington, IN: Indiana University Press, 1988), and Suzanne Rodriguez, *Wild Heart: Natalie Clifford Barney and the Decadence of Literary Paris* (London: HarperCollins, 2003).

16. Brophy, *PN*, p. 366.

17. Natalie Clifford Barney, *A Perilous Advantage: The Best of Natalie Clifford Barney*, ed. and trans. Anna Livia (Norwich, VT: New Victoria Publishers, 1992), p. 97.

18. These circumstances are fully recorded in Benkovitz, *Ronald Firbank*, and Brophy, *PN*.

19. Brophy, *PN*, pp. 326–34.

20. Ibid., pp. 493–4.

21. Ibid., p. 493.

22. Ibid., pp. 498–9.

23. See Robert Crawford, *The Young Eliot: From St. Louis to The Waste Land* (London: Viking Penguin, 2015), pp. 149–50.

24. All in Meryle Secrest, *Between Me and Life: A Biography of Romaine Brooks* (New York: Doubleday, 1974).

25. Brophy, *PN*, p. 360.

26. Ibid, p. 360.

27. <https://en.wikipedia.org/wiki/Zeno_of_Verona> (accessed 22 September 2017), is helpful; the fullest account is in Revd S. Baring-Gould, *The Lives of the Saints, volumes 1–16* (London: John Hodges, 1872–77; available through Project Gutenberg, <http://www.mirrorservice.org/sites/ftp.ibiblio.org/pub/docs/books/gutenberg/4/6/9/4/46947/46947-h/46947-h.htm> (accessed 17 October 2017).

28. <http://catholicsaints.mobi/calendar/23–june.htm> and <http://ortho-christian.com/94821.html>; (both accessed 22 September 2017) are helpful. The fullest account is in Baring-Gould, *The Lives of the Saints*.

29. Revd S. Baring-Gould, *Cambridge County Geographies: Cornwall* (Cambridge: Cambridge University Press, 1910), <http://www.ajhw.co.uk/books/book203/book203.html> (accessed 17 October 2017). I am surmising familiarity with this travel book, admittedly, though with Firbank's familiarity with Baring-Gould's *The Lives of the Saints* surely being beyond question, the probability of his having discovered other titles by the author surely follows.

30. For a detailed account of the interrelations between these men, see Max Egremont, *Siegfried Sassoon: A Biography* (London: Picador, 2005). The

guests attending Firbank's reading are identified in Benkovitz, *Ronald Firbank*.

31.  <https://en.wikipedia.org/wiki/Saint_Senara> (accessed 24 September 2017) is helpful; the fullest account is in Baring-Gould, *The Lives of the Saints*.
32.  Brophy, *PN*, pp. 326–34.
33.  Firbank, *TPZ*, p. 716.
34.  Brophy, *PN*, pp. 327–8.
35.  Ibid., pp. 196–7; Ronald Firbank, 'An Early Flemish Painter', *The Academy*, 73 (28 September 1903).
36.  Firbank, *TPZ*, p. 716.
37.  Brophy, *PN*, pp. 331–4.
38.  Ibid., p. 327.
39.  Ibid., p. 327.
40.  Ibid., p. 332.
41.  Henry Wotton: details drawn from Logan Pearsall Smith, *The Life and Letters of Sir Henry Wotton* (Oxford: Clarendon Press, 1907).
42.  Rodney Bolt, *As Good as God, As Clever as the Devil: The Impossible Life of Mary Benson* (London: Atlantic, 2011), and Ros Black, *A Talent for Humanity: The Life and Work of Lady Henry Somerset* (Chippenham and Eastbourne: Anthony Rowe, 2010) inform the account of the Somersets' life and scandal. The photograph is at <https://en.wikipedia.org/wiki/Lady_Henry_Somerset#/media/File:Lady_Henry_Somerset_with_Hannah_Whitall_Smith,_Mary_Brenson,_Logan_Pearsall_Smith,_Karin_Stephen_and_Ray_Strachey.jpg> (accessed 17 October 2017).
43.  Firbank, *TPZ*, p. 765.
44.  All in Morris B. Kaplan, *Sodom on the Thames: Sex, Love, and Scandal in Wilde Times* (Ithaca, NY: Cornell University Press, 2005).
45.  Rollo St Clair Talboys, ALS to RF, Crowthorne, 15 April 1904, Berg Collection, New York Public Library.
46.  Brophy, *PN*, p. 328.
47.  Oscar Wilde, *The Picture of Dorian Gray* (1891 edition), <https://www.gutenberg.org/files/174/174-h/174-h.htm> (accessed 12 October 2017).
48.  Oscar Wilde, *A Woman of No Importance* (1893), <http://www.gutenberg.org/files/854/854-h/854-h.htm> (accessed 15 October 2017).
49.  Brophy, *PN*, p. 328.
50.  Firbank, *TPZ*, p. 717.
51.  Ibid., p. 718.
52.  Ronald Firbank, ALS to Carl van Vechten, London, 10 June 1922, Berg Collection, New York Public Library; cited in Brophy, *PN*, p. 328.
53.  For Crowley's circumstances, I draw throughout on Lawrence Sutin, *Do What Thou Wilt: A Life of Aleister Crowley* (New York: Saint Martin's Press, 2002).

54. David Cannadine, *G. M. Trevelyan: A Life in History* (London: HarperCollins, 1992), informs this summary.

55. See Ben Downing, *Queen Bee of Tuscany: The Redoubtable Janet Ross* (New York: Farrar, Straus and Giroux, 2013), pp. 108–10.

56. Firbank, *TPZ*, p. 757.

57. Ronald Firbank, *Inclinations* (London: Grant Richards, 1916); the edition cited here is Ronald Firbank, *Vainglory, with Inclinations and Caprice*, ed. Richard Canning (London: Penguin, 2012), pp. 179–293.

58. Brophy, *PN*, p. 363.

59. Ibid., p. 494.

60. Ibid., p. 496.

61. Ibid., pp. 491–2.

62. Ibid., p. 492.

63. Ibid., p. 229.

64. Charlotte Fell Smith, *John Dee: 1527–1608* (London: Constable, 1909).

65. Ibid., p. 15.

66. See <https://pontifexverus.wordpress.com/tag/the–book–of–soyga/> (accessed 20 September 2017).

67. Jim Reeds, 'John Dee and the Magic Tables in the Book of Soyga' (1996), archived at <https://web.archive.org/web/20070305174955/http://www.dtc.umn.edu/~reedsj/soyga.pdf> (accessed 20 September 2017).

68. Benjamin Woolley, *The Queen's Conjuror: The Life and Magic of John Dee* (London: HarperCollins, 2001), p. 226.

69. Ibid., p. 355.

70. All concerning Gervase Markham drawn from <http://spenserians.cath.vt.edu/TextRecord.php?&textsid=33046> (accessed 19 September 2017).

71. Firbank, *TPZ*, p. 765.

72. Ibid., p. 765.

73. For Emperor Zeno, <https://en.wikipedia.org/wiki/Zeno_(emperor)> (accessed 20 September 2017), is helpful; the fullest account is in Baring-Gould, *The Lives of the Saints*. For Saint Arcadius, see Baring-Gould's account at <http://www.mirrorservice.org/sites/ftp.ibiblio.org/pub/docs/books/gutenberg/4/6/9/4/46947/46947–h/46947–h.htm> (accessed 17 October 2017).

74. These and other references to the Golden Dawn draw from Ellic Howe, *Magicians of the Golden Dawn: A Documentary History of a Magical Order, 1887–1923* (London: Routledge and Kegan Paul, 1972).

75. Sutin, *Do What Thou Wilt*, p. 201.

76. See <https://londonist.com/2011/06/the–mystical–artefacts–of–john–dee–at–the–british–museum> (accessed 12 October 2017).

77. Firbank, *TPZ*, p. 743.

78. Brophy, *PN*, p. 204.
79. Firbank, *TPZ*, p. 720; Ronald Firbank, *The Artificial Princess* (London: Duckworth, 1934); the edition cited here is 'The Artificial Princess', in Firbank, *The Complete Firbank*, pp. 27–73; here, p. 66; Brophy, *PN*, p. 193.
80. Franco Cardini, *The Chapel of the Magi in Palazzo Medici* (Florence: Mandragora Press, 1999), informs this summary.
81. All informed by Woolley, *The Queen's Conjuror*.
82. Firbank, *TPZ*, p. 729.
83. See Thomas Wright, *Oscar's Books: A Journey Around the Library of Oscar Wilde* (London: Chatto and Windus, 2008).
84. Evelyn Waugh, 'Ronald Firbank', *Life and Letters* 2 (March 1929), pp. 191–6; reprinted in Mervyn Horder (ed.), *Ronald Firbank: Memoirs and Critiques* (London: Duckworth, 1977), pp. 175–99; here, p. 176.
85. Firbank, *TPZ*, pp. 722–3.

Chapter 6

# 'Shavian that she was'

*John Dixon*

Giles Cooper, the one-time agent of Brigid Brophy, wrote in his obituary of her that '[h]er greatest literary disappointment, I believe, was that Michael Holroyd, not she, was approached by the Society of Authors to write George Bernard Shaw's biography'.[1] The Society of Authors in the early 1970s wanted a biographer who had *not* known Shaw personally, but who had a proven ability in writing biography and who had demonstrated an interest in Shaw. This put Brophy in the front running. She had written widely about Shaw in essays and reviews, with more than passing mentions in her critical studies of Mozart, Ronald Firbank and two of Aubrey Beardsley, all involving research into a wide variety of sources – some abroad, and not all in English.

The two on Beardsley are particularly relevant. One was a critical appreciation (*Black and White*, 1968), and the other a biography (*Beardsley and his World*, 1976). Both upped the status of Beardsley, and in 1976, Kenneth Clark, the director of the National Gallery (and the boss of Brophy's husband, Michael Levey) was asked by the *New York Review of Books* 'to write a piece on Beardsley to coincide with the publication of a short, useful book by Brigid Brophy in which, unfortunately, she had repressed her gift of critical insight and has concentrated on the facts of Beardsley's life'. He added later: 'The facts of his early life have recently been collected in a scholarly manner by Brigid Brophy.'[2]

The combination of critical insight and factual accuracy comes across in Brophy's review of the biographer Miriam Benkovitz, who had also written a study of Beardsley (and Firbank): 'To write with complete accuracy to any set of facts is hard even for the diligent and self-critical. I think with rue of a couple of half-inaccuracies in my own recent book on Beardsley.'[3] This desire for accuracy of expression was in part derived from Shaw. She maintained that:

> His *Sixteen Self-Sketches* contains a clue which so far as I know Shavian biographers have not yet picked up, and which suggests Shaw must have begotten a child – though that is not to say it was born. Writing of his sexual experiences as a young man, Shaw asserts: 'I was not impotent; I was not sterile; I was not homosexual.' Unless this is the sole moment in history when Shaw used a word imprecisely, there seems only one way he could have known he was not sterile.[4]

This and other insights, together with her other biographical studies, show her fitness to have been considered for the Shaw commission. As it was, Michael Holroyd was the successful candidate. He invited her, meanwhile, to contribute to his symposium essay collection *The Genius of Shaw*, which she did, with the essay on animal rights 'The Way of No Flesh'.[5] When he completed his monumental four-volume biography, Holroyd acknowledged Brophy's support and insight.

Without underestimating Holroyd's achievement, how can we begin to assemble Brophy's unwritten biography? Her commitment to Shaw – not uncritical – stretched throughout her life. There was almost a pre-destined affinity: Irish ancestry, vegetarianism (Brophy became a vegan, however; Shaw never did), a hatred of vivisection (Brophy called Shaw's preface to *The Doctor's Dilemma* (1911) '[t]he classic statement of the case').[6] They shared a love of music, particularly opera, and especially Mozart. They both opposed censorship and fought for the rights of authors. They set great store by the precise use of language, shared aspects of spelling (Brophy always spelled the word 'show' as 'shew') and an interest in shorthand. They were left-wing oriented; Brophy was a trades union and Labour Party member; Shaw was a Fabian. They were both feminists of sorts. Shaw liked watching boxing; Brophy, tennis. Both disliked the countryside. They disagreed about tobacco and alcohol.

Brophy reviewed productions of Shaw plays and sometimes wrote programme notes, including for the Shaw Festival in Ontario, Canada. She reviewed books about him, the actresses he wrote for, and even about his vegetarian cookbook. Passing references to him appear in her biographies of Beardsley and Firbank; more substantial ones in her 1962 philosophical work *The Black Ship to Hell*. Influences, as well as references, are apparent in her play *The Burglar*, in a couple of her early novels, in what she considered her most Shavian novel, *The Adventures of God in His Search for the Black Girl*, and in her last, *Palace without Chairs*.[7] All this could have been reassembled, expanded and made to inform a conjectural biography. It would have resulted in a challenging, if truncated, biographical essay. If she had gained the Shaw commission, however, it would have taken her years to complete. Given her state of health, she might never have finished it.

In this essay, I concentrate on a few key Brophy works, to discern less what she thought of Shaw and more about how he and his writings influenced her.

## Novels

Brophy's first novel, *Hackenfeller's Ape*, was published in 1953, just three years after Shaw's death. Brophy uses the Shavian spelling 'shew' for the more usual 'show', as she had in her first publication, the story collection *The Crown Princess*. The novel is in three parts, the first two set over four days, with a short postscript the following year. It concerns the rights of animals – a Shavian topic in itself – and tells of a victory of sorts for one particular animal, Edwina, and the posthumous non-achievement of one human space scientist, and the almost accidental success of a slightly ineffectual but well-meaning zoo scientist.

The novel includes a few bars of musical score – as does Shaw's play *Heartbreak House*. There is one direct, if passing, reference to him:

> 'At the time of Byron and Shelley, incest was the thrill of the day.'
> 'It was still a live issue', Darrelhyde put in, 'when Bernard Shaw began writing plays.'[8]

Brophy observed in relation to one of Shaw's early novels how the language used for scene setting was more appropriate to plays than novels, and argued that he was unconsciously feeling his way towards playwriting. The same perhaps could be said of Brophy's novel in relation to the appearance of a new character. Take the first meeting of Professor Darrelhyde and Kendrick. Brophy introduces Kenrick, albeit in the past tense, rather in the manner of a summary stage direction, a first onstage speculation as to how the newcomer might turn out:

> He had the appearance of a practical man, who would enjoy an electrician's work. He gave also an impression of physical courage; he had an air force look. The Professor associated him with some dangerous and individual sport, like sailing or climbing, in which he would depend – obviously with justification – on the neatness of both his limbs and his calculations.[9]

Another instance is the first meeting with Gloria: 'She was a girl of gentle bearing, self-contained and well-bred, but not without vivacity; she wore one of those printed cotton dresses which, to the Professor's view, turned all women in summertime into girls of eighteen.'[10] Both examples are from the Professor's point of view, and have the ring of a stage direction from a Shaw play: *The Doctor's Dilemma* would be a prime example. However, Brophy's description of the unborn ape is more detached and very sensitively imagined, and surely the reference to 'an over-bloated epicure' prefigures the situation in her later novel, *Flesh*:

> The embryo stored up the surplus food in fold after fold of lardy flesh that had never seen the light of day. It grew swollen and gross. A need to take exercise came upon it, not for any altruistic or utilitarian reason, but simply to ease itself; the same need might have fallen upon an over-bloated epicure.[11]

Brophy's next novel, *The King of a Rainy Country* (1956), is also divided as a three-act play, with three settings – London, *en route* and Venice – serving almost in musical terms as exposition, development and resolution. The initial banter of Susan and Neale somewhat resembles the twins in Shaw's *You Never Can Tell* (1898). He is also specifically mentioned in Susan's job interview.

> 'Your shorthand is Pitman's.'
>     'Basically. That is, I use it as the basis of my system.'
>     '*Your* system?'
>     I was pleased at wringing a little surprise from her. 'I have my own system, rather as Bernard Shaw did.'
>     'Oh yes?'[12]

Brophy's *Flesh* (1979) contains no reference to Shaw by name, but there is a strong resemblance with the Pygmalion legend. Elsewhere, in *Mozart the Dramatist*, Brophy comments on the similarity of the Don Giovanni and Pygmalion legends:

> A theme very similar to the statue that moves, namely the legend of Venus's granting Pygmalion's request for the animation of the statue he has sculpted, has been documented as a great favourite with the enlightenment, much treated by librettists and dramatists (including Rousseau), versifiers (including Voltaire) and painters (Boucher and Fragonard) [. . .] Pygmalion represents enlightened man at his most daring [. . .] he has actually usurped God the Father's creative prerogative.[13]

All the versions she mentions – and she could have added Jean-Phillippe Rameau's 'Acte de Ballet' *Pigmalion* (1748) too – are 'loyal' to the original legend, in that the created figure becomes the creature or lover of the creator. There is no attempt to rework the legend or make the setting anything other than aristocratic. Shaw sets the legend on an earthly level, with no gods and no kings, making the myth applicable to a less exalted and urban society – particularly to the relations between the professional and working classes. More than this, Shaw's created figure 'rebels'. She does not want to go back to her roots, nor is she satisfied with simply being a convincing construct duchess. Nor does she feel particularly grateful to her 'creator', still less bound to marry him.

*Flesh* continues the loosening of the original legend. Against an ordinary backdrop – bookshops, galleries, a furniture store – a gradual transformation begins its journey to a surprise, but oddly inevitable, outcome. Marcus is gauche, self-conscious, Jewish, and wants to write a novel. He has travelled with his sister (whom he believes to be lesbian) to foreign galleries. He talks art, collects art books and likes Rubens. Nancy, Jewish, from a slightly less affluent background, likes organising – and wants to organise Marcus. She sees him as suitable clay, a suitable case for transformation. She teaches him the social graces, including dancing. Under her influence he looks better, fatter. Their relationship is open. They are not set on getting married, but they do: 'Laundered, shaved and aftershaved, Marcus looked very well at his wedding. He was, now that he held himself better, quite a well-built man, with quite a handsome face.'[14] The honeymoon in Lucca involves Marcus's first sex, but not Nancy's. She has a penchant for it. The wedding night is a remarkable piece of description. Marcus is changed utterly, in the process of knowing Nancy. He even begins to worry about his looks:

> 'Well, I suppose I could get a plastic surgeon to alter my nose.'
>     She caressed him. 'I wouldn't have a surgeon touch you.'
>     'A surgeon did touch me. When I was a baby.'
>     'He wouldn't, if I'd been down there to touch him,' said Nancy.
> 'I resent any diminution of you. Particularly, darling, *there*.'[15]

He begins to fancy his chances:

> 'If you're really such a sensualist, I should have thought you'd be raring to get at all your big blonde Rubens women. . .'
>     'I don't want Rubens women, if you don't want to share them.'[16]

Marcus has a job restoring antique furniture. Nancy feeds him up for work, but he works mainly from home, and furnishes the flat. Nancy gets pregnant, but it is Marcus who grows in size. Three au pairs, all German, form a kind of Rubens's *Judgment of Paris*. Marcus has sex with the one called Ilse (which is the original name of his lesbian sister). His sister comes to hear of his infidelity and offers herself to Nancy as a substitute for the loss of Marcus. This backfires and Nancy challenges Marcus:

> 'You're disgustingly fat,' said Nancy [. . .] 'Just look at yourself [. . .] Look at your thighs. Look at your chest. You've got pendulous breasts like a woman.'
>     He gave a chuckle. 'It's a process of empathy. I've *become* a Rubens woman.'
>     He repented it instantly and [. . .] he decided to hurry past her. But as he came up to her he recognised that her look was, in reality, desirous.[17]

Nancy has come to love what she has transformed, and Marcus is grateful not to have lost her love and attention. She will now share a big blonde Rubens woman – for that is what Marcus has become.

In Brophy's low-key, inverted version of the Pygmalion legend, the woman, not the man is the primary agent, the one who 'has actually usurped God the Father's creative prerogative'. It is not mere domesticity or the influence of a good woman. She homes in on a likely character – though both will affect the other. The change is not one-way and not totally about flesh. The belief is reaffirmed that people can experience role reversals, even change sex, and are not trapped in whatever stereotype they might be thought to 'belong' to. All this, perhaps, goes further than the social 'upgrade' of Eliza Doolittle from flower girl to duchess (and indeed of Doolittle himself from dustman to millionaire) or of Lickcheese in Shaw's very first play, *Widowers' Houses* (1898).[18]

## Plays

In the preface to *Mrs Warren's Profession* (1898), Shaw wrote: 'The drama of pure feeling is no longer in the hands of the playwright; it has been conquered by the musician, after whose enchantments all the verbal arts seem cold and tame . . . there is, flatly, no future now for any drama without music except the drama of thought.'[19] Many of Shaw's plays were based on musical forms. On this matter, Brophy notes:

> He was trying, he told one actress, 'to do fine counterpoint': in three parts in *Candida*, in seven in what he naturally called 'the finale' of *The Philanderer.* He knew that the emotions in his plays had to create 'new intellectual speech channels' and even perceived that 'for some time these will necessarily appear so strange and artificial that it will be supposed that they are incapable of conveying emotion'.[20]

This musical base struck a chord with Brophy: 'I have learned my stagecraft from thinking hard about the form of the great operas and not from ASMing for ten years in a provincial rep.'[21] She also incorporated her beliefs into her works, rather downplaying 'character' as a nineteenth-century compensation for the lack of original ideas. She was a great reader of plays, reading them as if following a music score. She admired Shaw's practice of issuing his plays before they were performed:

> For every gross that exists of person who can pick their way through musical notation, follow the full score of an opera while it is performed and enjoy the score of a work they know in silence of their own reading head, you would be hard put to find one who can form from the score of a work he has never heard a firm enough impression of what it would sound like in performance for him to judge whether or not he would enjoy hearing or seeing it performed.

As a matter of fact, although the skill required is less specialised and seems much lesser, something of the same is true of reading plays. Few great playwrights have followed Bernard Shaw's rational and patient act of publishing his plays in a form that makes them accessible to readers whose only accomplishment is that they read.[22]

A musical and theatrical impetus exists in all Brophy's works, though her output of actual plays was limited. This had not been her intention and for a time she had seen herself primarily as a playwright: 'Between the ages of 6 and 10 I was a prolific playwright, mainly in blank verse. An elderly widow in a London suburb where I lived, being anxious to foster the arts, appointed herself my impresario.'[23] The only surviving play from Brophy's childhood is *The Manor Farm*, set in the days of the Saxon King Harold, and undated.[24] *The King of a Rainy Country*, however, includes a description of a school play.[25] Brophy also wrote of an actual school production in which she had been involved:

> My mother introduced her pupils, of whom I was one, to *A Midsummer Night's Dream* and *The Tempest* which she produced, with me in the cast, as school plays. John Brophy, who was writing a novel about Shakespeare, took me to see professional Shakespeare productions in London and Stratford-on-Avon, and discussed the plays with me as though daughter and father were equals. Any ability I have had as an adult to write English prose I learned from him and from reading the masters he directed me to, Bernard Shaw and Evelyn Waugh.[26]

Elsewhere she writes:

> In 1961 I reverted to my original vocation as dramatist with a one-act play, *The Waste Disposal Unit*, and in 1967 with a full-length play, *The Burglar*. The play's commercial failure warned impresarios against me and brought my public career as dramatist to an end. I have naturally continued to pursue my vocation, enlarging and varying my expressive use of the theatrical medium, first to create an opera in words and then to incarnate, by expressionist means, metaphor of the unconscious wish to die. These experiments, however, remain private, because of the present shortage of elderly widows anxious to foster the arts.[27]

In the preface to *The Burglar*, Brophy anticipated that '[in] my next play, *Libretto*, the language is again a creation, but this time of purely poetic comedy. In *Libretto* it is the words which are the music.'[28] In fact, *Libretto* was never completed and *The Burglar* and *The Waste Disposal Unit* are her only extant plays.

*The Burglar*, as well as having a rather bland title, has the same set for all three acts. As in Mozart's *Così fan tutti*, two couples are set off by a single catalyst. In Brophy's version the catalyst is a prudish burglar, and the couples have already swapped partners. A further exchange of partners would be a reversal to what is familiar. For a time, the two women hit it off but that is as far as it goes; there is no possibility of a same-sex arrangement. A similar two-couple situation occurs in Firbank's only full-length play *The Princess Zoubaroff* (1920). In his version, however, the two women do pair off at the end, with a rather indefinite set-up for the men who have been offstage for over an act. *The Burglar*, as with Firbank's play and Wilde's first two, was not a success. However, Ronald Hayman was later to write:

> It is a very clever piece of writing which reads better than it plays [. . .] The structure is more musical and logical than theatrical. As a piece of argument for five voices it is witty and well-constructed. As a radio play it might work; in the theatre it is progressively disappointing [. . .] The play fails to involve the audience [. . .] not through lack of action but because the characters and the events fail to come theatrically to life [. . .] Brophy takes a Shaw-like delight in flaying the hide off sacred cows [. . .] But she is less expert at creating characters to involve the audience's emotions. There is no Captain Shotover, no Ellie Dunn to be saved from marrying a middle-aged industrialist, no Mazzini Dunn to be disabused from thinking himself to be in the industrialist's debt. If the cast of *Heartbreak House* were reduced to Hector and Hesione, Randall and Ariadne, and the burglar, no-one would be very involved.[29]

Of the earlier radio play, *The Waste Disposal Unit*, Hayman writes:

> [It] is thoroughly successful as a farce within its own non-visual terms. As in her novel *In Transit*, which it prefigures, the comedy and conflict are bedded in the language itself [. . .] Having made the mistake of moving into three-dimensionality, Brophy should have the courage to move back to radio, a medium in which her ingenuity comes near to genius.[30]

Getting hold of a copy of this play nowadays is not easy. The take-off of the American and Italian accents would work best on radio (or in print, as in the middle section of *The King of a Rainy Country*). On stage, there might be a temptation to accompany the accents with exaggerated gestures. The noises made by the Waste Disposal Unit itself, however, would be a gift to BBC Sound Effects.

## The Adventures of God in His Search for the Black Girl

The dust jacket of *The Adventures of God in his Search for the Black Girl* (1973) declares it to be '[a] novel and some fables'.[31] Nowhere else – title-page or blurb – is the claim of novel made. The fables are twenty short items, three published in magazines, no dates; the others with no indication of the date of composition. The items include single lines, paragraphs, stories, mini-essays, variants on myths and fairy tales ('Bluebeard', 'Actaeon', 'The Labyrinth' and 'The Frog Prince'), and several items on Shaw – in two of which Shaw, now 'The Sage', discusses Democracy and the Greatest Crime. In 'Variations on Themes of Elgar and Brahms' the insulting remark that Brahms makes of Elgar – 'He has the mentality of the house-keeper or domestic bursar at a minor public school'[32] – is a revamp of Shaw's comment on Brahms: 'Brahms is just like Tennyson, an extraordinary musician, with the brains of a third-rate policeman.'[33] Musical quotations are included – a feature of many of Shaw's works. In Brophy's case, the effect is somewhat undermined.[34] (The main theme from the first movement of Elgar's Cello Concerto is quoted three times, each time differently. In the first version the fifth note is on a bar line too high, and the quavers in the fourth bar have their tails round the wrong way. The second bar in all versions is different. Either this is an elaborate and inexplicable joke by Brophy or just careless proofreading.)

The main item, 'The Adventures of God in His Search for the Black Girl', is a self-conscious revamp of Shaw's *The Adventures of the Black Girl in Her Search for God*: '"Where is God?" said the black girl to the missionary who had converted her.'[35] Thus Shaw begins his fable, which appeared in 1932 along with 'some lesser tales', including several reprinted items that must have appealed to Brophy too: 'Don Giovanni Explains', a fragment from his play *Back to Methuselah* (1921) and an account of a disastrous country visit. Shaw's language is straightforward, with dialogues, three-way discussions and dramatised incidents. The search or quest is linear; once a character (or embodiment of a philosophy or institution) is encountered, interrogated and rejected there is no going back or reappearance. The characters range from the Old Testament God, 'good' Old Testament prophets, modifiers of the Gospel and Islam to Evolutionists, Imperialists and Pavlov – and Voltaire tending his garden.

In Brophy's version, the characters are drawn from different periods; they come, go and reappear as if on stage, very like characters in Firbank's novels. Brophy quotes Gibbon: 'I have sometimes thought of writing a dialogue of the dead, in which Lucian, Erasmus, and Voltaire should mutually acknowledge the danger of exposing an old superstition to the contempt of the blind and fanatic multitude.'[36] The device, as she acknowledges, resembles the epilogue of Shaw's *St Joan* (1924), in which the characters reunite five hundred years later to discuss amicably and hear how the events of their lives have been interpreted.

The opening lines in Brophy's revamp come from Voltaire and a psychoanalyst:

'As I've said before,' said Voltaire, 'if God did not exist, it would be necessary to invent him.'
'Brilliant,' a psycho-analyst commented, 'but pre-psychological. If God did exist, it would make not a scrap of difference. We have invented him anyway.'[37]

After the arrival of several other characters, including Gibbon, God's 'presence' is clarified, very frail and confused, and trying to find the black girl. He takes soundings from a range of atheists: 'You're all historical characters, whereas I'm a fictitious one [. . .] Only among unbelievers [. . .] can I be accepted for what I am, namely a fictitious character.'[38] An atheist tone is paramount in the discussions, in line with the initial Gibbon quotation: 'the danger of exposing an old superstition to the contempt of the blind and fanatic multitude'. The old superstition is God; the danger for Gibbon and Voltaire is in exposing it to the unnamed minor characters, the Humble Christian, the Theologian, the historian other than Gibbon, etc.

Many topics feature in the discussions: the authority of the Bible, New Testament translations, vegetarianism, *Treasure Island*, the British prejudice against literature, Public Lending Right, and also much on human–animal relations.[39] Some sacred cows give rise to memorable one-liners. On machines: 'Industrial societies are now full of latter-day Luddites and modern machine-breakers, people who have confused "doing their own thing" with baking your own bread.'[40] On socialism: 'Socialists propose to abolish the rich. What they should do, and would do if they were socialists instead of superstitionists, is abolish the poor.'[41] This latter sentiment echoes the story in the same volume, 'The Sage on the Greatest Crime', where the greatest crime is held to be poverty.[42] The paragraphs about 2 + 2 = 5 occur in another story in the same volume, 'Democracy'.[43] Brophy often repeats herself. She certainly takes up some of the topics that Shaw uses – for example on Pavlov, where it must be admitted his version is much livelier; Brophy just gets God to relate a little parable.

The variety (and repeat appearances) of topics is linked partly by the witty and amiable quality of the conversation, and often by chance association. The pace changes and keeps the attention; the characters come and go and reappear, the conversation(s) form duets, trios and chamber ensembles. It is not static, nor as with Shaw's version a linear quest, but peripatetic, and with suggestions of stage scenery:

> 'I haven't,' Voltaire confirmed, linking his arm with God's as they came to a hillocky patch in the Elysian Fields, 'the smallest idea, where the Black Girl of yours is to be found. But, I'm happy to take a stroll with you and put you on your way.'[44]

When Voltaire is seen inspecting the oleanders he explains his phrase from *Candide*: 'Il faut cultiver votre jardin':

> 'Cultiver' is a verb cognate with 'culture', and thus is in logical opposition to 'nature'. If you believe that to plant a garden is an act of God, you have been misled by the book of Genesis. A garden is an attempt to improve on nature.[45]

Shaw's appearance, two-thirds of the way through, is prepared, almost as a key modulation, by careful name drops. Several names in the cast list are just statues: Lucian, who is commented on, and Samuel Butler, who is waved to. Butler's book *The Author of the Odyssey* (1897), which speculated that the author was a woman, leads to a discussion on Shaw's championing of this belief, and his support of feminism. Shaw is spotted and at first thought to be the black girl, and then a statue in the water garden:

> A tallish, boney-hipped figure wearing narrow trousers and something resembling a Norfolk jacket (in which, God considered, he must surely be too hot) stood, with his back to God and Voltaire, looking towards one of the most elaborate of the jets, which was illuminated by indigo lights.[46]

After a preliminary introduction – with the characters now reduced to God, Voltaire, the psychoanalyst and Gibbon – Shaw is given a long speech about Ireland. Shaw's speech is presented as he would have written it, his contractions without apostrophes: 'didnt', 'wont', 'cant'. Apostrophes are only used in possessives. Other characters keep apostrophes with contractions. This is a new method surely of differentiating characters on the page.

In the delightful scene with the sheep and goats, Shaw is given some flak, as has Gibbon been by the psychoanalyst. And then Voltaire criticises *St Joan*, arguing that the epilogue is fine, but the rest merely a chronicle play – and about religion at that.[47] Again, this is Brophy recycling. On two other occasions she trots out the same criticism in almost the same words.[48] Ultimately, the search for the black girl is abandoned. God writes a reference for himself. A manifesto (a godifesto) is drawn up, with Shaw as shorthand scribe. It is not on the future of the black girl, but on God: '"I do not exist" signed with divine authority, God.'[49] It is to be dropped *en masse* from heaven on to Rome. This ends the main section of the 'novel'. It is discursive, imaginative and vastly entertaining. Brophy appears in her version, as did Shaw in his. The technique is theatrical. The stumbling blocks are perhaps the quotations, the translations and the church Latin; and there are sixty-eight footnotes, many referring to works of Shaw. These might militate against defining the work as a novel. Yet it is obviously hybrid, and none the worse for that.

Its epilogue is quite different. It is prefaced by a quotation from *St Joan*: 'Have you heard no tales of the Black Prince who was blacker than the devil himself?'[50] On this rather tenuous connection, the black girl becomes the Black Prince, studying medieval English history and recently back from visiting Orleans. His name is Hector Erasmus (Erasmus is the missing character from the Gibbon quotation) Mkolo. He is black, but not a prince. His father kept a thatched general store in Central Africa, and his mother kept hens which his father was forever having to shoo out of the shop (a possible reference to the non-laying hens in *St Joan*). He is visiting Rome when the manifestos are dropped, like snow. They prove to be blank on both sides. You must use your imagination.

All this – ten pages – is narrated. There is no speech or conversation, which are among the strengths of the earlier part of the novel. However, at the very end of the epilogue the crowds assemble on the piazza in front of St Peter's and shout 'Iddio. Iddio. Iddio.'[51] A pun, both visually and aurally, for idiot. Interlinguistic, as well. Comparable to *Fin* at the very end of *In Transit*.

## Palace without Chairs

*Palace without Chairs: A Baroque Novel* (1978) was Brophy's last and longest novel. The jacket description states that 'the crackling conversational style of the vividly-characterised inhabitants suggests that among their ancestors was Shaw's King Magnus'.[52] There are indeed obvious parallels with Shaw's *The Apple Cart* (1930) in the setting, characters, situation and form. The setting is an imaginary kingdom – Ruritanian, Mittel-European, quite probably Balkan – called Evarchia. The capital is Asty, the nearest airport is Vienna, and it has diplomatic relations with Bulgaria. It is very much the territory of Shaw's *Arms and the Man* (1898), which is set in Bulgaria. The main characters are His Most Catholic and Pre-Canonical Majesty King Cosmo III, the Queen, and the five children, Ulric, Sempronius, Balthasar, Heather and Urban. The name Sempronius had appeared in *The Apple Cart*. A passing character, a travelling entertainer, is called Bluntchsli, which is the same as the anti-heroic chocolate soldier of Shaw's *Arms and the Man*. Cosmo III has a drink called Chocolate Pot served to him every morning (shades, here, of the breakfast chocolate served in Richard Strauss's cross-dressing opera *Der Rosenkavalier* [1911]).

The situation in *Palace without Chairs* is not dissimilar to *The Apple Cart*. In the Shaw play, King Magnus is 'cornered' by his cabinet and threatens – if certain things are not done – to resign and stand for parliament, and almost certainly win handsomely. In Brophy's novel, the issue is the succession; the king is dying; who will succeed? Both works are about the nature of democracy and the inability to get things done; in Brophy's novel, to get chairs for the palace.

*The Apple Cart* was the first of what Shaw called his Political Extravaganzas; he had touched on the form in parts of *Back to Methusaleh* (1921). Brophy, in choosing to write a political novel, adopts a similar pattern, with events and locations that parallel and resonate with the current situation. In a novel, necessarily, the descriptions and scene settings are longer (uniforms, protocol, Royal Riding School, etc.), and the twist of events (assassination, abdication, suicide, accident, military intervention) becomes more frequent. That the setting is royal does not imply that Brophy was a closet monarchist. Many myths and fairy tales revolve around royalty; the private and public roles and expectations are intertwined; the handing-over of power is crucial. Brophy used this device in other stories, such as 'The Singularly Ugly Princess' and in the title story of her first publication *The Crown Princess*: 'The Crown Princess [of Retzel] was seeking the exact moment when a small girl had become Royalty. Not Royal, but Royalty.'[53] That she was using royalty as a device Brophy implies in the initial quotation: 'Thus, regardless of real rank, all the children he [Van Dyck] painted became princes and princesses',[54] and further: 'Thanks to the cognateness of royal and real.'[55] She acknowledges royalty's very ordinariness in the key issue of procuring chairs for the palace: 'Though the popular imagination chooses to picture us as ethereal beings, we in fact have bottoms and should welcome somewhere to put them.'[56]

Nor should it be implied that Brophy was against democracy. Shaw had encountered this misreading with *The Apple Cart*: 'In Dresden the performance was actually prohibited as a blasphemy against Democracy.'[57] In Brophy's novel, the royal family are themselves pretty tepid about the form of government they are supposed to represent:

'We are, in so far as our office is concerned, non-political; we are all, in so far as we are persons, democrat and socialists – and, indeed, republicans.'
    'And also militant atheists,' Heather added.
    'Except Papa. Papa is a Christian [. . .] Politically, he is probably a Christian Democrat and a Christian Socialist – which means, as you will realise, something very different from being a democrat or a socialist or even from being a Social-Democrat.'[58]

Mention of these 'imaginary' but familiar-sounding political groupings reminds us that *Palace without Chairs* is essentially a political novel using fairy-tale conventions. It was dedicated to Michael Foot, the former leader of the Labour Party, 'whom I have long admired as a writer and agreed with as a politician,' Brophy wrote, 'and who has become a dear friend'.[59]

Not only does it contain references to early twentieth-century events, such as the shooting by a lone imbecile of an archduke, an abdication (albeit kept quiet), and Cold War rivalries between countries, including spying, security procedures and discipline, but there are references to the labour strikes that were not uncommon in late 1970s Britain, when the book was written. These well-incorporated references fit neatly against a divided ruling family that has lost faith in itself, and is waiting for its last true believer to die. They also anticipate the growth of a lone Silent Grenadier who believes in discipline and who eventually takes over Evarchia by force.

The most capable member of the royal family, who might have averted or delayed the takeover, is Balthasar. He heads the attempts to procure more chairs. He is opposed by protocol, definitions, further meetings, difficulties in scheduling; this is the most Shavian section of the novel. He is, in effect, Boss Mangan and the burglar in *Heartbreak House* (1919) – 'the only two efficient businessmen';[60] they both get killed by the bomb. Balthasar similarly dies in a freak accident involving a seagull. Interestingly, at the end of the first meeting, the section – instead of rounding off as a scene in a play might – diverts into a short discussion on thriller novels. This is the direction the novel slowly pursues, never with the breakneck pace and cheap and obvious twists typical of that genre; but equally never really establishing a viable reason for the lack of chairs. (Is it, we might wonder, supply and demand, and/or some built-in glitch in the economic system comparable to Breakages Ltd in *The Apple Cart*?)

Brophy's novel is divided into four parts; Winter Palace (chapters 1–3), Dead March (chapter 4), Summer Palace (chapters 5–8) and Palace Revolution (chapters 9–11). Are these four acts or four movements? The length of each part is 133, 28, 86 and 35 pages respectively. Each chapter is divided into short scenes. Winter Palace is the exposition. Dead March is the shortest section, by implication the slow movement, almost an interlude, mainly interrogation, with no speech marks but Joyce-like indentations with dashes. The Summer Palace could be construed as a scherzo, with its island setting and delightful invented birds. The Palace Revolution is the short resolution: the pace is more urgent, the scenes shorter, and they go from personal to crowd in a filmic manner. Brophy does not descend to the level of political thrillers; where she needs to she will (as with her use of fairy tale) adopt a device, put on the pace or spring a surprise, but she does not forfeit opportunities to make telling points. The warning note has been sounded. At the end, we readers are still on an unresolved plateau. Heather's love life will round off the story.

These many examples from Brophy's hugely varied output only begin to establish the extensive links between her and George Bernard Shaw – and include some examples where Brophy's 'Shavian' outlook even led her, paradoxically, to criticise Shaw himself and his legacy.

## Notes

1. Giles Gordon, 'Obituary: Brigid Brophy', *The Independent*, 8 August 1995, <http://www.independent.co.uk.news.people.obituary.brigid-brophy> (accessed 23 August 2019). The title of this chapter is also taken from this source.
2. Kenneth Clark, *The Best of Aubrey Beardsley* (London: Murray, 1978), pp. 8, 12.
3. Brigid Brophy, 'Abbé Aubrey', a review of Miriam Benkovitz's *Aubrey Beardsley: An Account of his Life*, *London Review of Books*, 2–16 April 1981.
4. Brigid Brophy, *Baroque-'n'-Roll and Other Essays* (London: Hamish Hamilton, 1987), p. 92. Brophy cites George Bernard Shaw, 'On sex in biography', in *Sixteen Self-Sketches* (London: Constable, 1949), p. 128.
5. Brigid Brophy, 'The Way of No Flesh', in Michael Holroyd (ed.), *The Genius of Shaw* (London: Hodder and Stoughton, 1979), pp. 95–111.
6. Brigid Brophy, 'The Rights of Animals', in *Reads* (London: Sphere, 1987), p. 131.
7. Brigid Brophy, *Palace without Chairs* (London: Hamish Hamilton, 1978).
8. Brigid Brophy, *Hackenfeller's Ape* (London: Alison and Busby, 1979), p. 51.
9. Ibid., p. 25.
10. Ibid., p. 67.
11. Ibid., p. 120.
12. Brigid Brophy, *The King of a Rainy Country* (London: Virago, 1990), p. 18.
13. Brigid Brophy, *Mozart the Dramatist: A New View of Mozart, His Operas and His Age* (London: Faber, 1964), p. 237.
14. Brigid Brophy, *Flesh* (London: Secker and Warburg, 1962; this edn, London: Faber and Faber, 2013), p. 40.
15. Ibid., p. 89.
16. Ibid., p. 49.
17. Ibid., p. 122.
18. George Bernard Shaw, 'Widowers' Houses', in *Plays Unpleasant* (London: Penguin, 1961).
19. George Bernard Shaw, 'Mrs Warren's Profession', in *Plays Unpleasant*, p. 196.
20. Brophy, *Baroque-'n'-Roll*, p. 85.
21. Brigid Brophy, 'Preface' to *The Burglar* (London: Cape, 1968), pp. 7–56; here, p. 32.
22. Brophy, *Baroque-'n'-Roll*, p. 164.
23. Brophy, *The King of a Rainy Country*, p. 276.

24. Brigid Brophy, *The Manor Farm*, in the Brophy archive, <http://www.brigidbrophy.com/unpublished-work> (accessed 23 August 2019).
25. Brophy, *The King of a Rainy Country*, p. 72.
26. Ibid., p. 276.
27. 'Brigid Brophy comments', in Kate Berry (ed.), *Contemporary Women Dramatists* (London: St James Press, 1994), p. 27.
28. Brophy, 'Preface' to *The Burglar*, p. 33.
29. Ronald Hayman, 'Commentary', in Berry (ed.), *Contemporary Women Dramatists*, pp. 28–9.
30. Ibid., p. 31.
31. Brigid Brophy, *The Adventures of God in His Search for the Black Girl* (London: Macmillan, 1973), jacket blurb.
32. Ibid., p. 39.
33. George Bernard Shaw, autograph postcard to Pakenham Beattie, 4 April 1893, Bonhams auction catalogue, 2009, <http://www.bonhams.com/auctions/16811/lot/148> (accessed 23 August 2019).
34. Brophy, *The Adventures*, pp. 39–43.
35. George Bernard Shaw, *The Adventures of the Black Girl in Her Search for God, and Some Lesser Tales* (London: Constable, 1932; this edn, London: Penguin, 1946), p. 25.
36. Epigraph quotation from Edward Gibbon, *Memoirs of My Life*, in Brophy, *The Adventures*, p. 112.
37. Brophy, *The Adventures*, p. 113.
38. Ibid., p. 118.
39. See Robert McKay, 'Brigid Brophy's Pro-animal Forms', *Contemporary Women's Writing*, 12.2 (2018), pp. 152–70.
40. Brophy, *The Adventures*, p. 178.
41. Ibid., p. 154.
42. Ibid., p. 45.
43. Ibid., p. 38.
44. Ibid., p. 147.
45. Ibid., p. 177.
46. Ibid., p. 182.
47. Ibid., p. 207.
48. 'Hamlet', in Brigid Brophy, Michael Levey and Charles Osborne, *Fifty Works of English and American Literature We Could Do Without* (New York: Stein and Day, 1968), p. 11; Brigid Brophy, 'The Great Celtic-Hibernian', in *Reads*, p. 152.
49. Brophy, *The Adventures*, p. 210.
50. George Bernard Shaw, *St Joan* (London: Constable, 1924; this edn, London: Penguin, 1959), p. 60.
51. Brophy, *The Adventures*, p. 224.
52. Brophy, *Palace without Chairs*, jacket blurb.
53. Brigid Brophy, *The Crown Princess and Other Stories* (London: Collins, 1953), p. 7.

54. Brophy, *Palace without Chairs*, epigraph, in Michael Levey, *Gainsborough's Daughters Chasing a Butterfly* (London: National Gallery, 1975).

55. Brophy, *Palace without Chairs*, p. 42.

56. Ibid., p. 46.

57. George Bernard Shaw, *The Apple Cart: A Political Extravaganza* (London: Constable, 1930; this edn, London: Penguin, 1964), 'Preface'.

58. Brophy, *Palace without Chairs*, p. 77.

59. Brigid Brophy, 'Afterword', in *King of a Rainy Country*, p. 280.

60. George Bernard Shaw, *Heartbreak House* (London: Constable, 1919; this edn, London: Penguin, 1964), p. 160.

# Chapter 7

# 'Il faut que je vive': Brigid Brophy and Animal Rights

*Gary L. Francione*

## Introduction

On 10 October 1965, *The Sunday Times Weekly Review* inaugurated a series called 'Minority View'. The first entry in this series was an essay, 'The Rights of Animals', by Brigid Brophy.[1] In 1971, Brophy published an essay, 'In Pursuit of a Fantasy', in the collection *Animals, Men and Morals: An Enquiry into the Maltreatment of Non-humans*.[2] In 1979, she contributed an essay entitled 'The Darwinist's Dilemma' to *Animals' Rights – a Symposium*.[3] In these three essays, Brophy, a novelist, critic, and campaigner for feminism, peace and all manner of reforms, provided the seeds of an *animal rights* theory.

Brophy had published her first novel, *Hackenfeller's Ape*, in 1953 and the plot involved, among other aspects, rescuing an ape from a zoo to prevent the animal from being sent into space. So, Brophy's interest in how humans used animals for various purposes began much earlier. But there can be no doubt that her 1965 and 1971 essays establish her as the original animal rights advocate of the modern period. Others, such as Henry Salt[4] and Leslie J. Cross,[5] had written about animal rights. Lewis Gompertz condemned all animal use and made important improvements on the design of the bicycle because he opposed the use of horses for transport.[6] But, as Richard D. Ryder notes, Brophy provided a 'restatement of the animal rights ideal' as part of the revival of the animal movement in the 1960s and 1970s[7] and did so before modern philosophers showed any interest in the topic.[8]

In this essay, I will discuss how Brophy effectively if not explicitly rejected key components of the position that had become conventional wisdom in Britain (and most other places) concerning our moral obligations to animals. That position – the *animal welfare position* – maintained that it was morally acceptable to use animals for human purposes as long as we treated them 'humanely'. I will also discuss the position that ultimately came to define the modern 'animal movement'. Unfortunately, it was not Brophy's animal rights position that prevailed.

### The animal welfare position: our conventional wisdom about animals

Before the nineteenth century, animals were generally regarded as *things* that had no moral or legal significance.[9] They were considered as inferiors who lacked the cognitive sophistication of humans. Jeremy Bentham, a nineteenth-century reformer who was a key figure in the animal welfare movement, argued that, although a full-grown horse or dog is more rational and more able to communicate than a human infant, 'the question is not, Can they *reason*? nor, Can they *talk*? but, Can they *suffer*?'[10] Bentham argued that the only characteristic required for moral significance was *sentience*, or subjective awareness and the ability to experience pain and suffering. Since animals, or at least most of the ones humans exploited, were unquestionably sentient, they mattered morally and humans had moral obligations to take their suffering seriously.

This is not to say that, because animals mattered morally, it was morally impermissible for humans to continue to exploit animals. Bentham maintained that animals are not self-aware and they do not know what they lose when we kill them. They have an interest in not suffering; they do not have an interest in continuing to live. If we kill and eat them, 'we are the better for it, and they are never the worse. They have none of those long-protracted anticipations of future misery which we have.'[11] As far as Bentham was concerned, animals do not care *that* we kill and eat them; they care only about *how* we treat them and kill them. So, humans could continue to use animals; they just had to take more seriously animal interests in not suffering. Another important figure in the discussion about animal welfare, John Stuart Mill, maintained that, in assessing the interests animals have, it was important to keep in mind that animals lack 'a sense of dignity, which all human beings possess in one form or other'.[12] Moreover, humans have 'a more developed intelligence, which gives a wider range to the whole of their sentiments, whether self-regarding or sympathetic.'[13] As a result, '[i]t is better to be a human being dissatisfied than a pig satisfied'.[14]

Although the animal welfare position ostensibly represented a paradigm shift in our thinking about the moral status of animals and rejected the idea that animals were just things, and resulted in laws that supposedly protected animals from 'cruel' or 'inhumane' treatment, it failed to provide any significant protection for animals because the framework it established for evaluating their interests was unsound. The animal welfare position did not recognize that animals had rights; indeed, the primary thinkers behind the animal welfare movement – people like Bentham and Mill – were *utilitarians*, who rejected moral rights. Animal interests in not suffering, unprotected by claims of right, were to be balanced against the interests of humans. But fundamental human interests are protected by moral rights that are recognised by law. One of those human rights – arguably one of the most important – is the right of private property. *And animals are chattel property under the law.* So although the animal welfare position purported to reject the idea that animals were just things that had no moral value, the status of animals as property meant that animals remained as things. The animal welfare position required, in effect, that we balance the interests of cognitively inferior animals who are property against the interests of humans who have property rights in animals. This was a system that could not work and did not work to provide any meaningful protection to animals.[15]

The prohibition on imposing unnecessary suffering did not prohibit uses of animals that were unnecessary, but only prohibited imposing more suffering than was necessary to use animals for various purposes most of which could not be plausibly described as necessary. In applying this standard, legislatures and courts deferred to animal owners, who were assumed to be rational actors best positioned to determine what level of suffering was necessary in order to use animals for these purposes. Therefore, the prohibition on unnecessary suffering became, in effect, a prohibition only on *gratuitous* suffering. By the 1960s, humans were using more animals than ever before and in more horrific ways. Intensive agriculture was emerging and spreading rapidly, and the use of animals in experiments – vivisection – was increasing. This was the context and the framework in which Brophy encountered and addressed the issue of our moral obligations to nonhuman animals.

## Enter Brophy and animal rights

Brophy rejected this framework in favour of an animal rights position. Brophy did not provide, nor did she intend to provide, any sort of systematic refutation of the animal welfare position, which she did not really discuss beyond noting that '[s]poradic legislation and individual kindness protect animals from some atrocities at human hands' but did not result in 'a general and explicit recognition' of animal rights. She did not discuss the property status of animals explicitly but she noted that '[t]o posterity it may seem as anomalous that we supposed a dog could be owned as it seems to us that cultivated and rational ancient Athenians supposed that a human could.'[16]

Neither *The Sunday Times* essay nor the 1971 book chapter is very long. The former occupies a page of the newspaper and is seven pages in length when reprinted a book; the latter is twenty-one pages in length but only has about five pages devoted to general theory. The rest of the essay is devoted to a discussion about vivisection and is located in one of the two sections of *Animals, Men and Morals* that examined particular uses of animals and not in one of the two sections that dealt with theory. Brophy's 1979 essay, which was more of a reflection on her earlier thoughts, is ten pages in length. She was not trying to produce the sort of theory that might satisfy an academic philosopher. I have the impression that she did not think that such an approach was necessary; she saw the ideas as simple and indisputable, and not requiring more than she said. I also do not think that she appreciated that the implication of the seeds she was planting was the complete incompatibility of the rights/welfare positions and the counterproductive nature of the welfarist position – ideas that came into sharp focus only in the late 1980s and 1990s.[17] In any event, Brophy's essays contained ideas that challenged our conventional wisdom about animals as represented in animal welfare theory in at least three fundamental respects.

First, Brophy implicitly rejected the concept of necessity that had developed within that theory and maintained that, if animals mattered morally, we needed to reject *uses* of animals that are not necessary and not just focus on whether particular practices were necessary to accomplish those uses. She claimed that the conflicts or dilemmas that we think exist between humans and animals are, for the most, illusory. In her *Sunday Times* essay, she argued that '[t]he only genuine moral problem is where there is a direct clash between an animal's life and a human one.' She observed that most of our uses of animals do not involve any such clash. For example, we think of using animals for food as involving a dilemma because we assume that we need to eat animals for reasons of health and nutrition. She pointed out that she had been a healthy vegetarian for ten years, and that using animals for food does not involve a genuine moral problem. It is simply a matter of palate pleasure. She noted that genuine clashes between humans and nonhumans 'are much rarer in reality than in exam papers'.[18] She claimed that '[t]he most genuine and painful clash' involves vivisection but she concluded that she did not think that vivisection is morally justified:

> I can see nothing (except our being able to get away with it) which lets us pick on animals that would not equally let us pick on idiot humans (who would be more useful) or, for the matter of that, on a few humans of any sort whom we might sacrifice for the good of the many.[19]

In her 1971 essay, she repeated this idea that, with the possible exception of vivisection, our use of animals does not involve any moral dilemmas:

> Buying a sealskin coat doesn't represent a choice between evils. It is a simple choice of evil. (The choice is human; the evil is to seals.) Neither can anyone pretend that, in a confrontation between humans and the calves they propose to convert into roast veal, there is any question of Them Or Us. The conspicuous and healthy existence of human vegetarians makes it impossible to claim that taking the calf's life is necessary to sustaining human life.
>     [...]
> Vivisection temporarily apart, in all relationships between humans as a group and the other animals as a group, the moral position of humans is straightforward. We simply override the others. Arbitrarily and wantonly – without, that is to say, justification or necessity – we are tyrants.[20]

Brophy was absolutely correct to note that, although we claim to reject inflicting unnecessary suffering on animals, most of the suffering we inflict on animals *cannot* be characterised as 'necessary' in any remotely plausible sense. We assume that there is a dilemma that we must try to resolve in a 'humane' way when there is no dilemma in the first place. Much of my work has focused on how the property status of animals guarantees that we will think about necessity in a way that will contradict and undermine what we claim to be our acceptance of the moral principle that we ought not to inflict unnecessary suffering on animals.[21] The 'conflicts' between humans and animals are largely conflicts between the owners of animal property and their property. These conflicts are *created* by the institution of property and they must be resolved in favor of the property owner in order for the institution of animal property to exist. As I mentioned above, Brophy never discussed the property problem. She sought only to clarify that a coherent sense of 'clash' or 'conflict' between humans and nonhumans had to rule out any situation where there was not legitimate compulsion.

Second, Brophy rejected the idea that using and killing animals does not per se involve a moral issue because animals are not self-aware and care only about *how* we treat them and how we kill them, and not *that* we use and kill them. This idea was at the very foundation of the animal welfare position and, in many ways, Brophy's rejection of it is her most important contribution; she recognised that animals have an interest in continuing to live and that this interest is separate and distinct from their interest in not suffering.[22] She linked this interest in continuing to live with the notion of rights. In her 1965 essay, she maintained that the issue of causing animals to suffer was a different issue from whether we had the right to kill them: 'I don't myself believe that, even when we fulfill our minimum obligation not to cause pain, we have the right to kill animals.'[23] In her 1971 essay, she looked to the American Declaration of Independence, which characterised the right to the pursuit of happiness as 'unalienable'. She noted that this recorded 'a fact of my nature. As a live sentient being, I am bound to the pursuit of happiness and to its concomitant, the shunning of pain.'[24] She argued that sentience is an 'instrument' that keeps us alive: 'From the moment that I am alive, my being alive consists of an organisation towards staying alive.' She applied this framework to all sentient beings and maintained that '[a] living organism is, in being alive and being organised, a tacit assertion of "Il faut que je vive".' This is just a simple matter of fact: 'Any living individaul [sic] thing cannot help but tend to continue to live.' She maintained that 'my right to stay alive is something I claim independently of my right to shun pain.'[25]

Brophy characterised 'Il faut que je vive' as 'self-validating', in that one person's necessity cannot 'absolutely and of its nature over-rule another person's.' She argued that to respond, as did the aris-tocrat in Voltaire's story, 'Je n'en vois pas la nécessité' is to behave as a tyrant. She saw the Declaration of Independence as converting a 'perception of the *facts* about being alive and sentient into a dec-laration of the *right* to continue alive and obey the pleasure-pain principle'.[26] The interests of sentient humans must be a matter of protection by rights because there is no reasonable way of judging between the value of the assertion 'Il faut que je vive' on the part of different humans. That is, we cannot protect the interests of humans depending on the mode of being or sentience. We must treat all as equal in their self-validating assertion. The issue is not what value X's life has to Y; the only party who gets to judge the value of X's life is X. Brophy was clear: X values X's life even if no one else does. And that is the same for every sentient being. Therefore, our rights to our life must be 'taken as equal':

> My life may seem to you a poor and limited little affair, the loss of which you would reckon no great loss. That doesn't, however, entitle you to make me lose it. Since we are separate entities, the question is not what my life is worth to you, but what it is worth to me, whose only life it is and who am the only person who lead it.[27]

She argued that certain 'secondary' human rights (the right to vote, the right to an education, etc.) made sense only in a cultural context, and it made perfect sense to say that animals had a right to life, and to pursue pleasure and shun pain, but did not have other rights, such as a right to vote.[28]

Brophy's position explicitly vindicated the right of sentient beings to live. That is, hers was a position not about the welfare of animals we exploit but about the right of animals not to be exploited. In her 1979 essay, she explained that she titled her 1965 essay as she did 'by deliberate analogy with – or, more precisely and more pointedly, by deliberate extrapolation from – the title of Thomas Paine's book (of 1791 and 1792) *The Rights of Man*.'[29] She also explained that her claim of rights for animals was based on egalitarianism and social justice. In our relationships with other humans, we will never rid ourselves of our 'egocentric vision' that allows us to see a 'tremendous gulf between Me and All the Rest of You'.[30] But our imagination allows us to appreciate our similarity to each other so that we can discount the distorting effects of our egocentrism. The same imagination should allow us to overcome our anthropocentric prejudices and make an intellectual adjustment in how we think about other animals. She acknowledged that recognising egalitarianism between all species raised questions, such as whether humans are justified in stopping cats and tigers from killing other animals, or in breaking laws to save nonhuman animals, but, these questions aside, she saw the issue of animal rights as 'straightforward'[31] and that 'there is a necessary continuity between the rights of all animals, as animals, including human animals in with the others'.[32]

Third, Brophy rejected the idea proposed by Mill and others that animals mattered less morally because they supposedly had inferior cognitive capacities and that some qualitative distinction between humans and nonhumans justified denying rights to the latter:

To argue that we humans are capable of complex, multifarious thought and feeling, whereas the sheep's experience is probably limited by lowly sheepish perceptions, is no more to the point than if I were to slaughter and eat you on the grounds that I am a sophisticated personality able to enjoy Mozart, formal logic and cannibalism whereas your imaginative world seems confined to *True Romances* and tinned spaghetti.[33]

We cannot compare experiences in terms of judging some to be of greater moral value than others; the issue is what one's experiences and perception are worth to one, not what they are worth to someone else. She rejected the conventional wisdom that, because nonhuman animals were less intellectually sophisticated, their experiences were somehow 'dim' relative to those of humans. Indeed, if animals have 'dimness in [. . .] intellect and imagination', they may experience pain and suffering in a more profound way.[34] The whole enterprise of trying to rank sentience in some hierarchical way was necessarily doomed from the outset:

> Your pleasure may be more pleasurable than my pain is painful. You may have received a special revelation to that effect, and your special revelation might be correct. But as neither you nor I can enter into each other's being or sentiency, we shan't convince one another; and an impartial, reasonable third person, who can't enter into either of us, possesses no reasonable scale for judging between us.[35]

She returned to this theme in 'The Darwinist's Dilemma', when she wrote that the concept of 'higher animals' was nothing more than 'another distortion induced by our anthropocentric point of view: 'by "higher" we just meant "more like us".'[36]

Brophy dismissed the entire enterprise of weighing the interests of sentient beings against each other in order to determine who had more significant interests. This was the basis of the system of animal welfare, which, on one level, required a balance of human and animal interests but, on another level, as we saw above, involved only a balancing between the interests of property owners and their property. Brophy rejected the balancing on both levels. She made clear that most of our 'conflicts' with animals are manufactured, and that even in a situation of genuine conflict, we cannot resolve that conflict through the fantasy of balancing interests where such balancing assumed from the outset that animal interests had less value.

She noted that the fact that nonhumans cannot speak our language or reason in the way that we do does not mean that they do not have a fundamental right to life any more than human babies or the mentally disabled or impaired do not have a fundamental right to life. It did, however, mean that animals are exempted from having moral obligations to us or to each other, and that it is *our* moral responsibility to establish rights for animals:

> And we have to recognise their total exception from recognising any of *our* rights – or one another's. The tiger cannot be called immoral if he fails to limit his pursuit of happiness in deference to the gazelle's right to live. The other animals are exempted (or excluded) from our system of morality altogether, which is why a declaration of their rights has to be drawn up not by them but on their behalf.[37]

In making this observation, Brophy effectively rejected the argument – made often by those who oppose animal rights – that animals cannot have rights because they do not share our system of justice or cannot enter into a social contract with us.[38] She was clear that it was *only* their sentience that gave rise to their right not to be exploited by us, and our ability to reason required that we respect that right and ignore any differences between humans and nonhumans as a basis for denying that right. She was also clear that we could not recognise animal rights and still continue to exploit animals: 'That I like the flavour of mutton no more entitles me to kill a sheep than a taste for roast leg of human would entitle me to kill you.'[39]

As mentioned above, three-quarters of Brophy's 1971 essay concerned vivisection. She argued there that, although it was our only use of animals that was not transparently frivolous, vivisection still did not present a true dilemma or clash between humans and nonhumans because there were no efforts to avoid the dilemma by seeking alternatives or disseminating information about non-animal models, etc. But she was also clear that, in any event, vivisection is wrong as a matter of rights:

> If it is justified in declaring human rights irreducible, so that it will not trade one of them for a dozen others, it is justified in declaring all animal lives absolute and declining to trade a hundred of $x$ species for one of $y$ species.[40]

Brophy had served as a Vice-President of the National Anti-Vivisection Society. Sometime in the early 1980s, she was diagnosed with multiple

sclerosis, from which she died in 1995 at age 66.[41] In considering treat-
ments, she made it clear that she did not want to be the beneficiary of
the suffering of any animals.[42]

In sum, Brophy's essays presented, albeit in a form so abbreviated
that one would miss if one blinked, a nascent animal rights position
twelve years before the publication of Tom Regan's *The Case for
Animal Rights* (or eighteen years, if you measure it from her 1965
essay).[43] And her position was actually more radical than Regan's. He
had linked full moral status with preference autonomy and she had
linked it with sentience alone. Although it is certainly true that Brophy
did not present a fully-developed theory of animal rights – she did not
set out to do so – she did discuss animal rights in a way that had not
occurred up to that point. Indeed, Brophy very deliberately took head-
on the problem of trying to derive an 'ought' from an 'is' by arguing
that the fact of sentience gave rise to the fact of an interest in living and
obeying the pleasure-pain principle, and from these facts we could, as
had the Declaration of Independence in the human context, derive a
right to life based on the recognition that there is no rational way to
judge whose right to life mattered more.

## The modern non-rights 'animal movement'

Brigid Brophy suggested elements of a truly radical animal *rights*
position. There can be no doubt that Ryder was correct in identifying Brophy as being central to the modern articulation of the animal
rights position. Brophy was a motivating force behind the formation
of the Oxford Group, an informal and eclectic group of intellectuals
who discussed animal issues in the late 1960s and 1970s. She was the
only contributor to *Animals, Men and Morals* specifically mentioned
and thanked by the editors in the Introduction to the book.[44] Brophy's
work was on some level recognised as visionary. But the movement
that developed was not a rights movement and did not reflect Brophy's thinking at all. Why? The short answer: Peter Singer. Brophy's
ideas never really had a chance. The movement that developed was
based on and dominated by Singer's *Animal Liberation*, published
in 1975, and Singer's position was *very* different from Brophy's. As I
discuss below, Singer presented what was at most a more progressive
version of the welfarist position.

Although Singer was a graduate student at Oxford at the time,
he did not contribute an essay to *Animals, Men and Morals*. In
*Animal Liberation*, Singer credited discussions with Roslind and

Stanley Godlovitch, two of the editors of that book, and others, as helping to shape his views,[45] and Singer dedicated the book to, among others, 'Ros and Stan'. He claimed that the idea to write *Animal Liberation* came after he received an 'enthusiastic response' to a review of *Animals, Men and Morals* that he sent unsolicited to the *New York Review of Books* (which then published *Animal Liberation*).[46] In that review, which was published in April 1973, Singer discussed some of the essays in the book. Brophy's was not one he chose.[47] He quoted Brophy only once in *Animal Liberation* in the context of talking about moral consistency.[48]

Singer is often referred to as the 'father of the animal rights movement'. But he, like Bentham, is a utilitarian who eschews moral rights. Singer is Bentham's modern proponent and, in many respects, Singer's work on animal ethics can be seen as an elaboration of Bentham's position. Singer was careful to separate the issues of suffering and killing, and he avoided drawing any conclusions about the morality of killing animals: 'the conclusions that are argued for in this book flow from the principle of minimizing suffering alone.'[49] He did, however, say in the context of considering killing (as opposed to imposing suffering) that not all lives were of equal worth and that there were objective bases for making judgments about whose life was worth more. This statement from Singer is about as definitive a rejection of Brophy's 'il faut que je vive' position as one could imagine:

> [A] rejection of speciesism does not imply that all lives are of equal worth. While self-awareness, intelligence, the capacity for meaningful relations with others, and so on are not relevant to the question of inflicting pain – since pain is pain, whatever other capacities, beyond the capacity to feel pain, the being may have – these capacities may be relevant to the question of taking life. It is not arbitrary to hold that the life of a self-aware being, capable of abstract thought, of planning for the future, of complex acts of communication, and so on, is more valuable than the life of a being without these capacities.[50]

So, Singer, like Bentham, maintained that sentience was all that was needed to have morally significant interests in not suffering but that the lives of animals had lesser moral value because animals were not self-aware.[51] Although Singer did not adopt Mill's more categorical position that the pleasures of the human intellect are always to be given more weight, he came close in his analysis of the relative value of lives. He maintained that 'superior' human cognition may cause humans to suffer more than nonhumans in some cases but to suffer less in other cases.[52]

As a practical matter, Singer's position, both as to what we have a moral obligation to do in our own lives and what we should advocate as the position of an ethical/political movement for nonhuman animals, was unclear and confused. For example, with respect to eating animals, he maintained that both animal suffering and the inefficient use of resources meant that '[t]he case for a radical break in our eating habits is clear; but should we eat nothing but vegetables? Where exactly do we draw the line?' The answer: '[d]rawing precise lines is always difficult.'[53] Singer purported to offer only 'suggestions' and '[s]incere nonspeciesists may well disagree among themselves' about where to draw the lines.[54] He stated that 'the principle of equal consideration of interests requires us to be vegetarians'[55] but it was not clear what this meant. Not consuming factory-farmed meat involves a 'moral necessity'. This is the 'absolute minimum'.[56]

But what about meat that is not produced intensively? He maintained that it would be difficult to obtain or identify such meat unless one lived in a rural area. If, however, one could be certain that meat was not produced intensively, consuming that meat is apparently not prohibited by 'moral necessity' and is a matter of where one wants to draw the line. He suggested that refusing to eat any meat from slaughtered animals might be 'the next step' based on the idea that it is wrong to kill an animal for 'the trivial purpose of pleasing our palates' and because even if animals are not raised intensively, they still suffer. But this was based on the idea that this 'next step' would represent 'only a very small additional step, since so few of the birds or mammals commonly eaten are not intensively reared.'[57] If more 'humanely' raised meat were readily available, then he would presumably promote consuming only this meat as a normatively *good* thing and as not prohibited by 'moral necessity'. He certainly took that position in the case of fish. Although fish are 'down the evolutionary scale',[58] there is 'strong, if not quite as conclusive' evidence that they can suffer,[59] but they are not subjected to the sort of suffering that factory-farmed mammals and birds experience even if they are raised in fish farms, which more closely approximate a natural environment for fish than is the case with intensively-raised land animals. For reasons of the suffering of fish and out of concern that commercial fishing involves ecological disruption and adversely affects coastal fishing villages, 'we should avoid eating fish' but that if we eat fish but do not eat other animals, we 'have taken a major step away from speciesism'.[60] This, and his many references to factory farming, make it appear that intensive agriculture was Singer's primary concern, and although he expressed reservations about consuming animals that were not intensively raised,[61] that was not prohibited as a moral imperative.

Singer argued that our obligation not to buy or consume eggs produced in an egg battery is as strong as the obligation concerning factory-farmed meat because 'the egg industry is one of the most ruthlessly intensive forms of modern factory farming'.[62] But 'free-range' eggs involve only 'relatively minor' ethical objections. He ignored in this context the fact that male chicks are killed when they hatch. He claimed that 'free-range' hens 'will be killed when they cease to lay productively, but they will have a pleasant existence until that time.'[63]

Although even milk that is not produced intensively involves suffering because cows have to be impregnated at regular intervals to prevent their milk from drying up, and calves are taken from their mothers (with males usually sent off to be raised and slaughtered for veal) so that the milk is available for humans, not consuming milk is not a 'moral necessity' in the sense that not consuming factory-farmed meat or battery eggs is. Singer noted that '[i]n an ideal world, free of all speciesist practices,' we would not consume dairy products but '[i]t is more important to encourage people to stop eating animal flesh and factory farm eggs than it is to condemn them for continuing to eat milk products.' He acknowledged that although vegans were 'living demonstrations'[64] that it was possible to eliminate all animal products from one's diet, '[e]liminating speciesism from one's dietary habits is very difficult to do all at once' and if we promote the idea that there is no morally significant difference between eating flesh and eating dairy, 'the result may be that many people are deterred from doing anything at all'.[65]

He also maintained that, 'to be consistent,' we should 'stop using other animal products for which animals have been killed or made to suffer.'[66] He noted that there were alternatives to leather and fur, and to candles and soaps that were made with animal ingredients. We could also avoid wool although, 'since the sheep is not killed for its fleece, and is allowed to roam freely, perhaps this is not a major issue.'[67] In a footnote, he acknowledged that 'the annual shearing process does appear to be a terrifying one for the sheep' and sheep farmers poison animals such as coyotes.[68] Singer was clear that consistency did not mean 'a rigid insistence on standards of absolute purity in all that one consumes or wears.'[69] He urged that we 'temper our ideals with common sense' so as to avoid conveying the idea that 'we strive for the kind of purity that is more appropriate to a religious dietary law than to an ethical and political movement.' Singer warned against 'worry about such details as whether the cake you are offered at a party was made with a factory farm egg.'[70] But on the other hand, he argued that animal advocates 'must not be shy' about the refusal to eat meat from factory-farmed sources.[71]

Singer revised *Animal Liberation* in 1990, and he acknowledged more explicitly that animal exploitation could be morally acceptable if it was made to be more 'humane'. In the 1975 version, Singer rejected the argument that the people who ate meat were conferring a benefit on animals because, but for the desire to eat animals, those animals would never have existed in the first place. He pointed out that we do not bestow any sort of 'benefit' on factory-farmed animals. But he also rejected the idea that we could justify consuming meat from animals who are 'humanely' raised and slaughtered because it makes no sense to say that we can confer a benefit on a nonexistent being by bringing that being into existence and thereby obtain a moral justification for treating that being with less than equal consideration.[72] So although only factory-farmed meat and eggs were ruled out as a matter of 'moral necessity' and '[s]incere nonspeciesists' could differ about everything else, Singer's 1975 book favours pesco—vegetarianism if only because Singer believed that it would be difficult to identify meat that was not factory-farmed.

Singer changed his position in 1990, and maintained that, at least in cases in which an animal is not self-aware (i.e., has an interest in not suffering but does not have an interest in continuing to live), 'it is not easy to explain why the loss to the animal killed is not, from an impartial point of view, made good by the creation of a new animal who will lead an equally pleasant life.'[73] He cautioned that continuing to think of animals as food would encourage our disrespect and mistreatment of them, and reaffirmed that he continued to reject eating meat from factory-farmed animals. But he acknowledged that the argument he now accepted

> could justify continuing to eat free-range animals (of a species incapable of having desires for the future), who have a pleasant existence in a social group suited to their behavioral needs, and are then killed quickly and without pain. I can respect conscientious people who take care to eat only meat that comes from such animals – but I suspect that unless they live on a farm where they can look after their own animals, they will, in practice, be very nearly vegetarian anyway. [74]

It is not clear why Singer felt that such 'conscientious' people would have to raise the animals themselves and could not rely reasonably on the representations made by the producers of 'happy meat' who claim that they produce meat exactly in the way that Singer described, and who, as I discuss below, Singer now praises and promotes. In any event, Singer changed the language about vegetarianism being required by the principle of equal consideration and now qualified this obligation to exist '[f]or all practical purposes as far as urban and suburban inhabitants of industrialized nations are concerned'.[75]

He reaffirmed that conventional eggs are as objectionable as intensively produced meat but stated that the moral objections to free-range eggs 'are very much less' with the primary objection being that 'the male chicks of the egg-laying strain will have been killed on hatching, and the hens themselves will be killed when they cease to lay productively.'[76] The morality of consuming free-range eggs will depend on one's view of killing and he does 'not, on balance, object to free-range egg production.'[77] He retained that portion of the 1975 version advising not to worry about whether food we are offered is made with factory-farmed eggs.[78] With respect to dairy products, he claimed that we should avoid milk and cheese but that we should 'not feel obliged to go to great lengths to avoid all food containing milk products.'[79] With respect to wool, which he characterised in 1975 as not involving 'a major issue'[80] because sheep roam freely, he said that, although they do roam freely, 'there is a strong case'[81] for not wearing wool in light of the cruel treatment of sheep. The implication is that, if these cruelties were eliminated or even reduced, wool would not present a serious moral issue even though sheep used for wool are eventually slaughtered. He retained his statements about how difficult it is to be a vegan[82] and his argument that we ought to avoid 'purity'.[83] He also retained the position that animal advocates 'must not be shy' about not eating meat from factory-farmed sources.[84] Singer's more recent writing continues to promote the idea that killing and eating animals who are not self-aware is not immoral if those animals have a reasonably pleasant life and a relatively painless death (at least under the view that we should aim to increase the total net amount of pleasure without regard to whether we increase the pleasure of existing beings or increase the number of beings who exist).[85]

In Singer's popular writing and in his advocacy, where he has an arguably greater impact in terms of audience, he also makes clear that he does not recognize any moral imperative not to use and kill animals. He describes himself as a 'flexible' vegan who will eat dairy and eggs when travelling or when eating in someone else's house. He characterises being a conscientious vegan as 'fanatical' and stands by the warnings of *Animal Liberation* not to appear to be too radical or serious about maintaining a vegan position. If a vegan is dining with non-vegans in a restaurant and orders a vegan dish only to have it come with 'a bit of grated cheese or something on it,' the vegan should eat the food so that the others do not think that being vegan is too difficult.[86] His reasoning here would also support eating the meal if it came with a bit of meat on it as there is no morally coherent distinction between meat and dairy, and if the meat were not from a factory-farmed animal, there would be no 'moral necessity' to not consume it.

Singer maintains that, if our concern is suffering and not killing, he can

> imagine a world in which people mostly eat plant foods, but occasionally treat themselves to the luxury of free range eggs, or possibly even meat from animals who live good lives under conditions natural for their species, and are then humanely killed on the farm.[87]

He then states that, although he does not eat meat, 'if you really were thoroughgoing in eating only animals that had had good lives, that could be a defensible ethical position.'[88] It appears as though he thinks that although not consuming factory-farmed animals is a 'moral necessity', it is morally acceptable to do so if one does so only infrequently: If vegans go out to a 'fancy restaurant,' he doesn't 'see anything really wrong' if 'they allow themselves the luxury of not being vegan that evening.'[89] Singer celebrated[90] the Directive of the European Union that supposedly banned battery cages even though it allows continuing to keep hens in cages that offer no significant welfare benefits over the conventional battery cage.[91]

In 2005, Singer issued a public statement on his own behalf, and on behalf of many large animal charities, expressing 'appreciation and support' for the 'pioneering' efforts of a large U.S. retail grocery chain, Whole Foods Market, in developing 'Animal Compassionate' standards of animal exploitation.[92] When Singer was asked about his support for these standards and concerns that he was endorsing the use of 'compassionate' to describe them, he stated:

> There might be some people who say, 'You can't be compassionate if you end up killing the animals.' I just think that's wrong.
>     [. . .]

> I think as long as the standards really are compassionate ones, that do as much as they can to give the animals decent lives before they're killed, I don't have a problem with it.[93]

Singer's position may in certain respects be more progressive than the welfare position that existed in 1965, but it *is* a welfarist position – and, frankly, a most confused one that provides little definitive normative guidance. Although Brophy did not promote an abolitionist position explicitly – it would be some years before Regan and I developed that as an approach to animal ethics[94] – her writing makes it clear that her beliefs accorded with abolitionist principles.[95]

So, the reason why Brophy's animal rights position did not form the foundation of the movement is that her work was eclipsed by Singer's *Animal Liberation*. But that raises the further question about why those interested in animal ethics were attracted to Singer's position and not to Brophy's. Part of the answer is surely that Brophy did not write very much on this issue. As discussed earlier, she did not present any sort of developed theory that explicitly challenged the welfarist position. There is also a sense in which the implications of her position were not fully appreciated as a substantive matter.

Singer's *Animal Liberation* was initially received as, and continues to be misrepresented and misunderstood as, a book about 'animal rights'. Interestingly, even Brophy seemed to subscribe to that view. In the copy of the original 1975 version of *Animal Liberation* that I have, one of the endorsements on the dust jacket is from Brigid Brophy herself, who praises the book as arguing that 'we must stop hunting, hurting, enslaving, and eating our fellows. We are not the only species with a right to life, liberty and the pursuit of happiness. Peter Singer puts the case comprehensively and convincingly.'[96] These words certainly describe *Brophy's* position; they do *not* describe Singer's position. The position that animals have a 'right to life, liberty and the pursuit of happiness,' which Brophy attributed to Singer, is not the message of *Animal Liberation*. But that *exact* expression appears in Brophy's 1971 essay at the point where Brophy discusses what follows from a recognition that a sentient being claims a right to stay alive and not just a right to shun pain – ideas that Singer explicitly rejected.[97] So Brophy's endorsement is something of a mystery and may stem from nothing more than that the first edition of *Animal Liberation* was, as I discussed above, confused and unclear, and she may just have *most* generously given Singer the benefit of the doubt. There are, however, two related reasons that explain why Singer's position prevailed and would have done so even if there was a greater appreciation of Brophy's position, and these reasons highlight some disturbing aspects of the modern 'animal movement'.

First, Singer's position was less demanding and the one thing that is clear is that if people are confronted with two ways of supposedly discharging their moral obligations to animals, most will choose the less demanding way. The only thing that those concerned about animals have to avoid is factory-farmed meat and conventional battery eggs (unless one were to be out for dinner at a 'fancy' restaurant or the eggs were contained in a cake). Everything else is a matter of where one wants to draw the line.

Brophy's position led as a matter of logic and morality to veganism, and as a matter of animal rights and justice and not merely as a way of reducing suffering. That is, Brophy thought that what was necessary was exactly what Singer said was 'very difficult' and a matter of 'purity'. Brophy was a long-time and vocal vegetarian but, as I have been told by those who knew her, including her daughter, Kate Levey, she stopped consuming all animal products and became a vegan although no one knew exactly when that occurred.[98] In her 1971 essay, she mentioned that she wore plastic shoes, which indicates that she saw the problem of animal exploitation as not involving just meat.[99] In a letter that Brophy wrote in 1989, she referred to herself as a vegan although it is almost certain that she was a vegan many years before that.[100] Brophy's position was that we could not justify exploiting animals because we could not justify killing animals and not just because it made animals suffer. Someone who took seriously an 'animal rights' position as Brophy had presented it could not – as a matter of recognising animal rights – eat meat, fish, dairy, eggs, or wear clothing made from animals, or participate in activities in which animals were exploited – however 'humanely' the animals were supposedly treated. It is disturbing that a large number of 'animal advocates' – including those who claim positions as 'leaders' of the movement – are not vegan. These people for the most part are enthusiastic fans of Singer's work. That is not surprising. The modern movement is actually hostile to the idea of veganism as a moral imperative. None of the large animal charities, including, ironically, the Vegan Society,[101] promotes veganism as a moral imperative and as a matter of justice.

Second, Singer provided a business plan for animal welfare charities that allowed them to promote as 'progress' *anything* that supposedly reduced animal suffering. Singer described himself as an 'incrementalist' and maintained that 'we've got to reduce animal suffering where we can, and even if we're just doing it by taking small steps, which fall well short of our ultimate goal, that's a good thing to do.'[102] But just about *any* campaign can be characterised as representing a 'small step' in the direction of reducing suffering. This opened up the door for the emergence of a large number of new 'animal groups' and for what has become a billion-dollar industry of campaigning for – and seeking donations for – measures that they claim will lessen suffering and, so, represent 'small steps' of progress that those who care about animals are obligated to support and fund.

In the 1960s and 1970s, the traditional large charities, such as the Royal Society for the Prevention of Cruelty to Animals, the Humane Society of the United States (HSUS), and the antivivisection societies, including the National Anti-Vivisection Society (of which Brophy served as vice-president), were joined by 'animal rights' groups that were, for the most part, 'grassroots' groups that tended to reject corporate, hierarchical structure. But, as I have discussed in my writing, by the 1990s, the grassroots element had largely gone and the 'movement' – including the 'animal rights' groups – had become a collection of corporate charities that marketed 'compassion' – that is, they promoted supposedly more 'humane' animal use.[103] These groups claimed (and continue to claim) that even the most insignificant welfare reforms will lead incrementally in the direction of ending animal exploitation.[104] Singer was (and is) cited as the authority for this position. These 'reforms' not only fail to provide any significantly greater protection for animals, they actually perpetuate animal use by making people feel more comfortable about continuing to exploit animals. Singer supports these campaigns and the corporate charities that promote this marketing of 'compassion'. It is no wonder that these charities enthusiastically embrace him; he makes their existence possible and he helps them to flourish.

Brophy is not around to tell us what she thinks of the 'happy exploitation' movement that Singer leads, but I have a strong suspicion that she would, like myself and others, reject it resoundingly.[105] It contravenes everything that she promoted in her work. I believe she would reject the claim that principled veganism is 'very difficult' and is a matter of 'purity' more suited to 'a religious dietary law than to an ethical and political movement', and she would see veganism as a necessary component of a moral life and of a movement that *should* see animal rights as a matter of justice. To the extent that Brophy campaigned for single issues, such as opposition to angling or to vivisection, she was always clear that her position was based on principles of animal rights that did not admit of *any* animal exploitation.

It is true that, in her 1979 essay, Brophy described as 'allies' those who were concerned about animals but had a different perspective from her, and this, along with her own endorsement of *Animal Liberation* might be understood to suggest that she would not oppose Singer's movement to promote 'compassionate' exploitation even if she did not subscribe to it herself.[106] But at least three considerations militate against such a view.

First, in the 1970s – indeed, through the 1980s and into the mid-1990s – there was a sense in which most of those concerned about animals regarded themselves as part of a unified 'movement' even when there were significant differences in their views. It was only in the mid-1990s that it became clear that the notion of a 'unified' animal movement was a fantasy.[107]

Second, when Brophy talked about 'allies' who had different perspectives, it appeared that she was focused more on how different people got to the same point. That is, she developed an animal rights position as a matter of social justice but she regarded as 'allies' those who got to that position through religious or spiritual perspectives. As far as I can tell, she was not discussing people who promoted continued but supposedly more 'humane' exploitation.

Third, when walking around Whole Foods Market and similar sorts of places and seeing all the signs proclaiming that the corpses and other animal products they sell are to be celebrated as some expression of 'compassion' and 'respect' for animals, I cannot imagine Brophy having a reaction other than profound sadness and utter contempt.

## Conclusion

One cannot help but wonder whether Brophy's work was marginalised simply because she was a woman and, for all the virtues of the 1960s and 1970s, an appreciation of women as intellectual leaders, particularly amongst many male academics, was not one of them. When I got involved with this issue in the mid-1980s, it was Tom Regan who was my mentor on the topic of animal rights and he never discussed Brophy's work. I thought of Brophy primarily as an anti-vivisectionist campaigner and never became aware of her position on animal rights until many years later. Perhaps Brophy was rejected because she was not a philosophy professor. Although it is true that Brophy did not teach philosophy, she certainly *did* philosophy in offering ideas that challenged anthropocentrism in a way that had not been done up to that point.

But whatever the reason, there can be no doubt that, had those interested in animal ethics cultivated the rights seeds that Brophy sowed rather than embraced the neo-welfarist theory of Singer, who does not shun the ironic designation of 'father of the animal rights movement', we would have an animal rights movement today rather than the 'happy exploitation' movement that exists. Those of us who promote the animal rights position have to deal on a daily basis with claims that slightly larger cages for hens represent a monumental achievement, and that promoting the abolition of animal exploitation and veganism as a moral imperative is 'divisive', 'extreme', or a matter of 'purity'.

In so many ways, animals would have been so much better off with a movement that had one parent – a mother – Brigid Brophy.

## Notes

Thanks to Richard Canning for organising the conference on Brigid Brophy at the University of Northampton in October 2015, which, with an enormous amount of additional effort by Richard and Gerri Kimber, lead to this volume. Thanks also to my partner and colleague, Anna E. Charlton, and to Heledd Baskerville, Sam Earle, Kate Levey, and Frances McCormack for their helpful comments. This essay is dedicated to Finlay, our blind and deaf dog who sees and hears in ways that I never could and whom I am confident Brigid Brophy would have liked very much had she met him.

1. Brigid Brophy, 'The Rights of Animals', *The Sunday Times Weekly Review*, 10 October 1965. This editorial was reprinted in Brigid Brophy, *Don't Never Forget: Collected Views and Reviews* (New York: Holt, Rinehart and Winston, 1966), pp. 15–21. References to the 1965 essay will be to the book rather than to the newspaper so that the page references can be supplied.
2. Brigid Brophy, 'In Pursuit of a Fantasy', in *Animals, Men and Morals: An Enquiry into the Maltreatment of Non-humans*, eds Stanley and Roslind Godlovitch and John Harris (London: Victor Gollancz, 1971), pp. 125–45.
3. Brigid Brophy, 'The Darwinist's Dilemma', in *Animals' Rights – A Symposium*, eds David Paterson and Richard D. Ryder (Fontwell, Sussex: Centaur Press, 1979), pp. 63–72.
4. Henry S. Salt, *Animals' Rights Considered in Relation to Social Progress* (New York: Macmillan & Co., 1894).
5. Leslie J. Cross, 'In Search of Veganism-2', *The Vegan* (Autumn 1949), pp. 15–17.
6. Lewis Gompertz, *Moral Inquiries on the Situation of Man and of Brutes* (London: Westley and Parrish, 1824).
7. Richard D. Ryder, *Animal Revolution: Changing Attitudes Towards Speciesism* (Oxford: Basil Blackwell, 1989), p. 181.

8. Ibid., p. 5.
9. Gary L. Francione, *Animals as Persons: Essays on the Abolition of Animal Exploitation* (New York: Columbia University Press, 2008), pp. 1–9; Gary L. Francione, *Introduction to Animal Rights: Your Child or the Dog?* (Philadelphia: Temple University Press, 2000), pp. 103–113.
10. Jeremy Bentham, *An Introduction to the Principles of Morals and Legislation* in *The Works of Jeremy Bentham*, vol. 1, ed. John Bowring (New York: Russell & Russell, 1962), pp. 142–3 n.§.
11. Ibid.
12. John Stuart Mill, 'Utilitarianism', in *John Stuart Mill and Jeremy Bentham: Utilitarianism and Other Essays*, ed. Alan Ryan (Harmondsworth, Middlesex: Penguin Books, 1987) pp. 272–338 (p. 280).
13. Ibid., p. 324.
14. Ibid., p. 281.
15. Gary L. Francione, *Animals, Property, and the Law* (Philadelphia: Temple University Press, 1995); Gary L. Francione and Robert Garner, *The Animal Rights Debate: Abolition or Regulation?* (New York: Columbia University Press, 2010), pp. 25–61.
16. Brophy, 'In Pursuit of a Fantasy', p. 126.
17. Gary L. Francione, 'Reflections on Tom Regan and the Animal Rights Movement That Once Was', *Between the Species*, 21: 1 (2018), pp. 1–41, <https://digitalcommons.calpoly.edu/bts/vol21/iss1/1> [accessed 21 August 2019]; Gary L. Francione, *Rain Without Thunder: The Ideology of the Animal Rights Movement* (Philadelphia: Temple University Press, 1996).
18. Brophy, 'The Rights of Animals', p. 19.
19. Ibid., pp. 19–20.
20. Brophy, 'In Pursuit of a Fantasy', p. 125.
21. Francione, *Animals, Property, and the Law*; Francione, *Introduction to Animal Rights*, pp. 50–80; Francione, *Rain Without Thunder*, pp. 110–46; Gary L. Francione, 'Animals – Property or Persons?', in *Animal Rights: Current Debates and New Directions*, eds Cass R. Sunstein and Martha C. Nussbaum (New York: Oxford University Press, 2004), pp. 108–42.
22. For a similar argument made in the context of discussing the problem of animals as property, see Francione, *Animals as Persons*, pp. 129–47.
23. Brophy, 'The Rights of Animals', p. 19.
24. Brophy, 'In Pursuit of a Fantasy', pp. 126–7.
25. Ibid., p. 127.
26. Ibid.
27. Ibid., p. 128.
28. Ibid., p. 130.
29. Brophy, 'The Darwinist's Dilemma', p. 63.
30. Ibid., p. 64.
31. Ibid., p. 69.

32. Ibid., p. 72.
33. Brophy, 'In Pursuit of a Fantasy', p. 129.
34. Ibid.
35. Ibid., p. 128.
36. Brophy, 'The Darwinist's Dilemma', p. 67.
37. Brophy, 'In Pursuit of a Fantasy', p. 130.
38. Francione, *Introduction to Animal Rights*, pp. 122–6.
39. Brophy, 'In Pursuit of a Fantasy', p. 129.
40. Ibid., p. 138.
41. Several obituaries report that Brophy was diagnosed with multiple sclerosis in 1979. But I am told by her daughter, Kate Levey, that it was sometime after 1982 that the diagnosis was made. Email from Kate Levey to Gary L. Francione, 22 August 2019 (copy on file with the author).
42. Brigid Brophy, 'A Case-Historical Fragment of Autobiography', *Baroque –'n' – Roll and Other Essays* (London: Hamish Hamilton, 1987), pp. 1–27 (pp. 20–1).
43. Tom Regan, *The Case for Animal Rights* (Berkeley & Los Angeles: University of California Press, 1983). For a critique of Regan's position as reflecting species bias, see Francione, *Animals as Persons*, pp. 210–29.
44. Stanley and Roslind Godlovitch and John Harris (eds), *Animals, Men and Morals*, p. 8.
45. Peter Singer, *Animal Liberation: A New Ethics for Our Treatment of Animals* (New York: New York Review Books, 1975), p. xv (hereafter, Singer, *Animal Liberation* (1975)).
46. Ibid., pp. xv–xvi.
47. Peter Singer, "Animal Liberation" (review of Stanley and Roslind Godlovitch and John Harris (eds), *Animals, Men and Morals*), *New York Review of Books*, 5 April 1973.
48. Singer, *Animal Liberation* (1975), pp. 256–7. Brophy remarked that inconsistency in one's personal life (e.g., an anti-vivisectionist who is not a vegetarian) affected the ability to persuade others but did not refute the truth of position promoted. She noted that she was both a vegetarian and an anti-vivisectionist. See Brophy, 'In Pursuit of a Fantasy', pp. 132–3.
49. Singer, *Animal Liberation* (1975), p. 24.
50. Ibid., p. 23.
51. Francione and Garner, *The Animal Rights Debate*, pp. 6–25. Singer would claim that the lives of similarly situated humans are also of less value.
52. Singer, *Animal Liberation* (1975), p. 18.
53. Ibid., p. 183.
54. Ibid., p. 192.
55. Ibid., p. 257.
56. Ibid., p. 184.

57. Ibid., p. 185.
58. Ibid., pp. 185–6.
59. Ibid., p. 186.
60. Ibid., p. 187.
61. See, e.g., ibid., pp. 172–3
62. Ibid., p. 189.
63. Ibid., p. 190.
64. Ibid., p. 191.
65. Ibid., p. 192.
66. Ibid., p. 257.
67. Ibid., p. 258.
68. Ibid., p. 275, n. 22.
69. Ibid., p. 258.
70. Ibid., p. 259.
71. Ibid., p. 176.
72. Ibid., pp. 254–5.
73. Peter Singer, *Animal Liberation*, 2nd ed., (New York: New York Review Books, 1990), p. 229 (hereafter Singer, *Animal Liberation* (1990)).
74. Ibid., pp. 229–30.
75. Ibid., p. 231.
76. Ibid., p. 175.
77. Ibid., p. 176.
78. Ibid., p. 232.
79. Ibid., p. 177.
80. Singer, *Animal Liberation* (1975), p. 258.
81. Singer, *Animal Liberation* (1990), p. 232.
82. Ibid., pp. 176–7.
83. Ibid., pp. 232–3.
84. Ibid., p. 162.
85. See, for example, Peter Singer, *Practical Ethics*, 3d ed. (New York: Cambridge University Press, 2011), pp. 104–22.
86. Catherine Clyne, 'Singer Says: The *Satya* Interview with Peter Singer', *Satya*, October 2006, <http://www.satyamag.com/oct06/singer.html> [accessed 21 August 2019].
87. Rosamund Raha, 'Animal Liberation: An Interview with Professor Peter Singer', *The Vegan*, Autumn 2006, pp. 18–19 (p. 19).
88. Patrick Barkham, 'Alfalfa Male Takes on the Corporation', *The Guardian*, 8 September 2006, <https://www.theguardian.com/environment/2006/sep/08/food.ethicalliving> [accessed 21 August 2019].
89. Dave Gilson, 'Chew the Right Thing', *Mother Jones*, 3 May 2006, <https://www.motherjones.com/politics/2006/05/chew-right-thing/> [accessed 21 August 2019].
90. Peter Singer, 'Europe's Ethical Eggs', *CNN Global Public Square*, 12 January 2012 <http://globalpublicsquare.blogs.cnn.com/2012/01/12/singer-europes-ethical-eggs/> [accessed 21 August 2019].

91. Francione and Garner, *The Animal Rights Debate*, pp. 43–4.
92. The letter is available at https://i0.wp.com/www.abolitionistap-proach.com/wp-content/uploads/2013/05/support1.jpg [accessed 21 August 2019].
93. Clyne, 'Singer Says'.
94. See Francione, 'Reflections on Tom Regan'.
95. For a general discussion of Abolitionism, see Gary L. Francione and Anna Charlton, *Animal Rights: The Abolitionist Approach* (Newark, NJ: Exempla Press, 2015).
96. Singer, *Animal Liberation* (1975), dust jacket.
97. Brophy, 'In Pursuit of a Fantasy', p. 128.
98. Email from Kate Levey to Gary L. Francione, 10 December 2018 (copy on file with the author).
99. Brophy, 'In Pursuit of a Fantasy', p. 133.
100. Letter from Brigid Brophy to Mervyn Horder, 17 September 1989 (copy on file with the author).
101. Gary L. Francione, 'A Moment of Silence for Donald Watson, Founder of the Vegan Society', *AbolitionistApproach.com*, 1 July 2014, < https://www.abolitionistapproach.com/moment-silence-donald-watson-founder-vegan-society/> [accessed 21 August 2019].
102. Clyne, 'Singer Says'.
103. See Francione, *Rain Without Thunder*.
104. See Francione and Garner, *The Animal Rights Debate*, pp. 29–61.
105. For an example of another philosopher who promotes veganism as a moral imperative, see Gary Steiner, *Animals and the Moral Community: Mental Life, Moral Status, and Kinship* (New York: Columbia University Press, 2008).
106. Brophy, 'The Darwinist's Dilemma', p. 70.
107. See Francione, *Rain Without Thunder*; Francione, 'Reflections on Tom Regan'.

# Chapter 8

# Brigid Brophy's Phenomenology of Sex in *Flesh* and *The Snow Ball*

## Jonathan Gibbs

Ian McEwan's 2007 novella *On Chesil Beach* opens with a pair of young newly-weds, Edward and Florence, eating bad food in a Dorset hotel, prior to retiring to their room to consummate their marriage. When they do, in the book's calamitous climax, Edward suffers premature ejaculation: 'He emptied himself over her in gouts, in vigorous but diminishing quantities, filling her navel, coating her belly, thighs, and even a portion of her chin and kneecap in tepid, viscous fluid'.[1] McEwan, who made his name with stories that revelled in all manner of sexual perversion – child sex abuse and murder, incest, sadism – here seems to be suggesting similar depths of gothic horror in the most commonplace, even vanilla of sexual encounters: the heterosexual marital bed.

Edward and Florence are products and victims of Britain's post-war puritanism, a time when, as the novella's opening line has it, 'conversation about sexual difficulties was plainly impossible'.[2] They are unexperienced, unenlightened and unprepared. It is 1962, the year before, as Philip Larkin famously asserted, sexual intercourse 'began'. Before then it had been

> A sort of bargaining,
> A wrangle for the ring,
> A shame that started at sixteen
> And spread to everything.[3]

McEwan's novella is a dramatisation of this state of affairs, with its handbooks for young brides talking of mucous membranes and glans, and 'happily, soon after he has entered her's, and, for Edward, rumours of 'men and women in tight black jeans and black polo-neck sweaters [having] constant easy sex, without having to meet each other's parents'.[4] After the disaster of Edward's coming too soon, and Florence's appalled reaction, and the frightened, thoughtless words that follow, their marriage is doomed. If only, you think, if only one or other of them had read Brigid Brophy's novel *Flesh*. Tragically, however, Edward and Florence married in July 1962, and *Flesh* wasn't published until later that year, by which time Edward and Florence were definitively divorced.[5] But if *Flesh* can't save Edward and Florence, it can, at least, give the lie to Larkin. Sexual intercourse *did* begin before 1963, and Nancy and Marcus, Brophy's protagonists, are the proof.

Brophy is often celebrated for her novels' sexual non-conformism and what Carole Sweeney calls their 'delightful perversity',[6] an aspect of her writing entirely in line with the progressive views expressed in her journalism, which pushed for, among other things, gender equality, homosexual rights and animal rights. (It is worth noting, however, that her most celebrated feature articles on these subjects were not published until after the novels I will be discussing in this essay.) Books such as *The Finishing Touch*, *In Transit* and, in a more subdued manner, *The King of a Rainy Country* give us ingenious role play, gender bending and gender blending, the intricate dance of fantasy. These are features that the novels share with those of her contemporary, friend and lover Iris Murdoch, who, in books such as *A Severed Head* (1961), *The Bell* (1958) and *The Black Prince* (1973), explored the consequences of the loss of religious faith, and the flooding in of Freud's theories of the unconscious, and of psychosexual development, to replace it. Murdoch's novels can seem like a series of laboratory experiments, under the controlled conditions offered by the often enclosed communities of her settings, in which she tests for the presence and behaviour of morality in these (those?) psychologically determined times. But while Murdoch's characters fall in and out of love with alarming regularity, and as a consequence are habitually, even compulsively, adulterous, they don't often actually have sex. They don't have to. The libido, in Murdoch, is a psychological, even an intellectual or spiritual mechanism, rather than a physiological one. Nor, where sex is concerned, is she interested in depicting the act; when she does, it is more likely to be from the exterior, stumbled upon, and of an illicit, taboo nature. (I'm thinking particularly of the incestuous sex either interrupted or spied upon in *A Severed Head* and *The Time of the Angels* [1966].)

Like Murdoch, then, Brophy is interested in perverse, transgressive and anomalous sexual behaviour, and positively so, but she is also interested in the erotics of sex in its more conventional forms.

Twice in the run of three very different short novels she published in the early years of the 1960s, she describes heterosexual intercourse at some length, and makes it a critical element of the plot. These are Marcus and Nancy's first time in bed together, on their honeymoon, in *Flesh* (1962), and Anna and 'Don Giovanni's' one-night stand in *The Snow Ball* (1964). The first she writes from the man's point of view, the second from the woman's. In both cases she ignores the physical mechanics of the act, but concentrates entirely – and in detail – on the physiological and psychological experience: what sex feels like, and what goes through a person's mind when they are doing it.

Where Murdoch's novels are concerned with the social aspects of desire, then – how it spills out of the bedroom to other aspects of life – *The Snow Ball* and *Flesh* concentrate on the erotic, by which I mean the aesthetics of sexual appetite, desire and identity. (And I very much include under this aesthetic banner the squeamishness and horror expressed in the failed sexual encounter in *On Chesil Beach*.) In this they tread a perilous line, not just in terms of offending prevailing morality – *Flesh* was published only two years after the unexpurgated *Lady Chatterley's Lover* – but of upsetting critical sensibilities.

The problem with sex in any literary artform is to do with point of view, and this means it's a particular problem for the novel, which rather considers point of view its special province. The novel can show us a character from the outside and from the inside, can even, for example using the free indirect style, do both at once. But this trick doesn't work with the physical act of sex, for two reasons. One is that during sex the brain becomes hyper-stimulated with a flood of very particular sense data and a surge of neurochemicals, and our perceptual apparatus becomes overloaded. We feel a lot, during sex, but we're not always able to say what it is that we feel. The second problem is that although novels are good at showing characters from the inside and the outside, nowhere is that difference greater than in sex. There is a chasm between how sex *looks* – at once frantic and static, and variously brutal and ridiculous – and how it *feels*. Most sex goes on inside our heads, unvocalised. When we do vocalise it ('Yes! Yes! Yes!' or 'God!') we are pointing to a peak experience that is crying out for a means of expression, and to the inability of language to do just that.

This problem of how to depict sex in language is borne out by the existence of the Bad Sex Award, organised by the *Literary Review*, to regular controversy. The prize describes its purpose as 'to draw attention to poorly written, perfunctory or redundant passages of sexual description in modern fiction',[7] and it often picks out writers who founder in the attempt to bring metaphorical language to bear on the description of sexual intercourse. Brigid Brophy, I'd contend, would never have been nominated for the Bad Sex Award. Quite what she achieved in her descriptions of sex in these two novels, and what she intended by them, is what I will discuss in the remainder of this essay.

## Flesh

*Flesh* is the story of Marcus and Nancy, a newly married couple whose experience of sex stands in stark contrast to that of Florence and Edward in *On Chesil Beach*. Both couples are sleeping together for the first time on or just after their wedding night. They are doing so at more or less the same time in history. McEwan's book is set specifically in July 1962, while Brophy's novel is less exact – but, published in late 1962, with Iris Murdoch reading it in typescript in March of that year, I think we can safely say it is set at around the turn of the decade. Brophy's couple are older, 28 and 29 to McEwan's 22 apiece, and, crucially, Brophy's Nancy is sexually experienced, with four past lovers. More than that, she has, the author tells us, 'a talent [for] sexual intercourse'.[8]

There are other similarities between the couples. All are intellectuals, of the North London/Oxford type. Both women play the violin, though Brophy's Nancy is less accomplished than McEwan's Florence, who will go on to form a celebrated string quartet. Marcus, like both Edward and Florence, is a virgin, and, at the start of the book, easily as socially awkward as either of them. On the night they first sleep together, Marcus is, no less than Edward, 'terrified of making love to Nancy and also terrified of failing to'.[9] Like Edward, Marcus is too nervous to enjoy the pre-sex dinner, though the food in Lucca in Tuscany, where Brophy's couple go on honeymoon, is surely better than that in Dorset; and he too is embarrassed in his contact with the hotel staff, thinking that every waiter and clerk can intuit his deep anxiety about the act: 'He was convinced he would never be able to behave with the vulgar normality of the men illustrated in travel brochures.'[10]

What saves Marcus is Nancy's communication. It's a perennial standby of sex advice columns today, but in 1962 this might have been revolutionary. (Compare to McEwan, as Edward and Florence edge towards their calamity: 'She and Edward still held each other's eyes. Talking appeared out of the question.'[11]) Meanwhile, in *Flesh*:

> She talked to him. Marcus had always imagined that when he did at last make love to a woman it would be in terrible silence, interrupted only by such noises as their bodies might involuntarily make, which he had already conceived might be embarrassing. But Nancy talked to him about what he was to do, about what he was doing, in a low, rather deep, swift voice which provoked in his skin almost the same sensation as her hands. When he entered her body, he felt he was following her voice.[12]

It is the last line here that is typical of Brophy's approach to treating the sex act. On reading the novel in typescript, earlier in the year, Murdoch wrote to Brophy: 'You must be the first person who has described sexual intercourse beautifully and well in a book. I liked the fine fine sensuousness of it all.'[13]

What follows is two pages of lyrical description of what having sex, for the first time, *feels like*, for Marcus. This is part psychological, part physiological. What is written, what is eroticised, is not the act, but the experience of it, as if Brophy is sketching a phenomenology of sex. The description is general, the language abstract, not concrete and graphic. There are no body parts, or at least no genitalia. The only thing that is 'inserted' anywhere, in a comic touch coming at the end of the passage, is Nancy's finger, in Marcus's ear. The language is metaphorical, but the metaphors don't pertain to the physical, as in so many nominations for the Bad Sex Awards. For example, there is a grotto, but the grotto is not – or not primarily – a metaphor for the vagina:

> Where she led him was a strange world that was not new to him, since he had always known it existed, subterraneanly: a grotto, with whose confines and geographical dispositions he at once made himself quite familiar, as with the world of inside his own mouth: but a magic grotto, limitless, infinitely receding and enticing, because every sensation he experienced there carried on its back an endless multiplication of overtones, with the result that the sensation, though more than complete, was never finished, and every experience conducted him to the next; a world where he pleasurably lost himself in a confusion of the senses not in the least malapropos but as appropriate and precise as poetry – a world where one really did see sounds

and hear scents, where doves might well have roared and given suck, where perfectly defined, delightful loyal tactile sensations dissolved into apperceptions of light or darkness, of colour, of thickness, of temperature.[14]

Certainly, it is possible to read this grotto metaphor in two different ways: as Nancy's vagina ('with whose confines and geographical dispositions he at once made himself quite familiar'), but also as the dark, interior non-place of sex, as it is experienced, in the moment. The punctiliousness of Brophy's syntax, and her insistence on following a thought or a feeling to its utmost refinement of meaning, is reminiscent of Henry James, and in fact the phenomenology of sex would appear to be as important to Brophy as the deepest intricacies of psychology are to James.

Although this is 'straight' heterosexual intercourse, then, there is perversity implicit in it. If the grotto is a metaphor for the vagina, then Brophy's application of it to Marcus feminises him. There are no phallic metaphors at his disposition, no matter that Brophy elsewhere accepts these as an appropriate unconscious expression of Freudian truths.[15] The second passage of this extended sex scene does, however, recast Marcus in a more active role:

And yet, even as he felt drained, a climax would gather out of his pebbly dryness like a wave re-forming in its moment of being sucked back, and he would heave himself up, curling above her like a wave, and would snatch, rape, her into an embrace of bitter, muscular, desperate, violence, that could only, he felt, be resolved by a death agony.[16]

Two thoughts occur in response to this passage. First, that again Brophy supplies Marcus with a metaphor (an ocean wave) that is more generally applied to the female sexual experience – and in fact that Brophy herself applies to the female orgasm in *The Snow Ball*.[17] And secondly, that it is entirely characteristic of Brophy to use the – here – provocative word 'rape' in its original and correct but now archaic meaning of *to seize by force*, or *carry off*. This points both to her insistence on linguistic precision and variegation as part of the novelist's duty, and to her wilfulness as a writer, and her readiness to court controversy and misreading, even in the passage in her book where she has the most to gain, and lose.

The flowering of Marcus's perversity within the conventional domain of his married, heterosexual sex-life shows itself both in and out of bed. It is hinted that he and Nancy, while still on their honey-moon in Lucca, experiment with unusual sex acts:

> 'Nothing is perverse. Nothing at all, if you really want to do it.'
> They acted on her apophthegm.
> But presently Marcus reversed it and whispered, in an apprecia-tive voice.
> 'Everything is perverse. If you really want to do it.'[18]

Likewise, he is happy to sashay down the hotel corridor in his wife's dressing gown, 'not caring in the least if someone guessed or even glimpsed that beneath its flounced, flowery cotton skirt he was, and very masculinely, naked'.[19]

This queering or inversion of Marcus's sexual persona is intrinsic to the novel's plot, which is often described as a gender-swapped retelling of the Pygmalion myth, but is as much a response to George Bernard Shaw's 1914 play as to the original. Shaw's play's point of difference with the original myth – i.e. that the statue/pupil, Eliza Doolittle, outgrows and rejects her maker/teacher, the Professor of Phonetics Henry Higgins – is carried over into Brophy's novel, only for Brophy to engineer the happy ending for her couple that Shaw explicitly rejected for Higgins and Eliza.

In *Flesh*, then, Nancy takes up the shy, awkward, congenitally single Marcus and, in marrying him and 'teaching' him sex, makes of him a sensualist. He grows in confidence, getting a job that he loves and that Nancy resents, and then, when the two of them have a child, sleeping with their German au pair while Nancy is out at work herself. Marcus's sensualism expresses itself through gluttony as well as libido, however, and by the end of the novel he is, in Nancy's own words, 'disgustingly fat'.[20] The book's ambiguous resolution comes from her realisation that she desires him *because of*, rather than despite, the 'horror' of his fatness: ambiguous, because in the book's final scene – another, albeit more perfunctory sex scene – Nancy yields to Marcus in an entirely passive, stereotypically female man-ner: 'she groaned under the irresistible pleasure he caused her – and also because it *was* pleasure, because it *was* irresistible, where she might have preferred pain'.[21]

There is an irony here that runs counter to Brophy's prevailing image in her novels and journalism as a social and sexual provocateur – which is otherwise apparent in the novel's unfussed discussion and acceptance of homosexuality, both in terms of Marcus's sister, Elsie, considered a repressed lesbian, and Marcus's employer, Polydore, presumed 'queer'. Nancy starts out as an embodiment – even a herald – of the liberated women of the 1960s who, as Brophy later wrote in her 1965 *Sunday Times* article 'The Immorality of Marriage', are 'free to admit to themselves that they have a taste for sexual intercourse';[22] yet she ends up literally trapped beneath her overweight husband, and enjoying it. It's true that the *Sunday Times* article does allow for the possibility of equality in marriage:

> Modern married people are free to choose to go back to the 'natural' division of roles between the sexes – provided they can discern what on earth that is.
>     [. . .]
>     Men and women [. . .] can achieve imaginative identification, in which there can be no question of rivalry or a conflict of self-interests; the self-interest, ambitions and ideals – the very Ego – of each are those of the other.[23]

Nevertheless it is an unexpected ending to the novel, and perhaps one as much influenced by the aesthetic demands of the form (it is in some manner a 'twist' ending) as by the ethical or political stance of the author. As Michael Bronski correctly states, 'Brophy's [journalistic] writing explicitly critiques a culture that views the world through heterosexual paradigms predicated on traditional gender roles',[24] and yet *Flesh* pushes back against that critique, toying with the paradigms that Brophy elsewhere attacks. The novel's irony certainly precludes the idea that Nancy's submission to Marcus is a full-blown reactionary acceptance of traditional gender roles. For a more appropriate interpretation of the ending we can look to Marcus's fatness, which in the novel feminises him:

> 'Just look at yourself,' [Nancy] said. 'Look at your thighs. Look at your chest. You've got great pendulous breasts, like a woman.'
>     He gave a chuckle. 'It's a process of empathy. I've *become* a Rubens woman.'[25]

Earlier, Nancy had explicitly said that she loathes Marcus's sister (the presumed lesbian Elsie) because she looks like Marcus, but with breasts. In submitting to a version of himself *with* breasts, Nancy is essentially embracing her bisexuality, at the very moment Marcus is luxuriating in his newfound hermaphroditism. To a certain extent this prefigures Susan Sontag's 1967 essay 'The Pornographic Imagination', in which she raises an eyebrow at the 'questionable assumption that human sexual appetite is, if untampered with, a natural pleasant function' and that '"the obscene" is a convention, the fiction imposed upon nature by a society convinced there is something vile about the sexual functions'.[26] Rather, Sontag suggests, human sexuality is 'a highly questionable phenomenon, and belongs, at least potentially, among the extreme rather than ordinary experiences of humanity'.[27] The achievement of *Flesh* as a novel is that it buries this perversity at least a little way under the surface. Nancy and Marcus both are and are not a normal, happily married couple. They are certainly happier than Florence and Edward could ever have been.

## The Snow Ball

Like *Flesh*, *The Snow Ball* is ostensibly structured around a hetero-sexual seduction leading to sex, but whereas in the earlier novel the woman is the pursuer and the man the pursued, here the roles are returned to their default, heteronormative position. Anna K, guest of her older friend Anne at her exceedingly lavish New Year's costume party, is pursued throughout the party by a masked Don Giovanni. She evades him for a time, but then yields, in increments. First, they flirt verbally, then they share a clandestine embrace behind the cur-tains of the raised gallery overlooking the house's packed ballroom, and finally they, almost wordlessly, agree to go to bed together. Anna's first thought, to use the house's master bedroom, is thwarted when they stumble upon Anne and her husband Tom-Tom having sex there themselves; Anna agrees to return to Don Giovanni's flat, although she insists on them both keeping their true identities secret from each other.

Where McEwan's Edward and Florence were both inexperienced, and *Flesh*'s Nancy experienced compared with Marcus's virginal innocence, both Anna and her Don are experienced lovers. In this they are contrasted, in the novel, not just to Anne and Tom-Tom, the older hosts, but to a younger couple, Ruth and (another) Edward, who lose their virginities together in the back of Ruth's father's Bentley, parked outside, more or less at the same time as Anna and the Don are sleeping together at his flat.

As she does for Nancy and Marcus, Brophy treats Anna and the Don's sex seriously, as a pleasurable act founded on mutual respect and desire – in which, to use Brophy's own definition of an ideal marriage partnership, they both achieve 'imaginative identi-fication' with each other, with 'no question of rivalry or a conflict of self-interests'.[28] In other words, sex can be as fulfilling in a one-night stand as within a marriage – a sentiment in line with Brophy's journalism. And, as with Marcus in *Flesh*, Brophy uses the scene to focus on the experience, rather than the representation, of sex.

Again, there is no physical description of the act, and we are left to decide whether this shows coyness, self-censorship or a positive intent to ignore this aspect of sexual behaviour in favour of the physiological and psychological. Here is the start of the sex scene in *The Snow Ball*:

> Then his head plunged, and his face was lost to her. She lost the wish to see it, the memory even that it existed, in the response of her sensations to his labouring body: until she suddenly emerged, at the end of the same arc of sensations which had begun with the flutter of his laugh and of his body, to the knowledge that her sensations had passed the point up to which she was free to go back on them, and that she was now free to have thoughts again, since her voyage to pleasure was from now on involuntary.[29]

'[H]is labouring body'; 'her voyage to pleasure': the (for Brophy) triteness of the prose can perhaps perhaps be explained by Anna's lack of investment in the act, pleasurable though it is in strict terms. Earlier, she had complained to the Don how 'awful [it was] to be surprised by one's own [sexual] feelings, at my age', and now, during sex, she thinks of her coming orgasm as 'an act as unwilled as sneezing, falling asleep or dying'.[30] When it comes, it is, though pleasurable, described in less than positive terms. 'Suffering, sobbing, swelling, sawing, sweating, her body was at last convulsed by the wave that broke inside it.'[31]

This is not the almost spiritual experience that Marcus has. It is, by contrast, almost entirely physiological. Sex, for Anna, it seems, is – like the desire that preceded it – an inconvenient but entirely natural phenomenon: neither to be courted nor avoided, but to be dealt with as and when it occurs. This plays out also in the narrative technique applied to the scene. Whereas the description of Marcus's first experience of sex is narrated as it were from above, extrapolating, condensing and summarising thoughts he would not have been able to express in the moment, Anna in *The Snow Ball* is able to think as she fucks; she owns the thoughts laid out on the page.

Afterwards, she puts off her lover's entreaties to allow their relationship to extend, for, he says, he loves her. The short, final part of the novel is expressly anti-romantic, with Anna giving no good reason why they should not see each other again and get to know each other. It's certainly not his fault, as they seem particularly well matched in interests, intellect and character. If sex is part of a complex of human activities also including love and desire, then what is interesting about *The Snow Ball* is the ease with which it shows how desire and love can become uncoupled. Compare to the novels of Iris Murdoch, where desire is a perpetual motion machine, never sated or extinguished: if sleeping with someone ends your desire for them, then that desire will simply be transferred to another love object. *The Snow Ball* offers a particularly brutal rebuttal to this idea: sex is the consummation of desire, out of which love as likely *may not* as *may* grow, even if the sex is good, even if it's with someone one feels physically and intellectually attracted to and respects.

The novel ends darkly, with death entering both the party, when a random guest collapses and dies, and Anna's thoughts, in the chilling final line. If Marcus and Nancy's marriage triumphs through imaginative identification, and survives through the growth of a joint but not strictly shared perversity, then for Anna none of this is possible.

## Brophy's possible theories of sex

While Brophy nowhere sets out what she is trying to do in her writing about sex in these two novels, she does makes clear statements in her journalism and criticism about the treatment of sex in literature, from which it is possible to infer, if not a theory, then at least an attitude. These pieces, many of them collected in *Don't Never Forget* – and written, as I have said, largely after the novels – include discussions of obscenity and censorship, and reviews of writers who write about sex. Of the latter, she disapproves of Kingsley Amis (juvenile), the Marquis de Sade ('not graphic enough to be pornographic'),[32] D. H. Lawrence and Henry Miller; while she approves of Colette, Françoise Sagan, John Cleland and Ronald Firbank.

One might have expected Lawrence to meet Brophy's approval. Certainly she is *for* Lawrence to the extent that she is against the censorship of his work (but then she is pretty much against all censorship), and moreover she approves of his insistence on using simple four-letter words to describe basic human activities; but it is his mixing of sex with a nebulous pagan spirituality that, finally, bores her. Her discussion of Lawrence comes in a piece on censorship entitled 'The British Museum and Solitary Vice', which she ends by quoting from a section on the ideal marriage from Lawrence's essay 'A Propos of *Lady Chatterley's Lover*', only to break off:

> 'in the rhythm of days, in the rhythm of months, in the rhythm of . . .'
> I can't be bothered to copy out any more of this fake-Swinburne incantation. In fact, marriage is no marriage that is not linked up with human imagination ('the marriage of true minds'), and that's all that matters.[33]

That line about human imagination, with its nod to Shakespeare, could be taken as a vindication of Marcus and Nancy's physical and mental – though not ever quite spiritual – communion in *Flesh*, although it is unclear by the end of the novel whether their growing and evolving sexual compatibility is anything more than a union of convenience between two healthy perverts.

Lawrence turns up again in her piece on Henry Miller, in which she attributes to the British writer 'the effect of literary fastidiousness, which puritanism, perhaps by accident, lent to [him]'.[34] Literary fastidiousness is a quality that could equally aptly be applied to Brophy, it must be said, although nothing in her writing or her life marks her as a puritan. Miller's failings, by contrast, extend far beyond a lack of fastidiousness, as Brophy sets out at length:

> The idea of a woman as a personality by whose autonomous existence he might feel moved is beyond him. Curiously enough, so is the idea – the sexual idea – of the female body. Proclaiming that sex is everywhere, he seems insensitive to sexuality, so blunted that nothing less than a primary sex characteristic can force itself on his attention. He is no sensualist. He might have made a mechanical engineer. He sees the female body as an assembly of knobs, pipes and slots. The connecting passages of flesh mean nothing to him except as a containing wall, on which he might well chalk – he really feels no more about any woman than about that whore, Paris – 'Miller was here'.[35]

Misogyny, anti-sensualism and lack of literary technique are here synonymous, or at least compound one another. What links them is a lack of imagination or empathy, the factors that Brophy has already imputed to a genuine marriage of minds, but which here can be taken as the basic requirements for writing about sex, as opposed to the mere attention to 'primary sexual characteristics'.

In the same review she declares that Miller's 'anecdotes are wholly concerned with externals: accounts of the acrobatics of copulation', and that he 'lacks the skill of the commercial pornographer. The sensibility which is blunt to the poetry of the erotic cannot exploit the erotic either.'[36] It is this 'poetry of the erotic' that is the quarry of this essay. It can be found, clearly, in pornography, and it is there in Lawrence, but the underpinning philosophy, and therefore the metaphors, for Brophy, are wrong. To write sex well, then, you need imagination, empathy, focus and a sensitive literary technique – just as to *do* it well you need imagination, empathy, focus on the matter at hand and technique (or, as per Nancy, 'talent'). For Brophy, Lawrence's elevated incantation is as wrongheaded as the mindless sexual graffiti of Miller.

It is worth dwelling on the question of how and whether sex writing should explicitly describe the physical mechanics of sex, as it is something that Brophy avoids. In her piece on censorship she commends Lawrence for his use of four-letter words, for telling the basics of sex like it is. For Brophy, this devolves to syntactic probity:

> any phrase in which the man is or does something *with* the woman is linguistically inadequate – inadequate to the act which, of all acts, is transitive, with a male subject and a direct female object. If this seems to us coarse, if it even seems to hint at brutality imposed on the woman, the fault lies with our obsession with brutality. The act *is* so – and is, in fact, not the least bit of good to the woman if it isn't. As a matter of fact the verb *love* is also transitive; it has the same vowel sound as, and is neither coarser nor prettier than, the other four-letter verb which represents one of the act in which it may take expression.[37]

Reading this, it is impossible not to note that Brophy uses the word 'fuck' nowhere in these two novels – nor, in fact, very many transitive verbs at all. We must look for the 'poetry of the erotic' elsewhere.

In the discussion of sex, Kingsley Amis is an interesting case. Brophy's piece on him in *Don't Never Forget* is a blistering attack on his debut, *Lucky Jim* (1954), written on the tenth anniversary of its publication.[38] She does not really address the treatment of sex (not that there's much of it in that book), but does miss a trick when discussing 'Lucky Jim, Mark V', aka Roger Micheldene, in Amis's fifth novel, *One Fat Englishman*, published in 1963, right in between *Flesh* and *The Snow Ball*. This novel, while full of the sexism, racism and bigotry familiar from Amis's books, is at least a lot funnier than *Lucky Jim*, and does keep step with Brophy in terms of its recognition of the changing place of sex both in society and in the novel, as the permissive decade finds its feet. It also contains a sex scene that is particularly interesting for our current discussion. Roger spends the first half of the novel in a permanent state of frustrated desire for the married Helene Bang, who seems uninterested in resuming the pair's earlier liaison, but eventually relents.

One chapter ends with Helene agreeing to go to bed with him, and the next starts *in media res*, with Roger reciting Virgil to himself as a way of delaying orgasm:

> '*Conticuere omnes*,' Roger was saying urgently to himself half an hour later, '*intentique ora tenebant. Inde toro pater Aeneas sic fatus ab alto: "Infandum. Regina, iubes renovare dolorem* [. . .]
>
> What Roger was saying to himself might have struck a casual observer, if one could have been contrived, as greatly at variance with what he was doing. In fact, however, the two were intimately linked. If he wanted to go on doing what he was doing for more than another ten seconds at the outside it was essential that he should go on saying things to himself – any old things as long as the supply of them could be kept up.[39]

If we read this scene, like that in *Flesh*, as an exploration of the phenomenology of sex, then we can see first of all that sex, for Roger, involves a drastic distancing of himself from his experience. And also that Helene is absent. Where for Marcus, having sex with Nancy in *Flesh*, there is a he and a she, and a continuous attempt to characterise and valorise the sensations heaping up on him, and to map the virgin territory of his own sexuality, for Roger there is only a strategic self-blinkering. It is bleakly funny. When it ends – he has moved from Virgil to A. E. Housman – it is something more than that:

> After the weeping Pleiads had made half a dozen circuits he found things beginning to get easier. His mind stopped behaving like a motor with a slipping clutch and gradually withdrew into itself. He saw nothing; there were sounds, but he heard them less and less. He lost all interest in where he was and who he was with, in any part or aspect of the future. For perhaps a minute, though he himself could not have known how long, he came as close as he had ever done to being unaware of who he was. Then the minute ended and he began taking notice of things again, including who he was with.[40]

This is as good a description of the *petite mort* as you could imagine, and throws a new light on the reader's understanding of Roger.

Rather than being merely a self-serving, skirt-chasing arsehole, he is a tragic, self-destructive figure whose compulsive sexual desire is bound up in the wish to obliterate his own personality. It's as cogent and biting an exploration of the phenomenology of sexuality (or at least male sexuality) as anything in *Flesh*, but negatively rather than positively portrayed.

Where then should we turn for positive descriptions of sex writing? Brophy commends Françoise Sagan for showing her characters as sexually active but free from sex drive, which places them somewhat in the position of Anna K in *The Snow Ball*:

> In love, they are obsessed by the awareness that their love is not quite obsessive. Every act, even every sexual act, is performed in the emptiness where the actors can ask both, and equally, 'Why should I?' and 'Why shouldn't I?' They are all in the situation of Josée in *Les Merveilleux Nuages*: 'Elle était libre. Ce n'était pas désagréable, ce n'était pas exaltant.'[41]

Nevertheless, unlike Anna – but like Murdoch's characters – none of Sagan's characters are seen to have the sex they do have, though Brophy puts this down to the author's characteristic existential ennui: 'An author too tired to evoke a dinner party cannot be expected to evoke the ambience of sexual intercourse. She merely states that it has taken place.'[42] While approving of this in Sagan, Brophy clearly wants to go further herself.

There is more sex in John Cleland, author of the once-notorious *Fanny Hill* (1748), which Brophy approves for its eighteenth-century sensibility:

> It is to Watteau's landscapes that he casts back when Fanny calls sexual intercourse 'our trip to Cythera'. Indeed, Cleland's couples share with Watteau's a grave elegance and a courteous concern for each other. Even when the four pairs take turns on the couch, 'good manners and politeness were inviolably observ'd'. Cleland himself is as decent. Mercifully *not* 'robust' or Rowlandsonian, he is decorous not merely in vocabulary but down to the last cadence of his fine, plain prose.[43]

That 'decent' is unexpected, and perhaps points us back to Brophy's surprising reticence when it comes to the plain facts and acts of sex in her writing. After all, if she would have found herself unable to write 'fuck' in a *Sunday Times* piece about D. H. Lawrence and *Lady*

*Chatterley*, there would presumably have been nothing to stop her putting the word – and others like it – in her novels. Candid in her desire to put sexual activity centre-stage, and keen also to show it at its equitable, generous and perhaps only implicitly perverse best, she wants the poetry of the erotic to be neither 'robust' (for which read *debased*), nor incantatory (for which read *elevated*), and certainly nothing like Miller's blunt, violent scrawl. As with Miller, she equates the sexual behaviour described on the page with the linguistic and lexical behaviour of the writer. Miller the author is as brutal and pig-ignorant in writing about sex as his characters are in having it. Cleland is as decorous and decent as his. In fact Fanny's description, at the beginning of her second letter, of the right way to write about sex is of interest: she should write, she says, 'in a mean [i.e. middle way] tempered with taste, between the revoltingness of gross, rank and vulgar expressions, and the ridicule of mincing metaphors and affected circumlocutions'.[44] For the first, read Miller, for the second the worst of the nominees for the Bad Sex Award.

Brophy does neither, but, if anything, she leans more to the second charge than to the first. It is fair to wonder why she wasn't more forthright in her language and descriptions in her novels, as she had been in her journalism. For the combination of imaginative sensuousness *and* the four-letter words needed to shake society out of its puritanism we would have to wait for John Updike, later in the decade. Yet what Brophy still does better than Updike is the evocation in prose of the feeling of the experience of sex. Which is, after all, our reasons for engaging in it whatsoever. What we all get up to in our bedrooms may not look much like what people get up to in pornographic films, but at best it feels like how they look like they're feeling. *Flesh* embodies and enacts this ecstasy, in a positive way, invoking not the dubious synthesis of phallic mythology, as in Lawrence, but a sensuality shared through the faculty of human imagination, just as *One Fat Englishman* enacts its negative version, the longed-for annihilation of self experienced in orgasm.[45]

The painter Watteau turns up again in a short piece in *Don't Never Forget* on Ronald Firbank, of whom Brophy writes: 'Eroticism plays over [his] surfaces like sunlight on a Watteau sleeve; and because it is so evanescent, resting for so brief a space on each facet, the effect, as with Watteau, is of tragedy.'[46] This evanescence, and the tragedy associated with it, are equally applicable to Brophy's writing about sex, although obviously her surfaces are not exterior, but interior: the surfaces of feelings and sensations, rather than parts of the body. And that tragedy is implicit in sex is central to *The Snow Ball*, where in the aftermath to her orgasm, already described as 'suffering, sobbing', Anna experiences 'an outburst, a shower, of pleasure [and] in this most intense, least voluntary and therefore most death-imaging of pleasures there was – and also for the release – a wry sadness'.[47] The sadness, here, lies presumably in the fact – and this is the thing that Roger Micheldene doesn't quite grasp – that sex only ever detaches you from yourself temporarily. For the greater release you must wait.

## Notes

1. Ian McEwan, *On Chesil Beach* (London: Jonathan Cape, 2007), p. 105.
2. Ibid., p. 3.
3. Philip Larkin, 'Annus Mirabilis', in *Collected Poems* (London: Marvell/ Faber, 1988).
4. McEwan, *On Chesil Beach*, pp. 8, 40.
5. It was reviewed by the *New Statesman* and the *Times Literary Supplement* in November of that year.
6. Carole-Anne Sweeney, 'Why This Rather Than That? The Delightful Perversity of Brigid Brophy', *Contemporary Women's Writing*, 12.2 (2018), pp. 233–47.
7. <https://literaryreview.co.uk/bad-sex-in-fiction-award> (accessed 26 April 2019).
8. Brigid Brophy, *Flesh* (London: Secker and Warburg, 1962), p. 52.
9. Ibid., p. 53.
10. Ibid., p. 55.
11. McEwan, *On Chesil Beach*, p. 88.
12. Brophy, *Flesh*, p. 56.
13. *Living on Paper: Letters from Iris Murdoch 1934–1995*, ed. Avril Horner and Anne Rowe (London: Chatto and Windus, 2015), p. 223.
14. Brophy, *Flesh*, p. 56.
15. See the chapter 'Double Entendre' in Brigid Brophy, *Black Ship to Hell* (London: Secker and Warburg, 1962), p. 45.
16. Brophy, *Flesh*, p. 56.
17. Brigid Brophy, *The Snow Ball* (London: Secker and Warburg, 1964), p. 157. See also *Lady Chatterley's Lover*, discussed below.
18. Brophy, *Flesh*, p. 58.
19. Ibid., p. 60.
20. Ibid., p. 154.
21. Ibid., p. 155.
22. Brigid Brophy, 'The Immorality of Marriage', in *Don't Never Forget: Collected Views and Reviews* (London: Jonathan Cape, 1966), pp. 22–8 (p. 22).
23. Ibid., pp. 23, 24.

24. Michael Bronski, 'Brigid Brophy's *Black Ship to Hell* and a Genealogy of Queer Theory', *Contemporary Women's Writing*, 12.2 (2018), pp. 171–85 (p. 180).
25. Brophy, *Flesh*, p. 154.
26. Susan Sontag, 'The Pornographic Imagination', in *Styles of Radical Will* (New York: Farrar, Straus and Giroux, 1969), pp. 35–73 (pp. 56–7).
27. Sontag, 'The Pornographic Imagination', p. 57.
28. Brophy, 'The Immorality of Marriage', p. 24.
29. Brophy, *The Snow Ball*, p. 156.
30. Ibid., pp. 135, 156.
31. Ibid., p. 157.
32. Brigid Brophy, 'Justine', in *Don't Never Forget*, pp. 81–4 (p. 81).
33. Brigid Brophy, 'The British Museum and Solitary Vice', in *Don't Never Forget*, pp. 101–5 (p. 105).
34. Brigid Brophy, 'Henry Miller', in *Don't Never Forget*, pp. 231–8 (p. 235).
35. Ibid., p. 235.
36. Ibid., pp. 233, 236.
37. Brophy, 'The British Museum and Solitary Vice', p. 103.
38. Brigid Brophy, 'Lucky Jim', in *Don't Never Forget*, pp. 217–22.
39. Kingsley Amis, *One Fat Englishman* (London: Gollancz, 1963), p. 107.
40. Ibid., p. 108.
41. Brigid Brophy, 'Françoise Sagan and the Art of the Beau Geste', in *Don't Never Forget*, pp. 269–84 (p. 274).
42. Ibid., p. 280.
43. Brigid Brophy, 'Mersey Sound, 1750', in *Don't Never Forget*, pp. 76–80 (p. 80).
44. John Cleland, *Fanny Hill: Memoirs of a Woman of Pleasure* (London, 1749), Letter the Second.
45. It is interesting that although Brophy treats the relationship between Eros and Thanatos at length in *Black Ship to Hell*, she only discusses in passing the self-annihilation inherent in orgasm. See again, Part I Chapter 5: 'The Double Entendre'.
46. Brigid Brophy, 'The New Rythum and Other Pieces', in *Don't Never Forget*, pp. 243–8 (p. 246).
47. Brophy, *The Snow Ball*, p. 157.

# Chapter 9

# Letter to Brigid

## *Rodney Hill*

Dear Brigid,

Forgive me writing after all these years. It is a letter I wanted to write many years ago. I remember so clearly when you entered my life in October 1971 – going on for half a century ago.

I was in my first term at Cambridge University. I was lost and bewildered, anxious about my sexuality, sexual orientation, and struggling with my then Christian faith and generally confused about what I believed in. Cambridge felt an alien environment and my home life, as the only child of a mentally ill, alcoholic mother and a distant father, felt even more alien.

From an early age I have taken refuge in public libraries. The city centre library felt so much more inviting than what Neville Chamberlain was reputed to have called 'this magnificent erection' – Giles Gilbert Scott's University Library. On the returned book trolley was a collection of essays and reviews called *Don't Never Forget* by an author who, at that stage, I was unfamiliar with. I suspect you were considered too 'racy' for my English public-school library.

It changed my life. I was predisposed to like it. I was already a vegetarian and a devotee of Mozart. I had spent my teens obsessed by the English Aesthetic Movement. I adored Beardsley (my parents had bought me a monograph of the complete Beardsley drawings to celebrate my entrance Exhibition to Cambridge). I had also loved Wilde since an enlightened (and possibly lavender-inclined) English master had read *The Ballad of Reading Gaol* out loud to us, as an alternative to the set text (possibly one of your *Fifty Works of English Literature We Can Do Without*). From the age of 13, after a colonial childhood, my family home was in raffish 1960s Brighton, which has always felt a Brophy kind of town with its fantastical Nash Pavilion. It was only a matter of time before I would 'discover' you.

*Don't Never Forget* was a revelation. New doors were opened, offering journeys which I am still on. You gave me clarity, courage and consolation. Authors I had never heard of then – Firbank, Highsmith, Elizabeth Taylor and John Horne Burns – have become lifelong passions. Others I was familiar with, like Simenon and James, whom I read – and still do – with a new depth and appreciation. I had already fallen in love with Naples, but you brought Lisbon to my attention with the unforgettable opening line: 'If you must have an earthquake, 1755 is the year to have it: when you rebuild, you will get a full-blown eighteenth-century city.'

John Horne Burns became a particular quest. Even by 1971, after your plea in 1964 that it should not happen, there was evidence that his name was becoming 'writ in water'. It took a dogged search of the second-hand bookstalls on Cambridge market to dig out his three fictions of *The Gallery*, *Lucifer with a Book* and *A Cry of Children*. The paperbacks had covers very much of the period, and have remained in my library ever since.

I was especially delighted to discover *The Gallery*. In my formative teens I was starved of homosexual literature or, should I say, homosexuals in literature. Mary Renault's *The Charioteer* had been a transformational read for me aged 13, but the homosexual theme had been treated rather obliquely. Now I was reading a collection of essays promoting fiction with gay characters and gay writers, even proposing: 'The three greatest novels of the twentieth century are *The Golden Bowl*, *À La Recherche du Temps Perdu* and *Concerning the Eccentricities of Cardinal Pirelli*. It is possible that all three are by homosexuals.' This felt tremendously affirming to a bewildered young gay man in 1971.

My enthusiasm for BB was now paramount – even obsessive. A second-hand paperback copy of *Hackenfeller's Ape* (the first of your fictions I read) was quickly followed by *In Transit*, *Flesh*, *The Snow Ball* and my absolute favourite, which I read over and over again, *The King of a Rainy Country*.

My passion was now so raised I had to have hardback versions, preferably first editions. *The Finishing Touch* was my first: beautifully produced, it had to be read in hardback. And then over the years I acquired multiple first edition copies of *A Rainy Country*. If I see one I have to have it – like adopting orphaned children. Of course, I was able to purchase your later fiction on publication date: *The Adventures of God in His Search for the Black Girl*, *Pussy Owl* and *Palace without Chairs* each eagerly awaited from the first pre-publication announcements.

One of your fictions remained elusive. I even read that you were determined to destroy all copies of *The Crown Princess*, including those in libraries. I wonder if this is true? It felt a particular challenge: a race between me acquiring a copy and you pulping them all. I haunted second-hand bookshops throughout the country trying to find a copy – my adrenalin pumping as I made my way to the hardback fiction or short story collections. In the end my acquisition of a copy was an anti-climax. By this time it was the late 1990s, and somebody mentioned to me that there was a website (on the newly introduced internet) called AbeBooks. I rushed to access the site only to be disappointed that my Holy Grail was not that rare: at least 20 copies were available from various second-hand dealers from around the English-speaking world. Such was my disappointment that I didn't actually order a copy until several months later.

My collection of Brophyania is complete and has travelled with me on various house moves in London and Manchester.

Nowadays writers are so accessible: book tours, tweets, blogs, etc. Then they seemed more remote, even a comparatively high-profile campaigning writer such as yourself. I got glimpses and vignettes, which were treasured. I remember you appeared in a Sunday colour supplement in the early 1970s. You were photographed with husband

**Figure 1** Brigid Brophy books. Collection of Rodney Hill

Michael and daughter Kate. I think the article was by Hunter Davies. Its curiosity value was this bohemian household with an open marriage and a couple of intellectuals who enjoyed watching *Match of the Day* with a 'best friend' (I presumed Maureen Duffy). I felt a real connection as I too watched *Match of the Day* in the college Junior Common Room.

Old Brompton Road began to get an almost mythic quality – 'a beehive in Brompton'. I even had a fantasy of hiring a wind band to play an arrangement of arias from *Le Nozze di Figaro* outside your ground floor flat on your birthday as an early morning surprise. Perhaps just as well I didn't, as I suspect you were not 'a morning person'.

And then there were the photographs. I loved the one of you in a zebra print top: often used but particularly effective on the dust jacket of the *Prancing Novelist*.

At last I met you. I was working at Tower Hamlets libraries and assisted John Dixon in organising the Fiction Now conference in October 1980. You were an obvious choice and we were so delighted you agreed to attend and be one of the keynote speakers. My partner Christopher (whom I met at Cambridge – the best thing about it) and I organised a display of all your books with photos, articles and dust jackets.

I remember you kindly agreed to sign (in purple ink) some of our first editions. You were insistent on precision. You wrote: 'Brigid Brophy's inscription in Rodney Hill's and Christopher Wright's copy' and also 'Written with best wishes in the copy belonging to Rodney Hill & Christopher Wright by Brigid Brophy'. You said that just signing them would be open to the suggestion that you had given them to us! You explained this was something you had learned from your writer father, John. I remember you spoke of him with tenderness.

You and I had fun laughing at the list of your earlier publications in *Palace without Chairs*. The publisher had listed your previous titles including *The Finishing Touch?* – the errant question mark opened up the possibility of seconds!

I felt very protective of you. You reminded me of an owl blinking at the daylight (and this predates *Pussy Owl*). I organised a taxi for you, surreptitiously paying the fare in advance so you wouldn't have to be bothered at your destination. It never crossed my mind that the taxi driver wouldn't be honest about this. Of course he was – and in a few days John Dixon forwarded your postcard thanking the anonymous taxi procurer: a lovely, courteous thing to do.

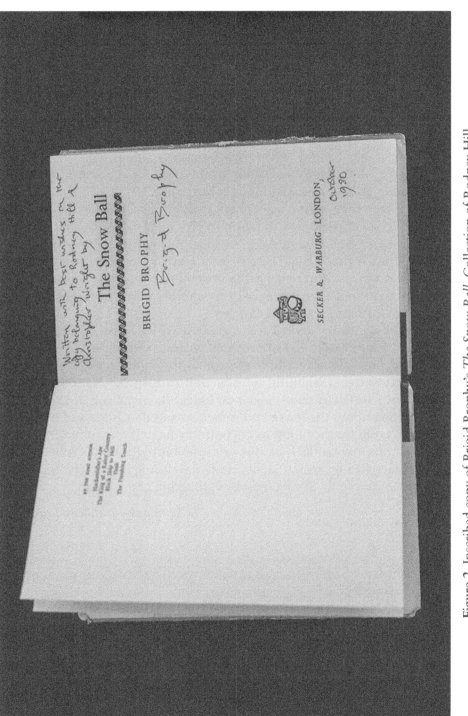

**Figure 2** Inscribed copy of Brigid Brophy's *The Snow Ball*. Collection of Rodney Hill

I remember reflecting on your gentleness and personal good manners. This seemed, on face value, to be in contrast to your sometimes barbed reviews. You could come across as aggressive in print and shy in life.

After that you began to disappear from view. The terrible news came out about your MS. By now we had left London and were living busy lives in the north-west of England. I read the 'Fragment of Autobiography' in *Baroque-'n'-Roll*. The opening pages I still find unbearably painful. There is a bitterness about 'ambushed by my closest ally', which shook me to the core. I hope you found some resolution and peace with this before you died.

I then read of Michael Levey's early retirement from the National Gallery and your move to Louth – I presumed to ensure better care for your long-term illness. And – in spite of Gay Men's Press and Virago reprints – your profile became shadowy in the wider, noisy, literary market place. You remained important to my personal growth from librarian to senior manager to psychotherapist and my life journey from Cambridge to senior citizen.

As I end this letter I feel a great sense of gratitude and sadness. For some reason Gainsborough's wistful painting of *The Painter's Daughters Chasing a Butterfly* comes to mind. I remember Michael Levey wrote a beautiful introduction to it in the National Gallery Picture in Focus series (alas I no longer have my copy). I recall him writing about the grave and somehow sad daughters and how happiness eluded them, just as the butterfly had. Trying to recall the past and pin it down feels as elusive as the butterfly and as transitory as a butterfly's lifespan. As I conclude the closing line of *The Snow Ball* comes to mind: 'She let herself in, thinking about death.'

With thanks and deep gratitude,

Rodney Hill

# Encoding Love: Hidden Correspondence in the Fiction of Brigid Brophy and Iris Murdoch

*Miles Leeson*

The relationship between Brigid Brophy and Iris Murdoch has had an interesting academic afterlife. At first considered a minor foot-note in the life of Murdoch, and unknown to many before the turn of the twenty-first century, it has, since the discovery of over a thousand letters from Murdoch to Brophy, gained greater prominence.[1] It is now clear that their relationship, which lasted from approximately the end of 1954 to 1967, should be considered one of the most important in Murdoch's life – of equal standing as those with Philippa Foot, Raymond Queneau, Frank Thompson, Elias Canetti and Franz Steiner; perhaps only her relationship with her husband John Bayley, and with her parents, exerted greater influence than these.

Although a full biography of Brophy has yet to be written, it would appear that she was far more stable in her same-sex relation-ships, throughout her life. Both she and Murdoch were in fairly open marriages, and both husbands were aware of their wives' activities with others; Murdoch, however, kept hers a secret from Bayley, whereas Brophy made it clear to her husband, Michael Levey. While Murdoch was involved with Brophy she had other ongoing relationships, ones that she would later term 'diffused eroticisms' in a letter to Brophy in 1967, whereas Brophy, it appears, did not.[2] The relationship broke down in 1967 as Murdoch would not com-mit to Brophy, nor would she give herself physically, both of which Brophy required, as she outlined over the course of many letters.[3] As a new lover, Maureen Duffy, came on the scene the relation-ship faded and became strained, although they kept in intermittent touch until Brophy's death in 1995. Their epistolary relationship has now been well documented in *Living on Paper: Letters from Iris Murdoch 1934–1995* (2015), although this collection contains only a fraction of the thousand or more letters that Murdoch wrote to Brophy.

It is the contention of this essay that their relationship becomes encoded in their fictional work of this period, although there are some caveats to this. I am not suggesting that their fiction becomes autobiographical, or a *roman à clef*, or diminished in some way due to this. I am not suggesting either that there are not a myriad other influences running through the work of both authors at this point in time; clearly, even a cursory reading of any of the novels published during this time would highlight a playfulness with genre, intertexts, form and other people (fictional or otherwise). I am also not suggesting that the mutual influence is fully aligned with Harold Bloom's definition in *The Anxiety of Influence*:

> 'Influence' is a metaphor, one that implies a matrix of relationships – imagistic, temporal, spiritual, psychological – all of them ultimately defensive in their nature. What matters most [. . .] is that the anxiety of influence *comes out of* a complex act of strong misreading, a creative interpretation.[4]

Both were strong personalities with different intellectual beliefs and approaches to writing. Murdoch saw herself in the lineage of the classic canon stretching back through Henry James, Dickens and Austen, to Shakespeare; Brophy to Bernard Shaw, Ronald Firbank, Wilde and Freud. Indeed, Brophy praises Shaw and Freud in *Black Ship to Hell* (1962), a critical text that she was working on during this time. It is also useful to note that Brophy highlights the work of Aristotle, whereas Murdoch would give him far less space, focusing in her philosophical work on the works of, and those derived from, Plato. Although this essay does not primarily comment on Brophy's non-fictional work, I believe the development of the premise in this work clearly demarcates her thinking from Murdoch's. As Brophy states in *Black Ship to Hell*:

> Fortunately, the twentieth century, as I have already more than hinted to my readers, provides us with two great mainstays: Bernard Shaw and Sigmund Freud [. . .] For intellect, and for the combination in it of range and grasp, Freud has no equal in the history of the world except Aristotle, whom he resembles.[5]

So, although their relationship (both personal and intellectual) was complex, the influence is limited, I believe, to the encoding of themselves within fiction, not with their personal aesthetic approach or the construction of their respective fictions. However, I am claiming that the relationship between the two, which has so far had little attention given to it in literary studies, may well open up new ways of reading their fictional works from this period. As both wrote so much during this time, I will primarily focus on Murdoch's *An Unofficial Rose* (1962), and Brophy's *Flesh* (1962) and *The Finishing Touch* (1963). During their relationship Murdoch wrote nine novels, along with works of philosophy, poetry and a play (the adapted version of her novel *A Severed Head* [1961]), while Brophy wrote four novels and a play (*The Burglar* [1967], a possible response to themes emerging from Murdoch's play-version of *A Severed Head* [1964]).[6] They also wrote to each other regularly, sometimes every day, and shared the details of their lives, as well as fantasies, arrangements for meetings and, crucially, some discussion of their published work.

Brophy and Murdoch met in Cheltenham for the awarding of the Cheltenham Literary Prize in 1954; Brigid won for her novel *Hackenfeller's Ape*, and Iris came second with *Under the Net* – both first novels. This was perhaps the only time that Brophy would be generally considered of greater critical stature. Although Brophy continued to write well-received novels, Murdoch's reputation soared after the publication of her fourth novel, *The Bell*, in 1958. After the ceremony both clearly felt an attraction, started to correspond, and began a relationship later that year. Kate Levey, Brophy's daughter, confirms this in her recent memoir of Murdoch:

> From the very start Iris Murdoch and Brigid Brophy disagreed about almost everything, yet the bond between the two writers survived in one form or other until broken after forty years by Brigid's death.
>
> My father Michael Levey was present when Iris and Brigid first met, in 1954. He was struck by their immediate rapport. Not long after, when Iris visited their London flat, Michael records the pair arguing uninhibitedly about Greek philosophers: Iris was for Plato's pre-eminence while Brigid argued for Aristotle's. My father remarks that to this he could 'bring nothing but attention to refilling the two participants' glasses'.[7]

In Murdoch's journal for this early period, pages have been removed by hand for unknown reasons. There is one page for 1955 (24 February) remaining, and it is here that we find the first mention of Brophy. They are clearly writing poetry to each other at this stage and this unpublished, indeed unknown verse by Iris (this is the first time it has been published) owes much to the seventeenth-century English metaphysical poet Andrew Marvell. Peter Conradi mentions it in passing: 'Soon they exchanged verses pastiching Marvell's "To His Coy Mistress"':[8]

> Had I but world enough and time
> I'd try to turn my uncouth rhyme
> And send you back ambiguous lines
> Like an exchange of Valentines
> I could not write so well. But then
> I'd trust you least I not my pen
> And love, in lines unmusical
> My honey metaphysical
> Were it not that I have bad dreams
> And at my back a maenad screams.[9]

Maenads are female followers of Dionysus, the Greek god of wine making, harvest, madness and fertility. Maenads literally translates as 'raving ones',[10] and it is clear, I think, that Murdoch was already in love. Clearly this private work was never intended for publication, but it is odd that Murdoch removed so much from her journals and yet left this intact. Although not proven, Murdoch scholarship currently holds that she bowdlerised the journals before handing them to Conradi, her official biographer. Perhaps she thought that, at some point, her personal writings would become public.

A poem in a later letter expands on Murdoch's desire for Brophy, clearly in response to a poem of Brophy's:

> Thanks for your poem (Freudian) received.
> I must confess I found it quite a tonic,
> And hope you will not be unduly peeved
> If I reply in spirit more ironic.
> I doubt in fact if you will be aggrieved
> At being greeted in a style Byronic,
> Since mixing of the sexes, which you prize,
> Dear Byron certainly exemplifies.
>
> How cleverly you write!
> It's quite confusing.
> You want me female, then you want me male,
> Or else hermaphrodite, to suit your choosing,

While for yourself you have some other tale
Of corresponding moves. ('You are amusing!')
To understand this stuff I simply fail,
Eschewing Freud and all his patter, for I
Don't make of sex a basic category.

Of course, one has a sex, I can't deny it.
For purposes of passports, clothes et cetera
I am a woman, and I don't decry it.
Since man has always done his best to fetter her,
A woman would be man, if she could try it,
In many cases – but this would not better her
In any deep respect, and as a spirit
Woman is man's superior in merit.

But I digress. Now turning from page one
I see you speak of locks where keys can go.
It's *most* obscure and I suspect a *pun*
Or some obscene and nasty *jeu de mots*;
And how can we be lock and key in one
And also wax? It's hardly *comme il faut*
To make your metaphors quite so inflated
Even when urging some things complicated.

And then this talk of *lying*. No, my dear,
Since something to your purpose in me lacks,
Or rather something not so (am I clear?)
I will be neither lock nor key nor wax,
Not closed, yet not for lying on I fear
(Or lying *with*. You make us sound like sacks!)
Nor by such entry to be prised apart
As rudely searching would not move my heart.

But why should I spend time to tell you this?
Your own ingenious spirit needs no lesson.
Nature denies us a consummate bliss
But gives us much to rest some happiness on:
Too great exactitude would come amiss.
Half sundered and in darkness we must press on.
For what it darkly is, then take my love,
And in the forest lost we still shall rove.[11]

Much could be said about this work; its concern with identity, gender and conflict. However, suffice to say that these issues will be
examined later, and will be found to be present in conversations in

the letters and, crucially, in the fiction of this period. The playfulness of both authors, and the discovery of this textual encoding, is only possible given the new material available to scholarship.

As mentioned earlier, little critical attention, thus far, has been given to their relationship. Conradi, in the (so far) only major academic biography of Murdoch, published in 2001, writes:

> The friendship grew when the Leveys visited the Bayleys at Steeple Aston, and Iris saw both in London; for years Brigid and Iris would go away for a weekend break. Neither husband felt excluded. This friendship was neither without astringency nor without resilience.[12]

The material that Conradi has on their relationship, some three or four pages out of 600 or so, comes primarily from interviewing Brophy's husband, Michael Levey. At this time the letters from Murdoch to Brophy were still in Michael's loft, and from reading these pages it is almost certain that Conradi did not have access to them.[13] Indeed, according to Kate Levey, her father did not want them made public until after his death.[14] If he had, no doubt the material would have made for a much lengthier chapter in Conradi's book in its own right. Later works, including Valerie Purton's *An Iris Murdoch Chronology* (2007) and Priscilla Martin and Anne Rowe's *Iris Murdoch: A Literary Life* (2010), mention Brophy, but again without knowledge of the letters the relationship was seen as one among many. Frances White's *Becoming Iris Murdoch* (2014) claims that the relationship 'fades out by February 1956', which new evidence disproves.[15]

While both women were in happy, yet unconventional, marriages, Murdoch was far more attached to conventionality in public than Brophy was. Although there are few, if any, representations of idealised marriage in Murdoch's fiction, Brophy rails against marriage in her non-fictional work. In 'The Immorality of Marriage' (1965) she states that 'Only on the subject of the relation between the sexes do reactionaries start citing "nature" as an ideal. They are to be heard nowadays complaining that our psychological and technological advances have produced an "unnatural state"';[16] and in 'Monogamy' (1965): 'There is of course no reason why we should be bound by nature and biology at all. Much of civilisation consists of overcoming them and setting ourselves free.'[17] It is no surprise then that Brophy was a noted member of the National Secular Society.[18] Murdoch was far more cautious about these kinds of ideas, longing instead for a workable, demythologised Christianity. It is clear, I believe, that Brophy's concerns are written out in the fictional works under discussion.

The most important work in Murdoch scholarship to emerge in the past five years has been Avril Horner and Anne Rowe's *Living on Paper*, which brings together a substantial number of publicly available letters to highlight Murdoch's ongoing relationships, friendships and correspondence with admirers; indeed this is the first work to publish a selection of the Murdoch–Brophy letters, with a section guide highlighting the importance of this relationship. The introductory material to three chapters in this work describes their evolving relationship and is the first sustained biographical material in this area to be published. The review of the collection in the *Observer* newspaper had this to say about the exposure of the relationship:

> Murdoch writes that she thinks of herself as a 'male homosexual in female guise', though what this meant in practice so far as Brophy was concerned had less to do with sex – 'I'm not in love with you, and don't want to be' – than with a peculiar role play involving Raffles, E. W. Hornung's gentleman thief: Murdoch assumed the role of the amateur cracksman, while Brophy was cast as his accomplice, Bunny, formerly his fag at school. But if this suggests their relationship had a certain levity, do not be deceived. It was tortured: sadomasochistic in an emotional sense, if not a physical one ('You are not a true classical sadomasochist like me,' noted Murdoch, having confessed that she had wanted to be beaten by those who interested her. 'You are just an abnormal perverted one.') Brophy was needy – too needy – and thus Murdoch is always apologising half-heartedly for her failings, her transparent insincerity shading swiftly into relief when her lover eventually moves on. It's striking that Brophy was open about her dislike of Murdoch's novels. As she (Iris) points out: 'I am, I think, rather like my books, so that it is at least odd (and a little unnerving) to find you detesting them.'[19]

Murdoch's journals are now in the public domain for the first time, housed in the Special Collections (of which the Iris Murdoch archive is a part) at Kingston University. Conradi had access to these for his biography,[20] but until 2017 they were not publicly available. Much has been excised, sadly, from the period under discussion, but what remains both confirms and complicates Murdoch's emotions towards Brophy. Brophy's letters to Murdoch are no longer in existence – Murdoch destroyed them either when she received them, or when she left her house outside Oxford to return to the city centre.[21] Her journal notes that she 'burnt a load of papers and such like' in her back garden before moving. Brophy kept carbon copies of letters to other literary figures she was in correspondence with, including Graham Greene and Patricia Highsmith, but there are no copies of those to Murdoch.[22] This is almost certainly because Brophy typed letters to almost everyone, but to Murdoch they were handwritten.

The only recent work that moves beyond the biographical to consider their personal relationship within and through their fiction is Pamela Osborn's article, '"Stop. That's Wicked": Sexual Freedom in Brigid Brophy's *The Burglar* and Iris Murdoch's *A Severed Head*'.[23] Here, Osborn states that 'Brophy's play is, to some degree, a response to Murdoch's work [*A Severed Head*]', and goes on to highlight the textual affinities between the two works:

> Murdoch envied those, like Brophy, who could write plays with apparent ease, because she found it very difficult [. . .] References to *A Severed Head* and its adaptation for theatre occur frequently in Murdoch's letters to Brophy. Often she is evidently responding directly to an enquiry from the latter about the progress of the adaptation.[24]

I agree with Osborn that this textual dialogue between the two writers is clear – indeed, it is rare for Brophy to praise a work by Murdoch as she did the play version of *A Severed Head*. Although there was mutual respect in their relationship, it did not extend to a love of each other's work. Murdoch was keen on Brophy's work, Brophy much less so on Murdoch's, as can be seen from a comment in Murdoch's journal for November 1958:

> A letter from BB attacks and rejects my work in a rather stupid way. She refers to my 'producing one more clay foot every year'. But BB's attitude merely irritates and can't in any way help. Her motives are not pure enough and I don't respect her enough (it would have to be a lot) – also she distinguishes me and my work, and the person who is to help me [improve] must not do that.[25]

This was in response to the publication of *The Bell*, which would make Murdoch far more visible to the general public. This was taken up by Murdoch in a letter to Brophy. The editors of *Living on Paper* believe this is from 1960 (the postmark is illegible), but it would seem more likely that it was written shortly after the journal entry above:

Dearest creature, your recently advertised efforts to amuse me certainly reached a new high in latest letter. I'm so glad about Adrian. I thought of you.

Until now I have taken the view that your odd attitude to my work was unimportant. Lots of my friends don't like that I write (eg Professor Frankel) but mostly they keep quiet about it, & it doesn't matter. I don't, by the way, dislike, or don't think I do interesting criticism, if devoid of spite. Interesting criticism one practically never gets, of course. My own debate about the merits of my work & how to improve it is one that I think no one else can contribute to. I believe I have a reasonably just estimate of my faults & virtues as a writer & know when & in what respect I am over-praised. I confess I am surprised that you altogether dislike my work, as I should have thought it was complex enough to have some things in it which wd [*sic*] touch your heart & mind. I am beginning now to think that your total rejection of it is important, & I'm not sure what should be done. It is not a matter of love me love my books. I feel no specially protective attachment to the completed things which recede at a great speed into the past. It is partly that I am, I think, rather like my books, so that it is at least odd (& a little unnerving) to find you detesting them. It is also that, more important, your dislike also touches the future, & touches my present activities, with a cold hand. In this role you seem destructive. I wonder why you so much insist on your feelings, instead of emulating the silence of Professor Frankel? You speak here of 'honesty' etc. But I don't think honesty is the same as ruthless self-expression. You want to do something by insisting. I wonder if we shouldn't perhaps discuss the whole matter sometime (an idea which before Sunday wd have seemed to me ludicrous.)

All my love.<br>I[26]

There is ample evidence, I believe (even though we only have one side of the correspondence), that both writers' fictional works cannot escape being encoded by their difficult relationship. Arguably this is more obvious in the work of Brophy, especially in *Flesh*, and in her subsequent novel *The Finishing Touch*, a novel indebted to Wilde, Firbank and, I would argue, her relationship with Murdoch too. Brophy dedicated *Flesh* to 'IM', and it is generally known by Murdoch scholars that Brophy gave her a copy, replete with changes to the paratext, the most telling being the alteration of the title from *Flesh: a novel* by Brigid Brophy to *Flash: A Navel* by Brigitte Bardot, as well as changes to biographical details as highlighted in figures 3, 4 and 5.[27]

**Figure 3** The front cover of Iris Murdoch's copy of *Flesh*, collaged by Brigid Brophy. Iris Murdoch Special Collection, Kingston University

Photo by          *Norman A. Chalk*

ANTONIA      and 34–26–35,
BRIGID/BROPHY, who is 33/ is married to Michael
Levey, art historian and/Assistant Keeper at the
National Gallery. They live in S.W.5 with their
guests, who sing;
small daughter and two statues. Brigid Brophy
which sees her   it not at all
writes non-fiction/as well as novels: her *Black Ship*
she conducts an endless
to Hell, published last year, is a psycho-analytical
herself
enquiry into war, and the *London Magazine* has
most of the results, mainly disguised
recently published two long extracts from her
as literary criticism. It is also going to publish her husband's poetry.
forthcoming book on Mozart's operas. She is
socially timid and inveterately literate: she would
always rather write a letter than telephone or go
there. (There are one or two rather intimate occasions of which this is not true.)
     Miss Brophy's previous books include: *The
Crown Princess*, a collection of stories ("exceptional
acuteness and penetrative power . . . a wit which
is unobtrusive but constant."—*Times Literary
Supplement*); *Hackenfeller's Ape* ("neat, original,
waspish, tender—an odd mixture of adjectives to
describe an oddly shaped and exciting woman."—
ISABEL QUIGLY, *Spectator*); *The King of a Rainy
Country* ("The Times is well written indeed . . . magnificently
Brigid Brophy
funny."—*The Times*).

**Figure 4** The back cover of Iris Murdoch's copy of *Flesh*, collaged by Brigid Brophy. Iris Murdoch Special Collection, Kingston University

After the problems of the selling of the family house and the acquisition of a flat, the question of a job for Marcus, who had never had one, became acute, not because he needed the money but because he had become active, vigorous,

*(continued on back flap)*

Figure 5 The front flap of the dust jacket of Iris Murdoch's copy of *Flesh*, collaged by Brigid Brophy. Iris Murdoch Special Collection, Kingston University

Association copies of novels are, naturally, not uncommon, but major changes, both playful and telling, are highly unusual. Murdoch had this to say about it:

> Dearest girl, I have never before received a novel dedicated to me wrapped up in silver paper. I am utterly delighted. The labour of love round the outside is much appreciated too and I hope represents many happy hours. The picture of you on the back rather turns my head. The hunched broad-shouldered appearance is just right [. . .] I shall treasure it. I also liked the account of you and your Keeper; and the mysterious 'go there'. (Where?) The dédicace gives me enormous pleasure. I feel very proud and want to go round telling everyone I know you. NB I adore the novel too. Thank you, Brigid. I embrace you, you dazzling creature. With great thanks and love, your much cheered up. Iris[28]

It is worth highlighting here that the 'labour of love' is designed both to amuse and to provoke. The reworking of Brophy's portrait on the back cover, for instance, highlights her intention to morph into James Joyce: for the Anglo-Irish Murdoch, a literary touchstone. More than this though, the playfulness with sexuality, gender and nationality is clear from these images, as well as the importance Brophy places on her epistolary relationship with Murdoch. The letters of this period are also replete with role play and gender transformation. The inclusion of the collaged contents page is by turns amusing and highly intimate, adding more weight to the received view that it was Brophy who wanted a fuller physical relationship, one that Murdoch was unable to provide. Murdoch wrote this to Brophy soon after publication: 'I'm very glad to hear of Flesh's success. Think of all those people reading my initials. Jolly good. You needn't, by the way, explain references to your texts (Pamela's telephone call.) I will recognise them!'[29] The references in *Flesh* must surely hint at more than intertextual jokes that could be picked up by any cultured reader.

The week after the letter quoted above Iris writes:

> I have read your novel with great delight. I do think it's good, a handsome lovely clever book, with excellence on every page, as proper books should have. You must be the first person who has described sexual intercourse beautifully and well in a book.[30]

The relationship between Nancy and Marcus in *Flesh* is not one of equals. However, although there is an element of the sadomasochistic to their life together, as Nancy moulds thin Marcus into a sexually

experienced Rubensesque figure, it was Brophy's novel of the following year, *The Finishing Touch*, that partly fictionalised her relationship with Murdoch. This is not to say that Brophy does not work
elements of their relationship into *Flesh*.

Clearly then, there is an interest on both sides on sexual relations in the novels of this period. Together with Osborn, I believe
that *A Severed Head* has elements of Brophy in it. This novel features a variety of interlocking relationships with a powerful female
enchanter, Honour Klein, that owes something to the fraught relationship between Murdoch and Brophy – how she interacts with
Martin Lynch-Gibbon in his basement may well reflect some of
this relationship.

It is *An Unofficial Rose* (1962), however, Murdoch's sixth novel,
written approximately eight years into her relationship with Brophy,
that contains her most obvious fictional portrayal of their relationship.[31] The novel opens with Hugh, a retired civil servant, standing
by the graveside of his recently deceased wife, Anne; alongside him is
his son, Randall, and other members of the family. Standing at some
distance from the mourners we are introduced to Hugh's former mistress, Emma Sands, and her secretary, Lindsay Rimmer. Randall, we
later find out, is having a relationship with Lindsay, while Hugh is
contemplating returning to his former lover. The relationship between
Emma and Lindsay is not clearly defined until the concluding chapters
of the novel, where it becomes clear that it includes domination and
sadomasochism. The hint at a sexual relationship is made by way of
euphemism to begin with: '"Her secretary, companion person"';[32] but
it later becomes clear that there is far more occurring:

> 'Terrible as my lot is here', said Randall, 'I assure you it was even more
> terrible there.' 'I don't think his lot is so terrible, do you?' said Lindsay.
> 'Certainly not,' said Emma, 'Considering how bad he is, we let him off
> very easily on the whole.' 'We hardly ever beat him,' said Lindsay.[33]

The darkly comic moment here is followed up towards the end
of the novel. Lindsay has left Emma to be with Randall as they
travel Europe together, and Emma has appointed a new companion, Jocelyn: obviously Murdoch in fictional form, down to the
educational background:

> 'Would you like to see a picture of her?' [. . .] Hugh saw a dark tou-
> sled boyish-looking girl with an arrogant ironical face. He laid the
> photo down. 'Well, I think you might –' 'I wanted to be sure she'd

come,' said Emma, speaking quickly. 'I always ask them to send photos. She's handsome, isn't she? Such a clever face. And her dossier is
good too. Second in Mods and a third in Greats. That seems all right,
doesn't it? Somerville, of course. I like them to be well educated. I
took Lindsay *plutôt pour ses beaux yeux*. But Jocelyn is really well
cultivated as well, and awfully nice.'[34]

We then get the full admission of the relationship that Emma will
have with Jocelyn, as she did with Lindsay: 'I shall manage. I shall
be happy. I shall be beating Jocelyn';[35] an element present in the
Brophy–Murdoch relationship.

There is more at play here, but the fictional relationship between
an older woman and a much younger female is one we see repeated
in Brophy's *The Snow Ball*. As a recurring character, the *ingénue*
figure also appears regularly in the works of Murdoch. *The Snow
Ball* includes the unequal relationship between the younger Anna
and the older Anne, the closeness of their names highlighting the
closeness between them and perhaps the interchange of identity that
Murdoch and Brophy also shared. Anne, for example, asks Anna:
'Listen, dearest. Do you believe there are intimacies of married life
one ought not to reveal even to one's best friend?'[36] This highlights,
I think, Murdoch's divide between her London life of friendships and
affairs, and her comfortable Oxford life of writing and John Bayley.
Anna, obsessed with Mozart, sex and death, clearly reflects the passionate nature of Brophy.

There is also the small inclusion of Brophy in Murdoch's *The Red
and the Green* (1965):

> He made a detailed study of the origins of monasticism in Ireland
> and formed a strong attachment to Saint Brigid, generous, gentle,
> miraculous saint, and went on devout pilgrimages upon her tracks.
> He projected a book entitled *The Significance of Brigid* as the first
> volume of his *oeuvre*. It seemed like the good life.[37]

This is the last evidence I can find that could be considered a reference to their ongoing relationship. Brophy's copy of the novel,[38]
which contains a few marginal notes on the text, does reference the
page before this section but has no direct link to it. Brophy seems
more interested in the links to Dublin locations specified in the novel.
Murdoch's next novel, *The Time of the Angels* (1966), is more densely
philosophical, and this was the last novel she wrote during their relationship. Murdoch dedicated her novel *The Good Apprentice* (1985)

to Brophy, but it seems that this was an act of friendship when Brigid was diagnosed with multiple sclerosis in the mid-1980s, rather than an act of erotic communication. However, Murdoch never liked to lose friends, and although the close relationship came to an end, her affection for Brigid did not: after a fashion Brigid was happy to be in communication with Iris.

If Murdoch's *An Unofficial Rose* highlights the sadomasochistic elements of their relationship, Brophy's novel *The Finishing Touch* highlights the drama of their speech. It was described by Brophy as 'a lesbian fantasy' (and without a dedication, which is unusual), and concerns two middle-aged women, Miss Antonia Mount and Miss Hetty Braid, who are in charge of a finishing school on the French Riviera. Early critics, indeed Brophy herself, connected it to the Soviet spy Anthony Blunt. Is Blunt in the novel in disguised form? Certainly, the most recent edition from Faber in 2013, with a foreword by Peter Stothard, takes Brophy's introduction to her work from 1986 (reproduced in this edition) at her word: 'What my imagination did, when it picked him up by the scruff of his neck, was change his sex and make him the headmistress of a finishing school for girls [. . .] he also retains his name.'[39] However, given the new material outlined above, I believe the thin veneer of Blunt has been applied to a fictionalised version of Brophy herself: we should not forget that her middle name was Antonia. The relationship between Antonia (Brophy) and Hetty (Murdoch) is rather more the restrained Iris and (less so) Brigid. In a letter written shortly after publication Iris praised the novel and said: 'Thank you very much indeed for Antonia. (So I shall always think of her.) We are delighted to have that delicious book – & I shall immediately read it again, & that will cheer me up very much.'[40] Supporting this claim is a greetings card, from a much later period, on which is written 'For darling Antonia from Old Faithful'.[41]

Clearly then this cannot now be overlooked. On second, or indeed third, reading with this in mind, our perspective on the novel changes significantly. The relationship between the two women in the novel is, once again, unequal and not without a sense of powerplay and gender ambiguity. The following extract highlights this, and also provides a vision of Brophy's Murdoch:

Astonishing, ran Antonia's train of thought as her eye took what would be, for the time being, its last glance at the back of Hetty's neck . . . that women who chose to dress like men always chose for their model the most careless, the most thorn-torn, the most ash- (or was it dandruff-?) spattered type of man . . . The drive would have been so much less fatiguing had Hetty modelled herself on some really sprucely, though not, of course, flashily, uniformed chauffeur.[42]

Hetty is also described using images connected with Murdoch's own appearance – 'not even the eye of affection could see in Hetty a shepherdess; but their sheepdog, sturdy, reliable, brisk'[43] –while 'Antonia had dressed to provoke' later on in the novel.[44] There is something rather arch about this I think, clearly a private joke between the two of them placed in plain sight in fiction, but also one that denigrates, albeit comedically, Murdoch.

As Osborn has stated, 'Brophy and Murdoch's dialogue about what constitutes a civilised approach to sex and sexuality [. . .] has taken on a new relevance in the twenty-first century',[45] and it is arguable that Brophy accepted this challenge more completely than Murdoch in her published essays. Both, however, undertook to explore sexuality and gender in their work by importing their own relationship, laid out in letters and journals, on to the page. For neither woman was this the most defining relationship of their lives, but it was certainly a formative, intense, near-decade lived out in London, in regular romantic short breaks, and on paper. I am sure that the material here is not the final word on their 'fictional' relationship; others will surely undertake deeper, singular readings of the novels and there may be more evidence that will come to light to enhance this reading.[46] However, it is the case that the works of both authors from this period benefit from a sustained bio-critical reading, and the encoding of their relationship on the page cannot be ignored.

## Notes

1. The letters are now housed in the Iris Murdoch archive at Kingston University, London.
2. Avril Horner and Anne Rowe (eds), *Living on Paper: Letters from Iris Murdoch 1934–1995* (London: Chatto and Windus, 2015), p. xvi.
3. Sadly only the correspondence from Murdoch to Brophy survives.
4. Harold Bloom, *The Anxiety of Influence: A Theory of Poetry* (Oxford: Oxford University Press, 1997), p. xxiii.
5. Brigid Brophy, *Black Ship to Hell* (New York: Harcourt and Brace, 1962), pp. 131, 134.
6. Murdoch's novels are *The Flight from the Enchanter* (1956), *The Sandcastle* (1957), *The Bell* (1958), *A Severed Head* (1961), *An Unofficial Rose* (1962), *The Unicorn* (1963), *The Italian Girl* (1964), *The*

*Red and the Green* (1965) and *The Time of the Angels* (1966), and the adaptation (with J. B. Priestley) of *A Severed Head* (1964). Brigid Brophy's novels are *The King of a Rainy Country* (1956), *Flesh* (1962), *The Finishing Touch* (1963) and *The Snow Ball* (1964). Her play, *The Burglar*, was written during this time but not published until after the end of their relationship in 1968.

7. Kate Levey, 'Iris and Brigid: A Sketch', in Miles Leeson (ed.), *Iris Murdoch: A Centenary Celebration* (Yeovil: Saberstorm Fiction, 2019), p. 61.
8. Peter Conradi, *Iris Murdoch: A Life* (London: HarperCollins, 2001), p. 487.
9. From Murdoch's journal (1955–onwards), housed at Kingston University. KUAS202/1/9
10. In Greek mythology Orpheus, the legendary poet and musician, is torn to pieces by maenads.
11. Horner and Rowe (eds), *Living on Paper*, pp. 206–7.
12. Conradi, *Iris Murdoch*, p. 487.
13. Conradi correspondence with Michael Levey in 1998.
14. Kate Levey, in conversation with the author.
15. Frances White, *Becoming Iris Murdoch* (London: Kingston University Press, 2014), p. 49.
16. Brigid Brophy, *Don't Never Forget: Collected Views and Reviews* (London: Jonathan Cape, 1966), p. 23.
17. Ibid., p. 29.
18. Other noted members of the NSS at the time included A. J. Ayer.
19. Rachel Cooke, '*Living On Paper: Letters from Iris Murdoch 1934–1995* review – ruthless in affairs of the heart', *The Observer*, <https://www.theguardian.com/books/2015/nov/08/living-on-paper-iris-murdoch-letters-review> (accessed 5 January 2019).
20. Murdoch gave him these in the 1990s when he began to write his biography.
21. Murdoch burnt Brophy's letters at her request, but also destroyed other correspondence at the same time.
22. Brigid Brophy's archive – amounting to several boxes of material – remains with her daughter, Kate Levey.
23. Pamela Osborn, '"Stop. That's Wicked": Sexual Freedom in Brigid Brophy's *The Burglar* and Iris Murdoch's *A Severed Head*', *Contemporary Women's Writing*, 12.2 (2018), pp. 222–32.
24. Ibid., p. 226.
25. From Murdoch's journal (1955–onwards), housed at Kingston University. KUAS202/1/9
26. Horner and Rowe (eds), *Living on Paper*, pp. 215–16
27. The copy was rediscovered by the author in Murdoch's former home at Charlbury Road in Oxford in 2017. It is now in the archive at Kingston University.

28. Letter to Brophy from Murdoch. Kingston University Archive. KUAS142/5/24.
29. Letter to Brophy from Murdoch. Kingston University Archive. KUAS142/5/168.
30. Letter to Brophy from Murdoch. Kingston University Archive. KUAS142/5/21.
31. It is dedicated to Margaret Hubbard, a fellow don at St Anne's College with whom Murdoch had a difficult relationship, one that ultimately led to Murdoch being asked to leave the college and the university. She subsequently worked at the Royal College of Art in London.
32. Iris Murdoch, *An Unofficial Rose* (London: Vintage, 2000), p. 33.
33. Ibid., p. 38.
34. Ibid., p. 267.
35. Ibid., p. 271.
36. Brigid Brophy, *The Snow Ball* (London: Sphere Books, 1990), p. 39.
37. Iris Murdoch, *The Red and the Green* (London: Chatto and Windus, 1965), pp. 108–9.
38. Owned by the author. The notes on the first blank endpaper may well be for a review, although I have not been able to trace this.
39. Brigid Brophy, *The Finishing Touch* (London: Faber and Faber, 2013), Introduction.
40. Unpublished letter to Brophy from Murdoch. Kingston University Archive. KUAS142/6/199.
41. Unpublished letter to Brophy from Murdoch. Kingston University Archive. KUAS142/7/77.
42. Brophy, *The Finishing Touch*, p. 43.
43. Ibid., p. 25.
44. Ibid., p. 43.
45. Osborn, '"Stop. That's Wicked"', p. 231.
46. It may be that Murdoch's unpublished novel *Jerusalem*, written in the late 1950s, will provide more evidence for this.

# Chapter 11

# 'Heads and Boxes': A Prop Art Exhibition Collaboration by Brigid Brophy and Maureen Duffy

*Jill Longmate*

An attentive reader of *The Times* on 21 April 1969 would have been intrigued by this announcement in the entertainment small advertisements:

> Heads and boxes: Prop Art. Brigid Brophy and Maureen Duffy, 19 to 31 May. Mason's Yard Gallery, 14 Mason's Yard (off Duke Street), St James, London, SW1.

Rather than featuring among other West End galleries in the Art Exhibitions section, this appeared under Exhibitions and Lectures, between the Buxton Antiques Fair and a London University science lecture, as if confirming the challenge of categorising a fresh departure by two established writers, each known for literary originality but not for visual art. The purpose was serious, the execution of it fun, but to launch a conceptual art exhibition, complete with manifesto about the Brophy–Duffy invention of Prop Art, was also daring. *Tribune* published the first advertisement, on 11 April, alerting progressive friends and sympathisers, but to announce it in *The Times*, then the newspaper of record, essential reading for opinion-formers, was to assert the claim of 'Heads and Boxes' to be taken seriously by a wider intellectual audience, including colleagues and contacts of the art historian Michael Levey, keeper of the National Gallery, to whom Brophy was married.

Despite the optimistic and innovative artistic climate of 1969, where experiment was welcomed in theory, any surprising initiative ran risks in practice, as Brophy was aware:

To be any kind of artist is a dangerous profession. There is a constant attempt to place limitations on the intellect and the imagination, and if someone comes up with something new – not newness of form which can become immediately fashionable, but newness of concept, people find this disturbing.

So they say that what you have done is a joke, or that you are not equipped, or that you are deliberately trying to shock, or that you ought to stick to what you know. And in our case, there is always one objection to fall back on, the one which says: you are a woman.[1]

There was, however, no risk of being ignored. As the *Guardian* explained, both creators were newsworthy:

Brigid Brophy and Maureen Duffy, novelists, playwrights, vegetarians, friends and Irish both have novels due, Duffy's in June, Brophy's in September. They live in the same area of London, and share the courage to defy convention. Miss Brophy advocated a love philosophy before hippies and flower children were invented. Miss Duffy wrote a serious novel about lesbianism before it was fashionable.[2]

As was sometimes hinted, but not said, in the press, they were also in love with each other. These were the heady early years of Brophy and Duffy's relationship.[3] 'Michael and Brigid's union was styled on freedom', as Kate Levey recalls. 'Relationships with other people were simply part of the fullness of the lives my parents had jointly created, from the outset. They did not conceal their feelings for others or lie to each other.'[4]

Brophy's Shavian farce, *The Burglar*, had appeared at the Vaudeville Theatre in 1967, attracting Peggy Ramsay to become her dramatic agent;[5] and Duffy's play *Rites*, inspired by the Bacchae myth, set in a ladies' toilet and produced by Joan Plowright, was opening at the Old Vic on 27 May 1969. Brophy's new novel *In Transit*, an experimental work centred around a narrator uncertain of her or his gender, was packed with puns (as the exhibition was to be), and had just been completed before the idea of 'Heads and Boxes' first occurred to her in late 1968.[6] Three years after the success of *The Microcosm*, Duffy's forthcoming fifth novel, *Wounds*, followed a diverse range of Londoners, interspersed with bedroom scenes between two lovers.

It was Brophy, the older and longer-established author of the two, who, Duffy recalls, was 'quite famous' as 'a brilliant reviewer and polemicist as well as novelist'.[7] In 1969 Brophy was known as much for her journalism as for the twelve books and two pamphlets she then had to her name. Asked for more press articles than she had time to write, she was able to pick and choose those she most wanted to do,[8] and was frequently published in the *Sunday Times*, *The Times*, *The Listener* and *New Statesman*, among others.

An outstanding intellectual, celebrated for her controversial opinions, logic and wit, 'during the sixties, Brophy was briefly known in London literary circles as the brainiest woman in Britain'.[9] In favour of vegetarianism, animal rights, pacifism and atheism, Brophy was a Freudian who also argued for open marriages, legalising same-sex marriage, and contraception being available to young people. She favoured comparative religious education, including humanism, rather than compulsory Christian teaching.[10] All this made her a *bête noire* for critics of the permissive society, and for those alarmed by feminism; and a gift for newspapers seeking quotable copy. In 1968 she inspired such *Daily Mail* headlines as 'Why does this woman attract so much wrath?' and 'Banned on Smith's shelves [. . .] the new Brophy', but she was also cited as an inspiration for freedom-seekers. When a young character in a 1969 episode of the ITV sit-com *Father, Dear Father* declared that she wanted to leave home and 'drink deep the cup of life [. . .] and fulfil myself as a woman', her father responded, 'You've been reading Brigid Brophy again.'[11]

## What was Prop Art?

Prop Art began, Brophy said, when she wanted to produce poems on paper that could be folded into the shape of the poem, creating a new artistic form that combined poetry and sculpture.[12] Though not known, or describing herself publicly, as a poet, Brophy's papers show that she privately wrote poems, very occasionally in this period, and particularly in later life, but rarely submitted them for publication.[13] Duffy was an experienced, published poet, whose work Brophy knew well.

As Brigid explained to the *Guardian*, her initial idea of sculpted paper poems evolved through discussion with Maureen into the use of small objects, such as children's toys, and other 'props' to create scenes in transparent plastic boxes, where the choice of (often punning) title was key to the meaning. They also wanted to use heads, but for some time couldn't source them, until they found white, life-size, polystyrene wig stands in Peter Jones, the department store in Chelsea's Sloane Square. Kate Levey confirms that these were sold loose, not in the plastic boxes, which were sourced

**Figure 6** [WOMAN]IFESTO of PROP ART. Credit: Brigid Brophy

elsewhere.[14] Duffy recalls that it was mainly Brigid, in her enthusi-asm for wordplay, who came up with the puns, and Maureen, the more practical of the two – experienced in making furniture and hanging wallpaper – who 'did the making'.[15]

The fullest theoretical explanation of this creative initiative appeared in what *Arts Review* called their 'exceptionally sober and accurate manifesto', which was pinned up at the exhibition and cir-culated to the press.[16] The following, slightly edited version covers all the theory: mentions of precise artworks are in a separate section below about the exhibits. It is thought that Brophy drew the woman in the title (Figure 6).[17]

**[WOMAN]IFESTO**
of
**PROP ART**

Catequizm
   Q. Why 'PROP'?
   A. Because it's composed of props (from the property cupboard of toy shops, chainstores etc.) which are propped-up (without con-cealment, pretentiousness or the use of machinery) on the everyday repertoire of the stationer's. And it is sometimes propagandist.
   Q. Which ART?
   A. It's a visual form of literature and a literary form of the visual arts.

2. Readymages
   Works of PROP ART are equivalents, in another medium, to poems: lyrics, epigrams (slightly in the ancient-world sense), satires, squibs . . . marseillaises or metaphysical extravaganzas.

The props of which PROP ART is composed are visual ready-mades. PROP ART is applying to 3-D objects the method of literature. For literature has always used oral readymades: words.

Like words, visual readymades are undivorceable from meaning.

The result is that works of PROP ART, while they assert themselves in their own right as objects, are also images which require to be (figuratively, and often literally as well) read.

### 3. Icontemplation

So: PROP ART is putting the literary or iconographical element back into the visual arts.

PROP ART is concerned with narrative – like television commercials or Giovanni di Paolo [a fifteenth-century Italian painter of biblical stories]. It is myth-obsessed – like Leonardo. . .

In purely literary works, like poems and novels, the material format (binding, type-face, etc.) is irrelevant: merely convenient and, with luck, decorative or evocative. But in PROP ART, which is literary plus, the character of the format is integral and indispensable.

Indeed, the format dictates how the image is to be read.

The boxed works, though not drama, resemble theatre: tableaux non-vivants.

The head works resemble icons (in modern idiom, pin-ups).

In both, the image invites not involvement but contemplation or even devotion.

### 4. Dramatic Works

That is because the image is objectified by the format.

The spectator is held off, and the image is enclosed in its autonomy as an object, by the impersonal and inexpressive character of the plastic materials of the format.

The head, unindividualised, endlessly reduplicable, itself a readymade (a wig stand), thrusts its bodily presence into the company but, thanks to its non-individualisation, only as a prop for displaying the emblem of the image.

The box's transparent smoothnesses, which eye or finger can pass across so glidingly, seals the image into its own logic and its own (often illogical) scale.

The box establishes the tableau as a tableau from a dream.

The obsessions – and particularly the myth-obsessions – which many of the boxes express are equivalent to recurrent dreams.

### 5. Selexpressionism

However, works of PROP ART are deliberate works, not involuntary symptoms.

In working them, the artists too, are to some extent excluded from involvement. The material can be contrived and manipulated but not wrought. Direct expressionism (e.g. by knocking up an impasto) is out.

The materials themselves are often inexpensive, and the ready-mades, when they are expressive at all, express someone else's, not the artists', intention.

The act through which the artists express emotion is, therefore, selection from readymades.

Colour, texture and pattern create mood. . .

6. Poemages

Not only is each work a PROP-ART equivalent to a poem: two works (Totem and At Court) incorporate poems. . .

Several of the images make satirical points. Some have (again, the dream-scene) a surrealist absence of point.

Some are the propaganda of (egalitarian, pacific, vegetarian) protest.

Vultures is a literary simile visually executed.

Sometimes some of the satire is turned against the character of the readymades themselves. . .

7. ♩♩♩ on the Pun.

Several of the images turn on puns.

Why do people draw sharp breaths, metaphorising that their teeth have been set on edge, at a pun as they do at a sour note?

Because a pun is sour, like an acid belch. It is an eructation from the unconscious. Puns are important parts of speech in the vocabulary of the unconscious. PROP ART puns because dreams pun.

As dreams know, a whole nexus may be condensed into a pun. . .

Sour notes, unacceptable to the rational scheme of traditional tonality, are useful to modern composers and listeners. In modern literature and in PROP ART, puns serve the same purpose in the texture of the work as the chords which used to be thought dissonances now serve in the texture of music.

8. The Dreamaturges

PROP ART was invented, and some fifty Heads and Boxes in it executed, in 1968–9 by Brigid Brophy, a novelist and dramatist, and Maureen Duffy, a novelist, dramatist and poet.

## 'Heads and Boxes': the exhibits

### Selection

There were 55 exhibits in the final exhibition list, with boxes grouped together in the first section, followed by heads. Fifty was aimed at as a satisfying number, which would look deliberately chosen (the principle Kate Levey recalls being used in *Fifty Works of English and American Literature We Could Do Without*, Brophy's 1967 book with Charles Osborne and Michael Levey).[18] How many were produced is unknown, but it was a prodigious number in a few months. Surviving photos, and a mention of 56 planned exhibits in March 1969 – when the exhibition was intended to be in late April – suggest that a few were omitted from the final display, but that any which met the artists' standards were included.[19] While connections can be drawn between the themes of some exhibits, they were intended, as Duffy explained, as 'small separate acts, very condensed'.[20]

## Content

While the two most unifying features of the exhibition were its – sometimes hard-hitting – humour and its dream-like, Freudian-influenced imagery, many of the most memorable exhibits also made political points. Those on animal rights were particularly striking. 'Tête d'Homme Garnie' (Figure 7) depicts a human head on a dinner plate with knife and fork, among leafy garnishing, ready for consumption, with a carrot on its head, onion in its mouth, and vegetables stuffed in eyes, nostrils and ears. Acknowledged as 'horrific', it 'makes the point that if you think liking the taste of meat justifies killing and eating animals, why not humans too?'[21] Similarly, in 'Aunt Eater' (Figure 8), a plastic anteater advances towards a small woman, respectably dressed in coat and hat. Brophy explained: '"This is simple revenge reversal. One is on the animal's side. One sympathises with the animal. Well, who would you like to eat?" "At another level," says Duffy, "we all want to destroy our mothers. So, any female relative substitute will do."'[22] Just as animal rights points were combined with Freudian psychology, they could also be provoked by literature. 'One of the boxes is a scene labelled with a sardonic variant on Blake's poem: "Little Lamb, Who Flayed Thee?"',[23] contrasting with a reference to Christ the Lamb as the creator in William Blake's 'Little Lamb who made thee.'

'Religious Headucation' is effective 'propaganda on behalf of freethought', displaying a head 'with padlocked brain, saying "Credo ergo non cogito." ("I believe, therefore I don't think")'.[24] Added to this reversal of Cartesian logic, an actual, not clerical, dog's collar, with lead, is around the neck. The words 'all things dull and dutiful' also appear, parodying the 'bright and beautiful' hymn. 'Headmaster' reflects similar scepticism of authority, with 'PUPIL' reduced to a small circular word in each eye, and the Head displayed on a plate stand, as

Figure 7  Tête de l'homme garnie. Photo: Euan Duff

Figure 8  Aunt Eater. Photo: Euan Duff

if endowed with more standing than he merits. 'HEADMASTER' is printed on the forehead, and 'SEE THE HEAD' across the neck. 'God-head', whose mildly menacing androgynous face has a black mask over the eyes, winged ears and crest on top of the head, owes more to Greek mythology. Plato is subjected to 'critical comment' in 'Platy-bust', a plastic platypus on a white Doric column and plinth, against a grandiloquent red wallpaper background.[25] 'Brainbox' also asserts the importance of engaging in rational thought for oneself: a model of the brain, apparently constructed from a kit, it has 'Thinks' added in a bubble. Creative thought seems to be celebrated in 'Egghead', where a chick hatches out from the top of the head.

A contrasting symbol of thought, 'Headquarters' (Figure 9) – a head cut vertically into four – featured on the invitation to the Private View. This exhibit was sold to James Brockway, a poet and translator

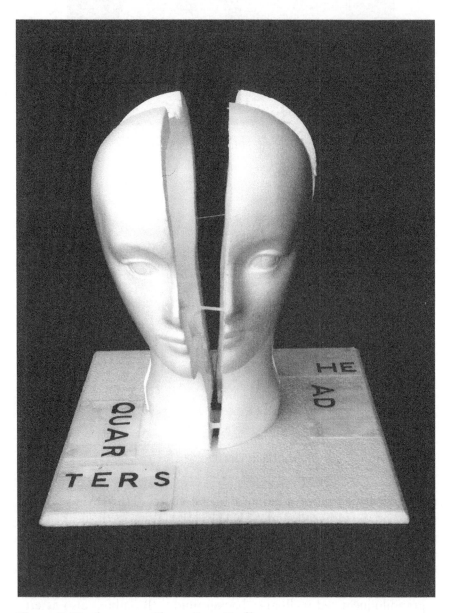

**Figure 9** Headquarters. Photo: Euan Duff

friend of Duffy's.[26] Though not immediately obvious, its intention was partly pacifist. Brophy explained: 'The head is where you do your thinking. If your head is divided into quarters your thinking will show cracks. Headquarters is also a military term and military thinking shows cracks.'[27] Pacifism features in other exhibits. Miniature hand-drums, like those once used to lead soldiers into battle, are hanging from the ears of 'Heardrums recalling the folksong *Johnny I Hardly Knew You*, its bloody bandage a sad comment on all those who have been gulled into battle'. 'The Human Race' 'shows soldiers of all ages running along the track towards a mythical goal',[28] the manifesto noting regretfully that 'the model human figures you can most easily buy in quantity and variety are model soldiers'. 'Treesons' is a pacifist pun on treason, showing scepticism about the supposed advances brought by evolution. The words 'Genialogy' and 'Apocalypse' accompany one ape on all fours, the next standing up, followed by a Roman centurion, a crusader and a parachutist.[29]

The monarchy undergoes witty Freudian analysis in 'Ma'soupappeal', in which a crowd of small figures gazes up at a baroque gold soup tureen, topped with cherubs holding a crown, balanced over the head of a maternal marsupial (kanga and roo), gazing back at the crowd. Another visual pun, 'Reign, Dear', features a reindeer, with a crown on its head, on a snowy plain with two dark pyramid shapes in the background, while 'Blockhead' is a head lying on its side, its neck stained with blood, like an executed monarch or royal victim.

Freudian metaphor, with a pacifist tinge, stalks 'Bipolarity', where two adult polar bears face each other aggressively from opposite sides of a dark carpet across the snow; an isolated small polar bear watches on. In 'Bosch!' the head is cut open to reveal small, grotesque toy animals, and an old man, smoking a pipe, sitting on a pig. A secularist response to Bosch, the artist's, depiction of hell, it is also a Freudian comment on the 'bosh' with which the unconscious may be filled.[30] Some exhibits have depths unsuspected by the casual viewer: 'Tip' – a tipper truck depositing a half crown coin on the dusty earth – the artists explained 'is about the psychoanalytical equation of money with excrement and also about the surreptitiousness and shame with which we both dispose of our waste matter (human or just broken artifacts) and give tips'.[31]

There are also jokes about the surreptitious business of selling sex. In 'Pornbroker', which *Arts Review* thought 'just for laughs',[32] two gold Christmas tree baubles are simply suspended together, a pun on the three gold balls of the pawnbroker. 'T'art' – a shiny red, heart-shaped tart, incorporating an image of three pink roses, encircled by twelve smaller roses, is arranged in a round, foil, food tray, on a

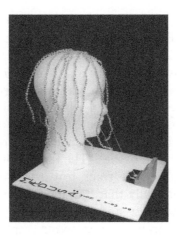

**Figure 10** Maedusa: with a view to. Photo: Euan Duff

background of red and gold velvet wallpaper of the kind associated with brothels in popular culture, a red-handled knife to the right of the tart. Greek mythology certainly features. A head of 'Polythenus' (alias Polyphemus) has a single cyclops eye added in black to the centre of his forehead, along with moustache and beard – the work was sold to Thea Porter, the fashion designer and retailer of hippie chic.[33] 'Maedusa: with a view to' (Figure 10) is a head of the Gorgon, the writhing snakes of her hair represented by thin foil dreadlocks, while two slender chains from her eyes, rather than turning people to stone, are attached to coins in a toy cash register below, perhaps in critical comment on capitalism's addiction to profit. Money also features in 'Danaegeld', with mobiles of gold coins surrounding a head, to represent Zeus coming to Danae in a shower of golden rain, as well as coins ceded to appease the Vikings.

In the best creative tradition, some works were inspired by other creators. 'Disposal', described as 'very moving' by *Arts Review*, depicted a circular, shiny black room, with matt silver doors, intended to imply 'lethalness'.[34] One exit is labelled 'Golden Lads', the other 'Girls', referencing Shakespeare's celebrated couplet about human mortality: 'Golden lads and girls all must, / As chimney-sweepers, come to dust'.[35] 'The Swan Around' was the first, and most expensive, exhibit to sell. Michael Levey bought it, saying it was his favourite. While this gave a supportive boost to the launch of the exhibition, this work of art was also one he kept for many years. It was based around the myth of Leda, incorporating 'a readymade' of Leonardo's composition 'in the Cesare de Sesto version' depicting Leda and her lover, the swan, and their offspring.[36] Mozart and his comic opera about infidelity are celebrated in 'Egg-Cosi Fantuttesy'.

Above an egg cup are displayed a white wig, blue fan, gold Cupids carrying a golden spoon, and the name of Da Ponte, the librettist.

Three exhibits are 'love poems'.[37] 'Paperwait' – small, domed and transparent – contains a day-by-day calendar, with sheets lifted to reveal the date of Friday 24. In 'Headlong', the title, on a heart-shaped sign, appears above a prostrate head on the ground. 'Head-ache' is a head sliced in two, vertically, with the open sides visible, one upright, the attached half horizontal with a transparent rect-angular box inside it labelled 'THOU' on the sides and 'U' on the ends. Others have related themes. Confidences, whether of friends or lovers, are exchanged in 'Tête à Tête', where the back of the head is removed to show a small angel with a halo inside it, whispering in the inner ear. There was some debate between the artists about 'Bed, Head', where two heads are lying under the sheets together, with swans' wings across the bedhead, each wing linked to half a masked head, in profile, at either side. '"That's pro-sex," said Duffy. "I thought it was pro-sleep," said Brophy. "Well, pro-sex and then pro-sleep," compromised Duffy.'[38]

Many of the rest seem to be primarily jokes. 'Old Phoques' Home' has three seals (*phoques*, in French) sitting on sea rocks/rock cakes, each surrounded by a tissue paper case, in marine whites and blues. In 'Dinosoar', a winged dinosaur flies above a green and yellow psy-chedelic circle. 'The patterned paper creates a pun within the pun: it is obviously a springtime earth from which the animal springs.'[39] A foam model of a poodle emerges from a bottle of spilt shampoo in 'Shampoodle'. Illuminated lightbulbs shine out from each eye socket of 'Headlight'. In 'Hedda', a football, signed by both artists, an implicitly feminist image, is attached to the top of the head at an angle. 'Tête Gallery' has a tiny cut-out head from a painting dis-played in each eye. The head of 'Headstrong' floats in a large glass of beer-coloured liquid, with a bottle of Guinness beside it; while 'Headline' consists of a head attached to a phone, with a stretched line on which 'LINE' is pegged like washing, reflecting how journal-ists phoned in copy.

## The significance of Heads and Boxes: Prop Art

How seriously should we take Prop Art? As Brophy put it, 'There are jokes in it [. . .] But it is not a joke to us. Just as one can write a farce without that being a farcical act. We did it as we write, because we wanted to do it. That is how the imagination works. It has ideas.'[40]

The exhibition was certainly serious to Brophy, who was 'an unstoppable creative force', Kate Levey recalls, unwilling to have her head confined in any one box, not even one marked 'writer'. Among Brophy's flow of creative ideas at the time was the possibility of writing a book about Prop Art, and making films, '*my* films. I would like to have the camera in my hands.'[41] While these ideas ended up on the cutting-room floor, such a fountain of aspirations suggests that it was a joyfully productive time for her.

Kate Levey recalls Brophy and Duffy thoroughly enjoying creating exhibits. She would 'come home from school to an attractive detritus of sellotape, spools of thin acrylic, full cake boards and plastic animals strewn over the large table in the front room. I found it stimulating and fun, an improvement on the sedate writing that normally went on' there. 'They were very excited . . . they caught fire. I hardly dare make the pun, it was a heady time!' Kate was given her own heads to experiment with, recalling that 'we were in confident, colourful times when creativity seemed natural'.[42]

Michael Levey, 'a staunch supporter of everything my mother did', also enjoyed the fun, and was quite taken with the concept: 'In Prop Art, Brigid and Maureen's creative synergy was quite infectious – both he and I were caught up in it.' He, Kate and Brigid went to buy extra heads in Peter Jones.[43] The artists were grateful to him for providing their first audience.[44] It was Michael who issued the invitation to the Private View at 8.30 p.m. on Sunday 18 May, and it was through him that various distinguished art historians were invited. Only one declined – Sir Kenneth Clark, who (along with Lady Clark, also invited) perhaps felt compelled to be at home for the final episode of *Civilization*, his landmark series on culture, broadcast on BBC 2 the same evening. (Other guests could catch the repeat on Tuesday.)

Kate Levey thinks it likely that Michael

was the impresario behind the great push it must have been to get Prop Art made public. I presume it was he who hired Mason's Yard Gallery. The exhibition was advertised, the invitations to the opening were professionally printed. It's pleasing if my father's working life among Old Masters helped fund the avant garde Prop Art event, but it was not out of character: he was generous with his money as well as catholic in his tastes. (Apparently he once rebuked an interviewer, who was tiresomely insisting that an art historian must have a field of special interest, saying 'I don't need a field; I am not a donkey.') So Brigid and Maureen could not have had a better advocate for this exceptional, original enterprise.[45]

The invitation was accepted by various prominent art historians: Dr Roy Strong, director of the National Portrait Gallery; Cecil Gould, deputy keeper, and Gregory Martin, assistant keeper at the National Gallery; Christopher J. White, director of Old Master sales at Colnaghi in London; and David Rodgers, director of Wolverhampton Museum. Journalists, some from publications that ran advance coverage of Prop Art, also accepted, including John Russell from the *Sunday Times*, and Suzi Gablik, with whom he had just written a book on Pop Art; Marina Warner, then in charge of features at *Vogue*, accepted but was unable to attend, though *Vogue* did cover the show.[46] Other journalists, editors and writers, including Kay Dick, Penelope Hoare, Catherine Stott, Margot Walmsley, Francis Wyndham, Sonia Orwell and Stephen Vizinczey, also accepted. Among Brophy's contacts who agreed to come were actress Fenella Fielding; Karl Miller, her editor at *The Listener*; her literary agent, Anne Graham Bell; her drama agent, Peggy Ramsay; Frank Dunlop, director of *The Burglar*; her mother, Charis; and long-standing friend and author Sally Backhouse. Some Labour politicians accepted, including cabinet minister Tony Crosland, then president of the Board of Trade, with his writer wife Susan, and Lord and Lady Annan. Noel Annan was then provost of UCL and Gabriele Ullstein, his wife, was a writer and critic.

Among Duffy's contacts, invitations were accepted by Euan Duff, the photographer, who took photos of the exhibits; her agent Jonathan Clowes; from Hutchinson's, her publisher, Brian Perman, the publicity manager, and Harold Harris; Hamish Hamilton; and the writer John Ackerman Jones. Other guests included spouses and friends of the above, and Thea Porter.

It was an inclusive list, with invitations also going to the Leveys' next-door neighbour and the Peter Jones saleswoman who sold them the wig stands.[47] While it is not certain who attended of the 46 who said they were coming – David Frost, Joan Plowright and Laurence Olivier certainly couldn't make it, with Iris Murdoch and John Bayley doubtful – it would have been a lively and distinguished gathering. Brophy, though shy and averse to small talk, enjoyed parties with a purpose like this, as Kate Levey confirms.[48]

So the overall aim was serious. Was the Prop Art exhibition an artistic success? The critics agreed that, as John Russell put it in the *Sunday Times*, 'the wit is on a level rarely met with in art galleries'. Michael Shepherd in the *Sunday Telegraph* characterised it as 'a do-it yourself fun thing' with a 'mixture of weakness and brilliance [. . .] a healthily infuriating [. . .] annihilation of tiny targets by 25-pounders

[. . .] and [. . .] a heady treat'.[49] The most detailed analysis came from Barbara Wright, in *Arts Review*, whose judgement was favourable:

> Funny, this 'prop art' undoubtedly is, and often light-hearted, but it is also profoundly serious [. . .] This art – and it *is* an art, though do not go expecting to find 'fine art' – is based on the readymade [. . .] One may think that each work makes only a small point [. . .] yet each is like a pinprick: 54 pinpricks can make quite an impression if they attain their target [. . .] It is amazing what variety of feeling there is in such basically simple constructions.

The manifesto also impressed *Arts Review* with its accuracy, among the plethora of art manifestos then associated with the counter-culture: the manifesto's description of exhibits as equivalent to poems and epigrams was 'not too much to claim'.[50] Manifestos had long been set forth at avant-garde Modernist exhibitions, but not always drafted by such experienced writers. While the occasional phrase – 'an elaborated metaphysical conceit' to describe 'Egg-Cosi Fantuttesy' – apparently sounds a note of parody, with Brophy one can never be sure. The invented word 'Poemage' has subsequently been used independently by others, with different meanings, though along with 'Prop Art', 'Dreamaturge', 'Icontemplation' and 'Selexpressionism', it has not yet made it into the *Oxford English Dictionary*.

Terms used by Brophy and Duffy also referenced earlier artistic movements – 'readymades' were used by Dada as early as 1913.[51] Other influences may have included the Cybernetic Serendipity exhibition at the ICA in 1968, which Kate Levey recalled her mother seeing.[52] It featured mobiles, and so it may have influenced 'Danaegeld', consciously or not. One version of 'The Compleat Vegetarian' image, a face made up entirely of vegetables, recently exhibited in Paris, appeared in the May/June 1969 issue of *The British Vegetarian*, possibly helping to inspire 'Tete de L'Homme Garnie' – or the carrots on its head may have been serendipitous coincidence. A more significant influence was kitsch. Duffy recalls having 'a Kitsch museum of absurd things'; and Brophy shared her enthusiasm, both of them entertaining Kate by showing her a book on the subject, probably the first one in English, which was published in 1969.[53]

The use of simple and affordable materials, taking a do-it-yourself approach where collaboration was encouraged, and references to music (as in Manifesto 6) were also a feature of the Fluxus movement, in which many avant-garde 1960s artists took part. They included Yoko Ono, who first met John Lennon at an exhibition of her work at Indica, the first conceptual art gallery in London in Mason's Yard – within a stone's throw of the gallery where Prop Art was later to be put on. Opened in 1965, Indica closed in 1967, but perhaps its memory lingered on in the mind of whoever booked the space at Mason's Yard Gallery.[54]

Fluxus was a democratic form of creativity, and it was entirely in the spirit of that movement that some Prop Art exhibits had a deliberately home-made appearance. While there were some technical feats that were impressive for the time – ensuring that 'Headlight' had large lit electric bulbs in each eye socket, for example, and achieving the secure balance of a football on a polystyrene head – some labels were hand-printed or typed, and other materials included High Street gift-wrapping paper and small plastic toy animals. Kate Levey recalled her youthful concern about the artists' use of sellotape, and 'flimsy', 'wonky' boxes.[55] Little attention was given to the long-term durability of exhibits. But that was not the point, and it is not unique – some art has deliberately built-in obsolescence. The point was the creativity of the moment, to express and share literary ideas through this verbal art with those who could be enticed to see it. 'This is art for the literate.'[56] While some jokes had to be explained to those with minimal classical education, that is hardly unique in the visual arts.

It is unclear whether the exhibition covered all its costs, but it raised enough through sales of exhibits (£42) to finance all the (known) advertising (under £22), and at least some materials, including all the wig stands (under £7).[57] Small ads appeared in *The Listener*, *Tribune*, *Private Eye*, *Observer* and *Sunday Times*, sometimes in two successive issues. A display advertisement in *Arts Review* gave the opening hours: 11.30 till 6, seven days a week.[58] The cost of hiring the exhibition space is unknown, although the reserved item, at 35 guineas (almost £37), would have narrowed or wiped out the gap between outgoings and income.[59]

Brophy had an established talent for getting publicity, and 'Heads and Boxes' achieved significant national coverage, with advance interviews and photos in the *Observer*, the *Guardian* and *Vogue*; and reviews in *Arts Review*, the *Sunday Times* and *Sunday Telegraph*. The name of this new artistic manifestation was memorable and topical. Brophy 'would have to keep restrained in interviews when people asked why it was Prop Art, not Pop Art', Kate Levey recalls.[60] The national press was more inclined to give it column inches than were newsletters published by Brophy's favourite causes, where space for art was much more limited. Targeted press releases were drafted for, but not used by, *The Freethinker, Humanist News, The British Vegetarian, Books and Bookmen* and *Peace News*. There was some pre-publicity in the final issue of the short-lived, subscription *Transmedia Newsletter*, produced by one of Brophy's then publishers, Donald Carroll.[61] Broadcasters do not seem to have been approached; local radio in London did not yet exist. Prop Art was noticed by Leeds City Art Gallery, where the City Librarian asked for a copy of the manifesto and list of exhibits, which were duly sent. Euan Duff's photographs, taken of most of the exhibits to preserve a permanent record, were kept in an album by Brophy, and some exhibits remain in private hands.[62] Both Brophy and Duffy proudly added the Prop Art exhibition to their respective entries in *Who's Who*, retaining it in subsequent editions. It was an enjoyable one-off project, though neither felt tempted to repeat the experiment.[63]

The artistic collaboration between the two writers worked well: 'We asked them if they ever argued when they were making their wig stands. Apparently not.'[64] Surviving handwritten papers suggest that Brophy took the lead in organising advertising and press contacts, but that Duffy contributed to press releases.[65] Storage of the burgeoning exhibits spread into both their homes.[66] The manifesto was their first known piece of jointly authored writing: others were to come later, during the long campaign for Public Lending Right.[67] All the signs are that they worked harmoniously together, sparking puns off each other, with Maureen's practicality complementing Brigid's self-confessed 'lack of manual dexterity'.[68] As Kate Levey recalled, 'I know Brigid and Maureen discovered as did I, that polystyrene had an unhelpful propensity to melt under the wrong glue and paint, and was the very devil to cut without its crumbling.' It was, typically, Duffy who found a solution to the glue problem in an alternative brand.[69]

'Heads and Boxes' remains a reminder of the importance of allowing free rein to creativity, and of what surprising outcomes can be achieved when established writers, or any artists, do not allow themselves to be pigeon-holed by the expectations of others. Intriguing art, it demonstrates, can be produced on a budget. It was a joyful, witty, yet serious tribute to the possibilities of collaboration between two women writers who sparked ideas off each other and complemented each other's strengths. Prop Art deserves celebration as a thought-provoking element of that mind-opening flourishing of creative free-thinking, laced with humour and challenging political points, so characteristic of late 1960s London, in which Brigid Brophy was a key figure.

## Notes

I am very grateful to Maureen Duffy and Kate Levey for permission to quote extensively from the Prop Art Manifesto and other sources, and for their patient responses to my questions; and to Euan Duff for kind permission to reproduce his photographs of the exhibits. I am also grateful to the British Library, the *Guardian*, and Stefan Dickers at Bishopsgate Institute Archive.

1.  Hannah Carter, 'Cracks at headquarters', *The Guardian*, 8 May 1969, p. 10.
2.  Ibid.
3.  Maureen Duffy, Interview by Sarah O'Reilly, Authors' Lives Series, British Library Sound Recordings, Track 10, March 2008. Avril Horner and Anne Rowe (eds), *Living on Paper: Letters from Iris Murdoch 1934–1995* (London: Chatto and Windus, 2015), p. 238.
4.  Kate Levey, 'Mr and Mrs Michael Levey', *Contemporary Women's Writing*, 12.2 (2018), pp. 149–50.
5.  Colin Chambers and Peggy Ramsay, *Peggy to her Playwrights: The Letters of Margaret Ramsay, Play Agent* (London: Oberon Books, 2018), p. 102.
6.  David Depledge, 'Juggling with Perspectives', *Books and Bookmen* (January 1969), pp. 8–9.
7.  Duffy, Interview by Sarah O'Reilly.
8.  Brigid Brophy, 'Preface', in *The Burglar: A Bedroom Farce* (London: Jonathan Cape, 1968), p. 20.
9.  Christine Brooke-Rose, 'Introduction', in Brigid Brophy, *In Transit* (Champaign, IL: Dalkey Archive Press, 2002), p. 1.
10. Brigid Brophy, *Don't Never Forget: Collected Views and Reviews* (London: Jonathan Cape. 1966), pp. 15–31; Brigid Brophy, *Religious Education in State Schools* (London: Fabian Society, 1967).
11. Peter Lewis, 'Why Does this Woman Attract so much Wrath?', *Daily Mail*, 27 February 1968, p. 6; Charles Greville, 'Banned on Smith's Shelves . . . The New Brophy', *Daily Mail*, 30 October 1968, p. 4; Matthew Freedman (@brownwindsor), 'A Topical Few Seconds from a 1969 Episode of Father, Dear Father', 30 October 2017.
12. Depledge, 'Juggling with Perspectives', p. 9; Carter, 'Cracks at headquarters', p. 10.
13. Kate Levey, personal interview, 6 October 2018.
14. Ibid.
15. Maureen Duffy, telephone interview, 16 October 2018.
16. Barbara Wright, 'Prop Art, Brigid Brophy & Maureen Duffy', *Arts Review*, 24 May 1969, p. 335.
17. Levey, personal interview, and Duffy, telephone interview.
18. Levey, personal interview
19. Donald Carroll, 'Unto us a Brainchild is Born', *Transmedia Newsletter* 5, March 1969, p. 2.

20. Carter, 'Cracks at headquarters', p. 10.
21. Brigid Brophy and Maureen Duffy, *Authors go 3-D – Press release* (1969), Kate Levey private papers.
22. Carter, 'Cracks at headquarters', p. 10.
23. Brophy and Duffy, *Authors go 3-D*.
24. Michael Shepherd, 'A Look on the Sunny Side', *Sunday Telegraph*, 1 June 1969, p. 12.
25. Brophy and Duffy, *Authors go 3-D*.
26. Kate Levey, private papers.
27. Carter, 'Cracks at headquarters', p. 10.
28. Brophy and Duffy, *Authors go 3-D*.
29. Wright, 'Prop Art, Brigid Brophy & Maureen Duffy', p. 335; Robert McKay, 'Brophy's Proanimal Thought and Aesthetics', *Contemporary Women's Writing*, 12.2 (2018), pp. 160–1; Kate Levey, private papers.
30. Duffy, telephone interview.
31. Brigid Brophy and Maureen Duffy, *Manifesto of Prop Art* (1969), p. 7.
32. Wright, 'Prop Art, Brigid Brophy & Maureen Duffy', p. 335.
33. Kate Levey, private papers.
34. Brophy and Duffy, *Manifesto*, section 5.
35. From 'Fear no more the heat of the sun' in *Cymbeline*.
36. Kate Levey, private papers; Brophy and Duffy, *Manifesto*, p. 3.
37. Brophy and Duffy, *Manifesto*, section 6, p. 5.
38. Pendennis, 'How to Get Ahead', *Observer*, 4 May 1969, p. 40.
39. Brophy and Duffy, *Manifesto*, section 5, p. 4.
40. Carter, 'Cracks at headquarters', p. 10.
41. Levey, personal interview; Pendennis, 'How to Get Ahead', p. 40; Depledge, 'Juggling with Perspectives', p. 9.
42. Kate Levey, 'A Radical DepARTure', received by Jill Longmate 10 October 2018, and personal interview.
43. Levey, 'A Radical DepARTure', and personal interview.
44. Carter, 'Cracks at headquarters', p. 10.
45. Levey, 'A Radical DepARTure'.
46. Marina Warner, email to the author, 10 October 2018.
47. Levey, personal interview, and Carter, 'Cracks at headquarters', p. 10.
48. Levey, personal interview.
49. John Russell, 'Talent on a Large Scale', *Sunday Times*, 25 May 1969, p. 59; Shepherd, 'A Look on the Sunny Side', p. 12.
50. Wright, 'Prop Art, Brigid Brophy & Maureen Duffy', pp. 335–6.
51. Tate, Art Terms, <https://www.tate.org.uk/art/art-terms/r/readymade> (accessed 27 October 2018).
52. Levey, personal interview.
53. Duffy, telephone interview; Levey, personal interview; Gillo Dorfles, *Kitsch. An Anthology of Bad Taste* (London: Studio Vista, 1969).
54. Terry Kirby, 'Where John Met Yoko: The Gallery that Broke the Mould', *Independent*, 21 November 2006.

55. Levey, 'A Radical DepARTure', and personal interview.
56. Brophy and Duffy, *Authors go 3-D*.
57. Kate Levey, private papers; Carter, 'Cracks at headquarters', p. 10.
58. *Arts Review*, 24 May 1969, p. 346.
59. Kate Levey, private papers.
60. Levey, personal interview
61. Carroll, 'Unto us a Brainchild is Born', pp. 1–2; Julian Norridge, 'Donald Carroll Obituary', *Guardian*, 3 February 2011.
62. Kate Levey, private papers.
63. Duffy, telephone interview; Levey, personal interview.
64. Pendennis, 'How to Get Ahead'.
65. Kate Levey, private papers.
66. Carter, 'Cracks at headquarters', p. 10. Levey, 'A Radical DepARTure'.
67. Jill Longmate, 'Brigid Brophy's Role in the Struggle for Public Lending Right 1972–79', *Contemporary Women's Writing*, 12.2 (2018), pp. 186–206.
68. Depledge, 'Juggling with Perspectives'.
69. Levey, 'A Radical DepARTure', and personal interview.

# Chapter 12

# Prancing Novelist and Black and White: Experiments in Biography

## Peter Parker

Ronald Firbank, Aubrey Beardsley and Wolfgang Amadeus Mozart provided Brigid Brophy, who described herself as 'a natural, logical and happy atheist', with an alternative Trinity.[1] These three short-lived geniuses are the presiding deities in Brophy's writing: they not only became the subjects of several essays and four works of non-fiction, but are palpable presences in other books. Brophy had started her career as a writer of fiction in 1953, and her earliest work of non-fiction, *Mozart the Dramatist*, was not published until 1964, the same year as her fifth (and most consciously Mozartian) novel, *The Snow Ball*, in which several people attending an eighteenth-century-themed fancy-dress party adopt the guises (and behaviour) of characters from *Don Giovanni*. A similarly fruitful exchange between fiction and non-fiction occurred in the case of Firbank, whose *The New Rythum and other pieces* she reviewed in the *London Magazine* in October 1962. This article was complemented, as it were, by *The Finishing Touch*, which was published the following year. This novel was described by Brophy as being written 'in a superficially Firbankian idiom', but it in fact pays homage to Firbank in its subject matter and its many allusions quite as much as in its language and style.[2]

One of the things that characterises Brophy as a writer is this sense that her work is all of a piece, even though the books themselves are very different in form and genre. It seems clear that she was thinking of her own career when she wrote of a novelist in her other more than superficially Firbankian novel, *Palace without Chairs* (1978), that he developed

a technique for dealing with his imagination when it, uninvited, proffered nuclei of fictions: a few he compressed into short stories, which took a day or two to imagine and write down, but most, even more cleverly, he distorted into sometimes rather brilliant critical perceptions about other writers' work.[3]

As a biographer, Brophy was as keen as anyone to hunt down facts and turn up hitherto unseen documents, but it is her unusual approach to her subjects, and the brilliant critical perceptions that result from her research, that make her studies of Aubrey Beardsley and Ronald Firbank so outstanding and unusual.

It might seem that these two books are very different. *Black and White*, published in 1968, is a very brief study of an artist who was at the time extremely fashionable; *Prancing Novelist*, published in 1973, is a very long study of a writer who, though admired by the elect, was fashionable neither then nor now. There was, however, a great deal that Beardsley and Firbank had in common, which no one before Brophy appeared to have noticed. Both men, in their personae as in their art, were supreme exemplars of the high-camp dandy style. Both were interested in portraying unorthodox sexuality, and both produced their work with the twin spectres of illness and mortality hovering over their shoulders. Both had oppressively close relationships with their mothers, and had sisters who played a significant role in their lives. ('I can find no evidence they so much as met', Brophy parenthetically remarks in *Black and White*; 'but if poetic justice exists, surely Mabel Beardsley had a love affair with Heather Firbank.')[4] Both men died young, abroad, and as Catholic converts. Sometimes mistaken as being unserious or merely decorative, their work was in fact highly innovative and ushered in Modernism.

Brophy's two books are not biographies in the usual sense of the word: instead they are works of polemic, a form in which Brophy always excelled. Indeed, *Prancing Novelist* bears the famously elaborate and nicely combative subtitle 'A defence of fiction in the form of a critical biography in praise of Ronald Firbank', and is a virtual *vade mecum* of Brophy's recurring themes: Mozart, Freud, Beardsley, the eighteenth century, the baroque, opera, homosexuality, vegetarianism, animal rights and the proper remuneration of writers. Both *Prancing Novelist* and *Black and White* carry 'Brief' or 'Outline' chronologies, placed at the front or back of the book, where the essential biographical data can be consulted without it clogging up the main text. Neither book follows the customary chronology of biography in the way Brophy's other, later book on Beardsley does. *Beardsley and his World*, published in 1976, was presumably written along guidelines set out by its publisher, Thames and Hudson, for their series of lavishly illustrated brief lives. Even so, it begins with one of those opening flourishes of which Brophy was so fond: 'Middle-class England in the 1870s was probably the most inhibiting and philistine environment a great artist could be born into.'[5] Note that 'great': on the first page of *Black and White*, Beardsley is similarly stamped 'a very great artist', and the whole vast edifice of *Prancing Novelist* is constructed on the premise that Firbank was not only 'a very good writer' but that his writing can be held up as primary evidence that 'works of art have and need no justification but themselves'.[6] Far from being an insignificant sport, Firbank is for Brophy 'the novelist who freed fiction from naturalism'.[7] His novels were works of pure imagination rather as Beardsley's pictures were. Sometimes felt to be interesting though minor relicts of the enervated *fin de siècle*, both men are instead presented by Brophy as avant-garde exemplars of 'pure style, pure image'.[8] When Firbank wrote in 1924 'I am all design', he might well have been echoing Beardsley.[9]

Brophy also believed that the work of both men had been underestimated, or disregarded, less as a result of their challengingly modernist form than because of a puritanical distaste for their subject matter. As an example of this, Brophy quotes the *New York Times*, which declared a fortnight after Beardsley's death at the age of 25 that his work was 'already [. . .] well-nigh forgotten'. The newspaper, Brophy suggests, 'was simply telling a lie, in the way moralistic people seem to feel justified in doing when they can see no other hope of diverting public attention from something they disapprove of'.[10] Oscar Wilde's patronising view that 'dear Aubrey's designs are like the naughty scribbles a precocious schoolboy makes in the margins of his copybooks' was an early example of attempts to banish the young artist to the realms of infantilism; but Brophy shows how it was precisely Beardsley's ability to remain connected to the 'polymorphous perversity' that Freud considered characteristic of childhood that makes his work so startlingly modern.[11] Firbank had been similarly ticked off by a schoolmasterly Evelyn Waugh for what, in an otherwise honourably praising 1929 article, he called 'silliness [and] coy naughtiness about birches and pretty boys'.[12]

Accusations of immaturity and silliness were often a kind of code for 'homosexual', and it probably didn't much help matters that both Beardsley and Firbank, as it were, *looked* the part. Glancing at himself in a mirror once, Beardsley murmured, 'Yes, yes, I look like a Sodomite. But no, I am not that.'[13] Quite what he *was* is unclear, but in a 1982 BBC documentary to which Brophy contributed, a lugubrious figure simply labelled 'A Consultant Psychiatrist' was wheeled on to provide a professional diagnosis. He solemnly opined that Beardsley 'had not reached a mature, adult stage of sexual development [. . .] he was a schoolboy who hasn't grown out of his schoolboy preoccupation with obscene drawings'. He added that 'the interest in female clothing', which this supposed expert says was 'the thing that struck [him] most forcibly' on being confronted by Beardsley's work, 'is typically that of a transvestite'.[14] The sad truth is that, although Beardsley once boasted that he was going to attend a fashionable restaurant 'dressed up as a tart and mean to have a regular spree', his frail constitution almost certainly prevented him from any kind of sexual activity, sodomitical or otherwise.[15] Though they do not put it so bluntly, those who left their first-hand impressions of Firbank's manner and appearance make it clear that he too looked like a sodomite, and indeed the author triumphantly twinkles across the dust jacket of *Prancing Novelist* in boater and spats, hands on hips, in an almost parodic pose of the *Übernance*. (The unlikely background to this 1904 photograph, a snowscape at the Alpine resort of Chamonix, has been removed for the purposes of design.) Taking the then refreshing, though admittedly autobiographical, view that sexual heterodoxy was not merely morally neutral but actually something to be celebrated, in both books Brophy blasts through layers of accreted dismissive prejudice.

*Black and White* was based on an essay Brophy had written for the *Atlantic Monthly* in February 1968, to which she gave the (to her) morally neutral but defining title 'The Perversity of Aubrey Beardsley'. In *Black and White*, she describes Beardsley as 'the most intensively and electrically erotic artist in the world'.[16] The 'obscene drawings' so disdained by the BBC psychiatrist were not, she said, a 'schoolboy preoccupation' but an essential part of Beardsley's oeuvre, in which Eros and Thanatos are held in precarious balance. Similarly, by taking Firbank's homosexuality seriously, Brophy not only provided an unsurpassed account of his literary personality, but extended the scope of biographical-literary criticism in general. If this now seems not particularly novel or pioneering, it is worth considering what Firbank studies looked like before Brophy. Her most recent predecessor in this field, Miriam J. Benkovitz, seems to have been incapable of reading either the life or the work of her subject, writing for example that: 'Firbank disliked [his homosexuality], if his novels are an indication' – to which the only response is an eloquently Firbankian row of dots, question marks and exclamation points.[17] (Apparently undaunted by the lethal dismantling of her book in *Prancing Novelist*, Benkovitz unwisely went on to write a book on Beardsley, drawing forth one of Brophy's most magisterially blistering reviews.)

If *Prancing Novelist* is pre-eminently a work of close reading, then *Black and White* might be described as a work of close *looking*. In both cases, however, Brophy takes the now academically unfashionable view that the lives of those who create works of art are crucial to an understanding of that art. In the cases of both Firbank and Beardsley, she felt that it was especially crucial that they lived much of their lives in the knowledge or suspicion that they were likely to die young. 'I never lie down at night without reflecting that – young as I am – I may not live so see another day', Mozart wrote to his father in April 1787, when he was just 31.[18] For Firbank and Beardsley this kind of reflection was even more acute. Beardsley was first diagnosed with what was then graphically known as consumption when he was around seven years old. 'I shall not live longer than did Keats', he accurately predicted, and throughout his short life he carried the marks of his illness, describing himself at the age of 18 as having 'a vile constitution, a sallow face and sunken eyes, long red hair, a shuffling gait and a stoop'.[19] Firbank also had bad lungs and suffered from poor health all his life. He had seen both his brothers die young, at 20 and 25, and in light of this, Brophy writes, 'the conviction of Firbank's adult life that he might die at any moment' begins to look less like superstition and 'more like a rational calculation of medical probability'.[20] She suggests that both men became the kind of artists they were because of their precarious health, that their acute awareness of their own mortality was reflected not only in the subject matter of their work but also in the form that work took. Their 'economy of artistic means', she writes, 'was dictated by their not expecting to live long enough to go the long way round about perfecting their art'.[21]

In the book's subtitle Brophy described *Black and White* as a 'Portrait of Aubrey Beardsley' rather than a biography. It is in fact a lightning sketch wholly appropriate to its subject, whom it also resembles in being elegantly svelte – no more than 95 generously laid-out pages, many of these filled by illustrations. Sidestepping the then customary biographical starting point of birth, family and ancestry, it plunges straight into the essentials. This too is appropriate to a subject who was not granted time to dawdle. One of the symptoms of consumption, apart from coughing and spitting blood, is fever, and Beardsley often worked at fever pitch, both literally and metaphorically. The 'terrible, biological haste' (as Brophy puts it) that made Beardsley such 'a prodigious worker' was shared by Firbank, whose output of ten novels and a play in the eleven years between 1915 and

1926 should dispense once and for all any impression he may have given of being a dilettante.[22]

If the worlds of Beardsley and Firbank suggest a kind of Arcadia, in which characters inhabit enchanted groves, it is an Arcadia in which death holds sway. Beardsley's pictures frequently feature goat-footed and vine-wreathed Pan figures, but in a drawing he did for the eighth and last edition of the *Savoy* magazine in 1896, a dandy picking his way through a flowery mead is confronted with an urn on a plinth bearing the legend *Et in Arcadia ego*. It was Brophy who recognised that Firbank's novels, far from being (as some commentators thought) merely whimsical, could be divided into Pastorals and Tragedies. One of these tragedies, *Prancing Nigger*, even enacts the traditional Arcadian fall from grace when the Mouth family relocate from their paradisal rural village to the vice-ridden city of Cuna-Cuna, where they variously come to grief. What Brophy, invoking Shakespearean scholarship, calls 'the three late tragedies' (*The Flower Beneath the Foot*, *Prancing Nigger* and *Concerning the Eccentricities of Cardinal Pirelli*) are all haunted by death and loss.[23]

Alongside satyrs and putti, another frequent motif in Beardsley's work is that of embryos, either used as sinister decorative devices or as additional characters in his fabulously corrupt *charivari*. Most commentators regarded these images as merely indicative of Beardsley's unwholesome imagination; it took Brophy to point out their autobiographical significance. One of the sixty 'Grotesques' Beardsley was commissioned in 1892 to draw for three volumes of *Bon-Mots* by various authors was a repellent image of a foetus in evening dress and cape. This has been identified as a kind of *reductio ad absurdum* caricature of the famously precocious and exquisitely dandiacal Max Beerbohm, who published a volume titled *The Works of Max Beerbohm* when he was only 23. But it was more than that, Brophy suggests (and in so doing alludes to Beardsley's self-identification with the fatally tubercular John Keats):

> It was his own precociousness Beardsley drew in embryonic form, together with his physical unviability. The essence of embryo is the vast head on the feeble, unfit-to-live body of a crustacean snatched from its shell; Beardsley is expressing the consumptive poet's dread that his body's unfitness will make him cease before his pen has gleaned the teeming brain inside that huge foetal skull.[24]

Brophy further argues that Beardsley's 'genius', like that of 'many that are going to die young [. . .] hurried on in advance of contemporary taste' – and this too is true of Firbank.[25] One of the ways in which Beardsley was in advance of contemporary taste was his unfashionable embrace of the eighteenth century, specifically in his exquisitely rococo illustrations for Pope's *The Rape of the Lock* and the melancholy arcadian pierrots that Brophy suggests he derived from the paintings of his fellow consumptive Jean-Antoine Watteau. 'Now that Beardsley's revolution in taste has triumphed', Brophy writes, 'it is hard – but necessary too if one is to honour his courage – to remember how frowned on the eighteenth century was by the nineteenth.'[26] Similarly, she notices that in his 1915 novel *Vainglory* Firbank refers to 'a sumptuous *Stations of the Cross* by Tiepolo', an eighteenth-century painter more or less unknown – or, if known, more or less dismissed – at this period; and that *Caprice*, published two years later, features 'an advertisement on an omnibus for a performance of *La Clemenza di Tito*', Mozart's late eighteenth-century opera, which was not performed in London after its 1806 premiere until 1957.[27]

The work of both Beardsley and Firbank was as much in advance of their time as their taste, which is why it was so often misunderstood. Even during the Beardsley boom, Brophy was concerned that, like Firbank, this revolutionary artist might be 'mistaken for minor'.[28] It was the very explosion of his popularity in the 1960s, with his designs printed not only on posters, but on mirrors, mugs, vases, lamps, tea-towels and other domestic furnishings, that made it all the more urgent for Brophy to argue that Beardsley was more than a merely decorative artist. She points out that during his lifetime Beardsley was often underestimated precisely because his work was made for reproduction and thus available to all. Because Beardsley did not paint on canvas but instead had his work published using new reprographic processes, he did not create what was usually understood by the word 'pictures', which is to say works 'done in oils, or at the least, colours of some sort'.[29] He was instead deemed an 'illustrator', though in fact his 'illustrations' not only stand on their own but sometimes have only the most tenuous relationship to the text alongside which they appeared. Indeed, what remain perhaps his most famous pictures – certainly the ones that made his reputation – were those for the first English edition (1894) of Oscar Wilde's *Salomé*, which Beardsley more accurately called 'decorations'. It was precisely this creation of what are undeniably pictures out of what would have been considered the restrictive materials of black ink and white paper that made Beardsley so revolutionary and modern. 'The tension that dominates all his compositions', Brophy writes, 'is entirely in the design and medium.'[30]

The close attention that Brophy pays in *Black and White* to the design of what in Beardsley's case was the page (rather than the canvas) carries over into *Prancing Novelist*. It is not merely what Firbank writes, but how he arranges his words on the page, another composition in black and white, of print on paper. 'The technique of isolating a single image in space', she writes, 'Firbank learned from his cult of the black-and-white drawings of Aubrey Beardsley – round so many of which Beardsley drew frames, either elaborately decorative or of the most exactly sited ruled lines.'[31] Also,

> Firbank's writing consists of his giving his images space to be contemplated in.
>
> His technique is to *aerate* his books.
>
> Indeed, his pages are quite visibly aerated by the deployment on them of white space.[32]

(It is worth noting parenthetically that these three sentences on Brophy's own page are themselves characteristically arranged into three short paragraphs in witty imitation and illustration of the technique she is describing.) Firbank's attention to the appearance of his text is apparent in his complaint upon receiving the proofs of *Inclinations*, in which there is perhaps more white space than in any other of his books: 'I wanted more capital letters & dots instead of dashes.'[33] Firbank, writes Brophy, used rows of dots to 'impose a rallentando that gives the reader time to contemplate the images' ambiguity . . . . At the same stroke, the dots ventilate the page, by their actual airy look. Dots are almost perforation.'[34] When, in 1924, Firbank wrote (with his customary disregard of orthography) 'I think nothing of fileing fifty pages down to make a brief, crisp paragraph, or even a row of dots!', he was not underestimating the importance of those dots.[35] 'The aerated look of his pages', Brophy writes, 'is a visible analogue of the aeration of his literary expression.'[36] Beardsley, too, deployed rows of dots, used to delineate the fall or flounce of the elaborate costumes in which he decks out some of his characters, dots that indeed aerate these images, evoking by the most economical of means the physical lightness, the sheer airiness, of muslin, lace or crêpe.

*Black and White* is not merely an obviously appropriate title for a book about an artist whose work was largely restricted to these two non-colours; it is also a persistent theme of the book, related by

Brophy to the artist's oncoming death. 'For black-and-white was in itself an image, for Beardsley, of the erosion of his life', she observes. 'In Beardsley the medium is, to an exceptional extent, the image. Strictly, his medium is black *on* white [. . .] Black was encroaching on, eating into, the white space' – and this is a process Brophy compares, in one of those irresistible imaginative speculations in which she specialised, to the encroachment of consumption, eating into the artist's lungs. ('Did he', she wonders, 'actually think of his lungs, in cockney or the language of offal-dealers, as his lights?')[37] The deployment of black and white, Brophy suggests, had similar *memento mori* associations for Firbank. What seems at first to be a failure of tone, as when in *The Artificial Princess* a royal personage gets 'hot and piggy', is wholly deliberate: 'Firbank introduces the perfect incongruous word "piggy"', she writes,

> in the way baroque statuaries introduce the bare buttocks of a mourning boy angel among the graven allegorical persons and draperies of a tomb.
>
> Like a baroque tomb, Firbank's design proceeds by contrasts. White marble and black marble, juxtaposed, afford each other a setting of irony. In the midst of high-life we are in the low comedy of flesh and its liability to death.[38]

It is not without significance that Brophy once said of her own novel *The Snow Ball* that it was 'deliberately constructed as a baroque monumental tomb'.[39]

Many people regard *Prancing Novelist* as an all too monumental construction in which the hapless Firbank is merely entombed. While *Black and White* seems as sprightly as the talent it describes, as well-tailored to its subject as a closely fitting dinner jacket, *Prancing Novelist* has been criticised as far too weighty to load on to Firbank's frail, consumptive shoulders. In fact, the sheer bulk of the book is part of its point. Yes, Brophy is proclaiming, Ronald Firbank is absolutely worth this amount of critical and biographical attention. And for those who find this undeniably long book a daunting prospect, it should be pointed out that it is nevertheless broken down into carefully arranged 'Parts' and 'Chapters' and short (often very short) sections within those chapters – aerated indeed by observations that solicit the reader's attention by being isolated in their own space.

When Brophy wrote the manuscript of *Prancing Novelist* in violet ink it was not merely a tribute to Firbank but an example of the imaginative empathy that illuminates every page of the book. She had immersed herself so thoroughly in the author's life and work that even her wildest speculations, one feels, can be taken on trust. And it is what she calls her 'irrepressible speculativeness' that leads to those elegantly assured imaginative leaps – leaps worthy of Firbank's beloved *Ballets russes*.[40] One mark of a good book is that it could not have been written by anyone else, and it is this that makes these two experiments in biography, characterised by the author's energy, wit, idiosyncrasy and combativeness, so exhilarating to read.

## Notes

1. Brigid Brophy, *The King of a Rainy Country* (London: Virago, 1990), p. 276.
2. Brigid Brophy, *Prancing Novelist* (London: Macmillan, 1973), p. 49.
3. Brigid Brophy, *Palace without Chairs* (London: Hamish Hamilton, 1978), p. 81.
4. Brigid Brophy, *Black and White: A Portrait of Aubrey Beardsley* (London: Jonathan Cape, 1968), p. 2.
5. Brigid Brophy, *Beardsley and his World* (London: Thames and Hudson, 1976), p. 5.
6. Brophy, *Black and White*, p. 11; Brophy, *Prancing Novelist*, pp. xiii, 70.
7. Brophy, *Prancing Novelist*, p. xiv.
8. Brophy, *Black and White*, p. 12.
9. Brophy, *Prancing Novelist*, p. 409.
10. Brophy, *Black and White*, p. 66.
11. Charles Ricketts, *Recollections of Oscar Wilde* (London: Nonesuch Press, 1932), pp. 51–2.
12. Donat Gallagher (ed.), *The Essays, Articles and Reviews of Evelyn Waugh* (London: Methuen, 1983), p. 56.
13. William H. O'Donnell and Douglas N. Archibald (eds), *The Collected Works of W. B. Yeats, Vol. III: Autobiographies* (New York: Touchstone, 1999), p. 253.
14. *Beardsley and his Work*, BBC Television, 19 January 1982, <http://www.bbc.co.uk/iplayer/episode/p02t77gl/beardsley-and-his-work> (accessed 4 October 2019).
15. Brophy, *Beardsley and his World*, p. 71.
16. Brophy, *Black and White*, p. 11.
17. Miriam J. Benkovitz, *Ronald Firbank* (London: Weidenfeld and Nicolson, 1970), p. 241.
18. Andrew Steptoe, *The Mozart–Da Ponte Operas* (Oxford: Oxford University Press, 1988), p. 84.
19. Brophy, *Beardsley and his World*, p. 56.
20. Brophy, *Prancing Novelist*, p. 116.

21. Ibid., p. 116.
22. Brophy, *Black and White*, p. 11.
23. Brophy, *Prancing Novelist*, p. 95.
24. Brophy, *Black and White*, p. 66.
25. Brigid Brophy, *Mozart the Dramatist* (London: Libris, 1988), p. 7.
26. Brophy, *Black and White*, p. 54.
27. Brophy, *Prancing Novelist*, p. 193.
28. Ibid., p. 248.
29. Brophy, *Black and White*, p. 70.
30. Ibid., p. 12.
31. Brophy, *Prancing Novelist*, p. 68.
32. Ibid., p. 396.
33. Ibid., p. 397.
34. Ibid., p. 397.
35. Ibid., p. 69
36. Ibid., p. 396.
37. Brophy, *Black and White*, p. 80.
38. Brophy, *Prancing Novelist*, p. 429.
39. Brigid Brophy, *The Burglar* (London: Jonathan Cape, 1968), p. 29.
40. Brophy, *Prancing Novelist*, p. 117.

# Chapter 13

# 'Monster Cupid': Brophy, Camp and *The Snow Ball*

*Allan Pero*

It would be foolhardy to dismiss Brigid Brophy's works as the witty artefacts of a Firbankian epigone, who, like Ronald Firbank, would seem merely to have aped the aesthetes and decadents of the 1890s; indeed, neither her work nor that of Firbank should be the stuff of dismissal at all. Rather, Brophy's oeuvre should be treated like a missal, as a mode of instruction, celebration and worship. More specifically, a sustained reading suggests that her devotion both to artists such as Firbank and Beardsley and to the baroque/rococo in general work to produce a *missale plenum* of experimental camp. I contend that camp is not trash, nor is it kitsch; I, like Brophy, insist that camp is a form of allegory – specifically, baroque and rococo allegory – that attempts not only to rescue allegory from the banality of being mere illustration, but also, crucially, to present it as a particularly apt form of modernist expression and critique.

As Brophy tells us in *Prancing Novelist*, 'Firbank is perhaps the inventor, certainly the fixer, of modern camp.'[1] The qualifier 'modern' is essential here. Modern camp, as a symptom of the limits of a taste for symbolism, for totality, through allegory produces a temporal gap between the beautiful and the sublime that seizes upon the failed moments of the baroque, of rococo, of aestheticism and decadence by, as Brophy suggests, 'pioneering backwards'.[2] Why? The reason is that camp allegory, in its steely fascination with artifice, ruins and excess, steadfastly does not produce an illusion of totality or of unity. Camp allegory ironises, critiques and escapes the limits of the illusion provided by beauty as symbol of totality. Camp allegory stands as a truth procedure, one could say, that explicitly acknowledges that there is no longer any seamless unity of the immanent with the absolute. The ruins, the absurdities, the extravagance, the very worldliness of the world form signposts on this often treacherous, mysterious, enigmatic path to the absolute – an absolute that Brophy contends is bound up in both psychological and classical truth.

More pointedly, since allegory always operates metonymically, rather than metaphorically from what is represents, it never makes a claim to totality. The worlds of allegory are broken up, fragmented, partial. In this sense, allegory is always already 'ahead' of symbolism. If we turn to essays such as 'Baroque-'n'-Roll', we see that Brophy's fascination with the baroque has political implications, implications that circulate through two of camp's primary concerns: wit and tragedy. Brophy makes the counter-intuitive claim that wit is, at its core, leftist in sympathy. As a form of wit, camp sensibility is, by Brophy's own lights, kept aflame by such avatars as 'Voltaire, Gibbon, Shaw, and Wilde', who are its guardians because they 'belonged to the (emotionally considered) left'.[3] For Brophy, the baroque is a study in ironic juxtaposition: 'In the midst of the high-life we are in the low comedy of flesh and its liability to death.'[4] Baroque allegory, like its architecture and its painting, prompts questions about structure, about possibility, about the ideological and spatial limits of realism. The baroque itself holds two contradictory precepts in tension; baroque logic 'stands for an alternate mode of rationality to the dominant trends in modernity, one that is centrifugal, disruptive vis à vis modern rationalism', on the one hand, while on the other rendering theatrical its centripetal claims to power or control over the margins.[5] In its modern, camp incarnation, the baroque maintains its centrifugal questioning, even as it attempts to give voice to those who are marginal or peripheral. (We encounter this questioning in novels such as *The Snow Ball* and the crumbling *Palace without Chairs* – indeed, the latter, about a royal family falling into ruin, and their country, Evarchia, lurching into fascistic chaos, is subtitled 'A Baroque Novel'.) Brophy's revolutionary camp does not seek to capture perfection, nor fact, nor balance, but like many baroque and rococo artists, it reveals psychological truth when it 'arrests and transfixes the explosion at the very point of disintegration'.[6]

But before we can fully appreciate the value of camp in Brophy's work, we must first turn to two of its antecedents – the baroque and the rococo. Early in *Mozart the Dramatist*, Brophy had argued that the art and culture of the eighteenth century, having been 'written off as frivolous, monotonous and worthless', re-emerged in the early days of modernism 'as a serious artistic revolution, nurtured half inside the mauve cloak of the "decadent" movement and half in reaction against it'.[7] She singles out three figures crucial to this revaluation: Richard Strauss (*Der Rosenkavalier*), Shaw (*Man and Superman* and *Candida*) and that master of sinister dreams in black and white, Aubrey Beardsley (especially in his illustrations for Pope's *The Rape of the Lock* and Jonson's *Volpone*). In their different registers, each of these artists explored what Enlightenment culture can still teach us about decay and ruin – not merely the ruining of young women like Richardson's Clarissa Harlowe (*Clarissa, or, the History of a Young Lady*, 1748), but also the drive to ruination that Voltaire, among others, perceived in the possibilities that bloom when, '[i]n that most thoughtful of centuries, *nothing* was unthinkable. The enlightenment was an enfant terrible, a Candide, who not merely said the unthinkable but insisted it was reasonable to do so and that the taboo embargo was unreasonable.'[8] In effect, if nothing is unthinkable, then the confusion and collapse of all values – in short, nothingness itself – become an object of study, however allegorically it might be enrobed.

This tendency towards a contemplation of the unthinkable is mirrored in how the period represented the sacred and the profane. Walter Benjamin tells us in his baroque study *The Origin of German Tragic Drama* (1977) that just as many constellations are themselves used in ancient cosmology as anthropomorphised forms of nature, as gods in human form, they also point to a continuity and conflation of nature, the human and the divine. But at the same time, they come down to us, in representation, only as fragments, devoid of what Brophy might name as their castrating power. For Brophy, the period reduces the devil to a toy, and 'God it left standing but hardly mythological any longer; blanched to an allegory, he is hardly more than an alternative name for nature'.[9] In Benjamin's view, the task of the baroque critic is, as he strangely puts it, 'the mortification of works' – that is, the critic's duty is to complete the artwork through criticism. But how? For the critic of the baroque, it means exploring the profanation of the sacred, the falling of the divine into ruin – in short, offering a fulfilling exegesis of the triumph of death; together, these objects of contemplation uncover the allegorical, though perhaps overgrown, path to redemption. (One could claim that Brophy's own monumental tome, with the baroque title *Prancing Novelist: A Defence of Fiction in the Form of a Critical Biography in Praise of Ronald Firbank*, is just such a critical mortification.) In their reclamation through the *Trauerspiel*, Benjamin, in his 'mortification' of baroque tragic drama, works towards stripping off and burning away all that remains of their ephemeral, transitory existence; in the plays, fate (through myth) gives way to sacrifice (death), which in turn yields the possibility of atonement (redemption).[10] Only in this manner can their beauty arrive at the 'altar of truth'.[11]

Brophy takes up a similar reading of the decay of the baroque into the rococo, contending that '[b]y the time of the rococo, to whose utmost development *Figaro* belongs, there is no telling sacred winged babies from profane; the air is thick with the decorative flights of indistinguishable putti and amoretti'.[12] This indistinguishability is endemic to what Christine Buci-Glucksmann calls 'baroque reason', in which 'the baroque signifier proliferates beyond everything signified, placing language', and, as she says elsewhere, images, 'in excess of corporality'.[13] But Brophy radically parts company with Benjamin in her reading of the period's attitude to redemption; in this, we see the emergence of a more camp relation to the baroque and rococo than the melancholic one put forward by Benjamin. The ironic attitude to God that Brophy sees in the Enlightenment can be summarised thus: 'The crime of killing God the Father had been so effective that God was no longer supposed capable of returning to avenge himself', and as a result, the Enlightenment 'believe[d] in miracles neither of redemption nor of punishment; it held that the original creation, nature, was competent to administer both'.[14]

What was once the rule of life, that the world was bound to the realms of the sacred and the profane, now gives way to the exception – to exceptions that trouble even the distinction between life and death. This is why, in the radical disconnection that has occurred between and among the realms of nature, humanity and the divine, it is only in the complete devaluation, the complete mortification of worldly values that the hitherto unthinkable has been made possible. That is to say, the mortification of history in the baroque is a necessary component of seeing the negative, allegorical path of redemption – one that, in its tragic mode, cannot be guaranteed or marked out by God.

In a sense, one could say that history constitutes the stars, and that redemption is revealed to us in the baroque and rococo through their constellations – but redemption is just as elusive in camp as it is in the baroque and rococo. The harmony of the constellations is akin to the harmony of the spheres; in their very distances from each other, they constitute a 'pure essence' in their representation, upon which their very existence depends. In the constellation, we discover the pledge and seal of their truth.[15] But the truth was not something the Enlightenment – or its plenipotentiaries, the baroque and rococo – could necessarily depend upon, because of the fragility of truth's certainty in an ephemeral world:

In art as in thought, the enlightenment knew itself to be imperma-
nent. Not that it doubted the truth or justice of the illumination it
gave, but the reasonable point of view had nowhere been put into
permanent practice. Moreover, the realistic calculation of reason's
small chances was deepened into a tragic doom whose source was
the unconscious certainty that, even though reason was justified, to
assert so deserved punishment.[16]

This 'tragic doom' that Brophy describes also informs Benjamin's
choice of the *Trauerspiel* as his object of study. He meditates upon
a form in which tragedy itself has already become subject to ruin.
The *Trauerspiel* is not tragedy proper; one must believe in the sacred
and the profane, but one must also adhere to a kind of pantheism
in which the natural, the human and the divine live in a rather confused harmony. Obviously, classical tragedy is not congruent with
the seventeenth-century *Trauerspiel*, nor are the baroque and rococo
variants thereof in the century that followed any more congruent.
The eighteenth century plays with the tragic, but does not trouble
itself to rise to tragedy in the classical sense. Brophy reminds us that,
unlike propaganda claims to the contrary, it is not that the baroque
and rococo had no sense of tragedy; rather, they present tragedy
from the perspective of irony, a perspective that redounds upon the
modern age:

eighteenth-century tragedy is the tragedy of intelligence in a block-
headed world (one of the great discoveries of the eighteenth century
was that intelligence is beautiful) and of the frail instinct of pleasure
in a world block-headedly going on committing old atrocities and
working up to worse ones: a poignancy to which our own world situation makes us more than ever vulnerable.[17]

It is as if we must sift intellectually through the ruins of tragedy
proper to find its essence; if, as Benjamin maintains (and here he
agrees with Benedetto Croce), one cannot proceed deductively – that
is, by accruing a mass of atrocities and then deducing from them,
through examples, through their existence as tragedies – then one
must proceed as if every atrocious idea or act must be treated indi-
vidually, in its positivity, as original, as distinct and separate. This
method respects ideas in their 'irreducible multiplicity'.[18] Although
Benjamin agrees with Croce that one should resist the reduction
of artworks to their generic elements, he offers one proviso: that
notions such as the comic and tragic need to be retained precisely

because they are structures, lending 'consistency and substance to any and every drama, without being in any way commensurable'.[19] For the purposes of understanding camp, perhaps we could view the logic in play here as being like the constellation: it is a structure, lending consistency to the representation, but it does not reduce the stars themselves to the mere elements of the constellation itself. It is in this way that allegory itself, as a structure, is the truth content of the *Trauerspiel*, but has implications for the species of camp that will transcend it. In this constellation of comic and tragic affects, this structuring impulse informs the *Trauerspiel*'s slow evolution into the psychological, even erotic truths of rococo modernist camp – truths that Brophy repeatedly turns to, in their commingling of comic and tragic affects.

One effect of this commingling is that modern camp produces affects that resist tidy generic or intellectual classification. Often, camp is mocked or shunned for having produced such elusive affects – remarks like 'Should I laugh or cry?' or 'What am I supposed to do/feel now?' reveal the arbitrary and constraining limits of what is aesthetically or culturally sanctioned. Eve Kosofsky Sedgwick has speculated 'that shame/performativity may get us a lot further with the cluster of phenomena called "camp" than the notion of parody will, and more too than will any opposition between "depth" and "surface"'.[20] To that I say amen. Camp has so often been subjected to what Sedgwick called 'paranoiac reading' that I would like to take the occasion of writing about Brophy to think about camp by way of what Sedgwick named as paranoiac reading's opposite: 'reparative reading'. By way of summary, paranoiac reading takes up the way in which the logic of a hermeneutics of suspicion first advanced by Paul Ricoeur had fallen regrettably into paranoia – a paranoia that had shifted from pathology into prescription, from pathology into methodology – a prescription that had virtually become coextensive with critical theoretical inquiry *tout court*.[21]

If you weren't reading paranoiacally, you just weren't reading hard enough. Sedgwick then turns to Melanie Klein (through Silvan Tompkins), and recapitulates Klein's distinction between what she calls the paranoid position (marked by envy, jealousy, anxiety and hateful projection on to part-objects) and the depressive position (marked by its limited ability to mitigate against anxiety, while opening up the possibility of reimagining or 'repairing' one's relation to part-objects). Not surprisingly, the latter position – that is, the depressive or melancholic position – is fuelled by love, a love that does not transform the part-objects into a coherent, seamless whole, but instead sets up a relation to them that, as reparation, provides emotional comfort and solace.[22] It helps to quell anxiety, and repairs melancholia by granting the depressive objects of desire that are phenomenologically and emotionally sustaining. This impulse, I contend, is a crucial dimension of Brophy's own work, variously informing her political activism, her concern for animal rights, her feminism and her critique of what is now called heteronormativity.

In effect, Brophy's fidelity to the camp value of objects and the alembicating of plots into fragments (at work, for example, in both the novels of Ronald Firbank and the personages of Aubrey Beardsley) are aesthetic and ontographic in their rococo natures. Both Firbank and Beardsley place aesthetic and affective responses to objects on the same level as the description of the being of *things*. In their works, the troubling of distinctions between figure and ground (a feature that the rococo and modernist abstraction share in common) evokes a peculiar logic in which objects – things – are granted an ontological, rather than ontic, status. It is one reason why reading Firbank can be frustrating or confusing, and why Beardsley titillates in such affective, indirect ways. This ornate levelling and layering of personages and things renders the former less important, and the latter more so. Characters are just as liable to be overheard as heard, as likely to be espied as seen. Occasionally, this way of being is staged through a frivolous *prosopopoeia*, but more often the affective relation to objects occurs between things, as opposed to it being shaped by a subject's response to a thing or place.

As we know, the rococo is generally conceived of as a period in art and design (though it had its impact on architecture too) coming after the baroque; in effect, the rococo is a late eighteenth-century phenomenon – encapsulated by such works as Watteau's *L'Embarquement pour Cythère* (1717) – which, for modernism, Giorgio Agamben claims, 'was to lead the artist not to the promised happiness but to a competition with the Most Uncanny, with the divine terror that had driven Plato to banish the poets from his city'.[23] But this is not the end point for art. Agamben follows Nietzsche to a point beyond this encounter with the Most Uncanny, into another kind of art, one produced for artists only. And this is perhaps why Cythera retains such a strong attraction for so many artists who came after Watteau.

As Ken Ireland has argued in his *Cythera Regained?*, the rococo returns in the nineteenth century, leaving its mark on art, literature, music and interior design, only to fade again in late 1910. But as Jane Stevenson has recently shown us, the rococo's predecessor, the baroque, itself returned during the interwar period, 'buggering' it with its 'queer style'.[24] Firbank's modernist recasting of the rococo, then, is as much a response to modernism as it is to the previous generation (those rococo elements of Théophile Gautier, Félicien Rops, the Second French Empire, Pater, Beardsley, Strauss and, of course, Wilde) and to the worlds of Venus's Cythera and Pierrot's Moon, or any of the other ebullient, pink-toned froths confected by Tiepolo and Watteau. Any sustained engagement with the rococo revival leads one to find oneself entangled in the fretwork and filigree of romanticism, aestheticism and decadence. If, in its first incarnation, rococo signals an end to the tragedy of the baroque, then its reincarnation points delicately, even decadently, towards the farcical elements of Victorianism – an attitude to which modernism, in general, is sympathetic – elements that figures such as Firbank and Beardsley persistently exploit. Incidentally, it is fitting that, in 1895, Beardsley referred to the cult of Watteau 'as [. . .] so entirely *modern*'.[25]

Given her deep interest in opera and in Mozart, Brophy's novel *The Snow Ball* comes to us as no surprise, since she transports the themes of death and sex in *Don Giovanni* to a costume ball with an eighteenth-century theme held on New Year's Eve in London. The house where the ball takes place is riotously camp. Grotesque, even sinister, the house is replete with crumbling profanations of cherub and putti alike:

> They swarmed in delicate flights over its ceilings and alighted wherever it offered them a plinth or a pinnacle; they were its genius [. . .] Three chased one another for a veiled purpose up the drawing room wall, fluttering round half a trompe l'oeil column: the whole, fragmented column and all but fragmented cupids – one of them lacked the last inch of fleeing heel – was a patch rescued, and transferred here, from a destroyed fresco.[26]

In this house, Cupid is a 'monster' who, from 'his niche above the grand staircase', oversees the female protagonist's adventure in erotic camp fantasy.[27] She is Anna, a woman entering a self-conscious middle age, who attends the ball unhopeful, but nevertheless prepared to immerse herself in the spirit of fantasy that pervades such evenings. She arrives dressed as Donna Anna from *Don Giovanni*, but, in this case, the question of her desire is not posed moralistically (will she be seduced, betrayed?), but as one of agency – will she find her desire, and, more importantly, what will she do about it? As we know, desire and fantasy are intimately linked; if desire is confounded by the enigma of the other's desire – *What does the other want from me?* – then fantasy is a means of answering that riddle.

At midnight she encounters a masked man, who kisses her, at first teasingly, then erotically, and finally with passion.[28] In a move that points to Brophy's command of desire's vicissitudes, Anna finds herself confused by the kiss, and retreats to the hostess's boudoir, itself a camp fantasia of a 'tart's rococo'.[29] In effect, when the masked man confronts her desire, she retreats not because it is not what she wants, but because it *is*. As Brophy is careful to tell us, Anna's mounting desire is propelled not by speed, but by its deferral.[30]

Her retreat, then, is not prompted by petit-bourgeois morality, nor is it the tired stratagem of the coquette; Anna is a woman of wit and experience. In the spirit of that deferral, I shall digress slightly to explore the implications of Anna's hesitation. By embracing his imposture as Don Giovanni, the masked man has taken on, for Anna, the status of what Jacques Lacan calls 'a woman's dream'.[31] Lacan means that in his utter willingness to take on the role of the other's fantasy, Don Giovanni is actually the embodiment of a 'pure feminine image' precisely because he is uncastrated in relation to the image of the father. He is a perfect object of desire because he is uncastrated – he lacks nothing.[32] In *Mozart the Dramatist*, Brophy refers to the suspension of castration as one of the previously 'unthinkable' possibilities that was made thinkable in the eighteenth century – in 'the political equivalent of parricide'.[33] So Don Giovanni's killing of Donna Anna's father, the Commendatore (he has no wish to commit this murder, but is challenged by the Commendatore to a duel), is itself a substitute for failed castration. The Commendatore functions, Brophy explains, as a 'quasi-father-in-law' who must stand in for the absent God.

Of course, this is a primary difference between Molière's Don Juan and Mozart's reimagining of him. In the latter incarnation, Don Giovanni is not the enemy of God, happily acknowledging His existence even as he thumbs his nose at God and at the consequences of his own sin; instead, Don Giovanni must make amends to the dead father in the same way as Brophy sees Mozart himself atoning for the recent death of his own father: 'The logical amends for a son to make to a father whom he has unconsciously wished dead is to bring him back to life in deliberate fantasy.'[34] This is why the Commendatore must, in his return as a statue, embody both memorialisation and animation, castration and the power of judgement.

With these insights in mind, we can now return to Anna's dilemma. After the fateful kiss, she discusses with the hostess and the hilariously named expert, Dr Brompius (whose Firbankian name implies that he will dispense pious bromides), the long-debated question of whether Donna Anna was indeed seduced by Don Giovanni. The problem is that, with the scene having occurred offstage, we cannot know whether Donna Anna is lying or Don Giovanni has simply failed. After a long, rather campy disquisition on the impossibility of inferring the truth one way or the other, Anna is assured that if Donna Anna had not been seduced, she never would have declared that she had been. 'Unless she just liked mischief', Anna replies.[35] And this is the problem – Donna Anna's desire remains a question in *Don Giovanni* because there is no room for it in the opera, outside of her love for her father, and of her anxiety about Don Ottavio's faith in her. In the novel, Anna cannot find the answer to her own desire through the plot of the opera proper. Instead, she must contend with the question of her desire on her own terms. In taking on the role of Donna Anna, she must traverse the fantasy, the particular mischief that has already gathered force in her earlier kiss with her Don Giovanni. Uncannily, this is why Don Giovanni reappears just at that moment to 'claim' her.[36] If we take his remark half in earnest and all in jest, Anna has yet to be claimed, and thus she has not been seduced. If she is to make mischief, then it is up to her to discover where her mischief takes her. In sum, it is she who must claim her desire – and Don Giovanni, the object of her desire, remains its vehicle, not its driver.

One compelling camp dimension in the novel sees Brophy place sexuality and image in conversation with each other. Camp, bristling as it does with forgotten knowledge, with its fascination for cultural history, for the bygone esoteric, for the fallen arcane, sees objects as *things* – as having a kind of being or ontology that we encounter. Essentially, it is a relation – a being-with. Camp objects are not just tools or baubles; they are strangely erotic relationships forged in the name of critical self-love, or in the name of constructing or exploring a particular myth of self. In her own clear-eyed take on her erotic thingliness, Anna decides early on that her idea of herself as sexual object is absolutely 'a question of taste, a question of style. Anyone who contemplated forming an intimate relation to this face must ask himself whether he possessed such a taste and, possessing it, was prepared to develop it.'[37]

As she makes her way through the house, she encounters her ageing reflection in a mirror, a surface and frame as ornate and filigreed as one might expect: 'She knew that to the eye of love its [her face's] spoiled prettiness presented hints, minimal but re-current, of the erotic, like the idea of an unfrocked nun. In the eye of self-love, the mirror, she had found its infinite rococo complexity infinitely interesting.'[38] One striking element here is the paradoxical play of minimalism and infinitude that Anna sees as she searches her face. A paranoiac reading would focus on Anna's narcissism and her longing to find comforting vanity amid her 'spoiled prettiness'. But I believe there is a richer inter-pretation to be found, one driven by reparative rather than paranoiac reading. Brophy, in her devotion to Firbank, is engaged in continuing his camp response to the minimalism that characterises much High Modernism. Several of Brophy's short, sharp works mirror Firbank's own dense, writhing, breviloquent novels (the longest of which, *Vain-glory*, is, by Firbank's standard, a staggering 197 pages; the remain-der, rustling around the 100–110-page mark, would, like Brophy's *The Finishing Touch* and *Flesh*, reasonably be called novellas). They are miracles of compression. If, like Beckett, Firbank meditates upon subjectivity trembling on the precipice of nothingness, then, also like Beckett, he eschews depth of meaning in favour of 'the materiality of the word surface'.[39] However, like Brophy, Firbank does so from the expressly opposite pole, turning our attention instead to the uncanny agency of objects that assume virtually the role of characters, and to the cosmos of ornament, in which glittering worlds can be discovered in glittering surfaces, and enjoyment promised in the blandishments of a modernist rococo – an aesthetic of ludic mirrors, reflecting the capriciousness of excess, and the anamorphic gaze lurking in what Firbank calls 'the truest lies' of language.

It is precisely this kind of encounter we are treated to in Anna's meditation upon her reflection – minimalism and infinitude coincide in the mirror's surface to produce new possibilities for her desire. The marks of finitude, 'the spoiled prettiness' on her face, do not lure her into despair, nor into the cynicism of decrying infinitude as the realm of the 'impossible'. Rather, she discovers the infinite in the finite; that is, she acknowledges that the fact that there is nothing outside the finite is to render it infinitely finite, as it were. The infinite is thus not something to be gained as compensation for ageing and death; rather, the infinite is always with us, in the spoils of enjoy-ment, or what Lacan calls *jouissance*. How so? We must return to the two things (apart from Mozart) that occupy Anna above all else: 'sex and death'.[40] In the mirror, Anna encounters something more complex than an ageing face. She confronts, in the slow ruination of her femininity, the image of the death drive – that is, the infini-tude of her enjoyment – that dogs her every reflection. In effect, sex and death – or, more specifically, the death drive – are one and the same. If desire, which would seem to be infinitely deferred, since no one object could ever satisfy it fully, is a kind of infinitude, it is, as Alenka Zupančič contends, 'a bad infinitude' because it is simply the failure to accomplish or fulfil one's desire. The 'good' infinitude is that of the death drive – which, importantly, is not a 'secret wish' to die because, in its infinitude, the death drive is already immortal.[41] Anna confronts in the mirror a complexity that troubles her desire: if she pursues enjoyment, then she is attempting to tame enjoyment for the purposes of desire. If she attempts to realise her desire, to bring it to an absolute end, a drive that is much more radical than pursuing her desire, she places herself on the side of enjoyment, or *jouissance*. Death, as opposed to the death drive, would be a path to ending the infinitude of enjoyment, since it is perforce bound to mortality. The question Anna faces is more complex than she realises, and as the novel proceeds, it is brought to an absurd climax: 'Am I prepared to realize my desire – that is, sacrifice the one thing I value above all else, in order to preserve its infinitude?'

The scene before the mirror also evokes Beardsley's *The Mirror of Love* (1895). In it, the mirror's surface already holds a reflection – the body of a hermaphroditic figure – surrounded by a rococo frame. As Brophy notes in *Black and White: A Portrait of Aubrey Beardsley*, the drawing was rejected by the publisher because of the gender ambiguity of the figure at its centre.[42] The figure's instability is not an excess or aberration; instead, it functions as a metonym for the infinitude of bodily enjoyment that we otherwise try to domesticate or legislate as 'sexuality'. Beardsley's image points to the infinite materiality of bodies that I alluded to earlier; as Buci-Glucksmann explains, with the collapse of received notions or forms of identity and appearance, 'we are left with an infinite regress towards a point that is always slipping away, a pure otherness of figure'. This decay, she continues, 'carries us towards Eros: the seductive, beguiling theatre of bodies induces an active and dynamic image of Eros through captivation or rapture, divine or human'.[43] If, as Brophy insists, part of Beardsley's revolution in art is staged in the mirror of camp, it is just as indebted to a polymorphous perversity that informs the bodies who march and pose in front of it: 'The polymorphism Beardsley preserved from infancy is not only mirrored directly in what he depicted. It is metaphored in the very eclecticism of his style.'[44] In effect, Anna's confrontation with the mirror is polymorphously perverse in the sense that, in typical camp style, she derives enjoyment from the rococo object framing her image, even as it metaphorically evokes the infinite appositions or reflections of enjoyment itself.

Yet another reason why Anna defers giving herself over to Don Giovanni is her desire for perfection. In shying away from intimacy (even with pets), Anna avoids the problem of having to live up to another's image of her. Implicitly she recognises that, in her position as woman, she is expected to rely upon an *other*, a man, to grant her the kind of completion she craves – but her desire, marked as it is by camp, casts her fantasy of completion in a particular light. She confesses: 'I'd like to be attractive not as a person but as a thing. Not to be made use of – no monetary value. I'd like to be a useless thing [. . .] an ornamental thing.'[45] In desiring to escape the demands, the guilt, even the comforts of other people, Anna imagines herself as an aesthetic object, one that requires nothing and is, in its uselessness, nothing, but in a positive sense. That is to say, Anna does not desire nothingness in the sense of negation; she wants to exist, free from the other's desire, free from the commodification of her gender, or the reification of objects, but paradoxically wants to be free of the finite world of her imperfection that is, for her, 'a sign of life', even as she wants to live in that world.[46] What she seems to be edging towards is not death, but an aesthetic stasis, vouchsafed by nothing as infinitude – one in which, through 'a kind of heretical-mystical and then baroque conversion, this "nothing of being" changes into an infinity of ecstatic delight [*jouissance*], a plethora of forms'.[47] She longs to escape the nothingness of being a woman – that is, to escape the tedium of being merely a symptom of man – into the nothingness of infinite enjoyment, one that is replete, complete and singular.

After his unmasking, and when Anna finally consents to have sex with Don Giovanni, she is granted the only kind of *jouissance* he can hope to provide – that of orgasm:

> as though by digging into his flesh, by pitting him, her fingers or teeth could actually lay hold on the paradox whereby so much thought and strategy in the vertical world went towards manoeuvring into this horizontal situation where pleasure consisted in something being imposed, in being carried beyond the point of no return, in suffering an act as unwilled as sneezing, falling asleep or dying. Suffering, sobbing, swelling, sawing, sweating, her body was at last convulsed by the wave that broke inside it: and the image which was dashed up on to the walls of her mind and deposited like droplets there, distinct but quite passive, was of the rococo cartouche which broke everlastingly over the walls of Anne's bedroom, perpetually but without moisture drenching the white satin with drops like drops of glycerine or sweat.[48]

Obviously, some may find this experience enough in itself. But what I want to draw attention to is the paradox she hopes to seize upon while coming. If we recall her earlier speech about her desire for perfection, what she desires is the experience of a *jouissance* that stands apart from seduction, 'manoeuvring' and the imposition of the other's desire, and instead moves towards a 'point of no return', of being caught up in the waves of infinite pleasure, and encountering there an image of that infinitude. Here Anna returns not to the image of Don Giovanni, but to the image of the 'rococo cartouche' that, significantly, breaks 'everlastingly'. But why a cartouche? More specifically, why a rococo one? As Brophy tells us, one of the neoclassical suspicions of the rococo was that it 'was an erotic style', promoting libertinism.[49] Like the mirror Anna encounters earlier, the cartouche is marked by rococo scrolling, and in its design evokes a peculiar paradox: the cartouche frames, but does not circumscribe. Generally, a rococo cartouche is fashioned around an ovular space, sometimes displaying a vignette, a mirror, or the empty convexity of plaster, but will break away from its circumference, defying gravity and completion alike. The waves or scrolls that meander away from the circumference of the oval are meant to evoke or capture infinitude.

But they do not. The rococo image can perhaps evoke, but not resolve, the paradox of *jouissance*. Anna's orgasm is, finally, just an orgasm, providing her with a glimpse of *jouissance*'s reflection – what Anna calls 'this most intense, least voluntary, and therefore most death-imaging of pleasures there was'.[50] *Jouissance* of the genital sort may haunt her, resisting her mastery of it; in its involuntary nature, orgasm is not the kind of *jouissance* she seeks because it is incomplete, because it throws her back into the melancholy, the 'wry sadness' of her imperfection, her finitude.[51]

When she rejects Don Giovanni's love, Anna remains consistent not only with Donna Anna of Mozart's opera, but also with her own fidelity to Cupid – he who watches over the house. She cannot push her intimations of another kind of *jouissance* to fruition, and turns back to her god. But since this is a camp novel, her god is also in ruins:

> Partly, of course, it was his age: an infant aged at least two hundred years – in the wood, that was to say; aged two millennia, probably, in the mythological conception. His gold was peeling off in great leaves, as though he had got sunburn, shewing the crimson ground beneath; his wing was chipped; worm had visited, and then left, him. But he was hideous, also, in the mythological conception, and all the restoration in the world could not have hidden it.[52]

The problem is that Anna is caught up in the paradox that Cupid represents; despite his mischief, he is finally bound to his fickle mother, Venus, and to her bidding, but is at the same time irretrievably phallic. He is as mortal and finite, in his way, as Anna is in hers. She fantasises about mothering him, restoring him, but relents, knowing he is too old, too hideous to save, and that he is a phallus that is finally impotent, that his bow and arrow remain but are rotting. Although Cupid is, as Brophy suggests in *Mozart the Dramatist*, the 'easiest to interpret in terms of natural allegory', he is allegorical no more because Anna understands that 'it was no good his veiling his mystery from women', even though she perversely, melancholically, but not polymorphously, continues to place her faith in him.[53] For Anna, the phallic allegory Cupid once embodied, one of love and desire, has been supplanted by banality: the phallic symbols of weaponry and death. Nevertheless, like the countess in *Figaro*, Anna raises her voice to Cupid, in a 'prayer to the only god she believed in', and melancholically cries, 'O Cupid, save the world.'[54] But unlike the countess in *Figaro*, her prayer receives nothing but a silent, dusty answer. With sex and Mozart having inevitably failed her, she returns to her flat at dawn, and her thoughts turn not to redemption, but to her other faithless love: death.

## Notes

1. Brigid Brophy, *Prancing Novelist: A Defence of Fiction in the Form of a Critical Biography in Praise of Ronald Firbank* (London: Macmillan, 1973), p. 171.
2. Ibid., p. 80.
3. Ibid., p. 406.
4. Ibid., p. 429.
5. William Egginton, *The Theater of Truth: The Ideology of (Neo) Baroque Aesthetics* (Stanford, CA: Stanford University Press, 2010), pp. 70–1.
6. Brigid Brophy, *Baroque-'n'-Roll and Other Essays* (London: Hamish Hamilton, 1987), p. 156.
7. Brigid Brophy, *Mozart the Dramatist: The Value of his Operas to Him, to his Age and to Us* (New York: Harcourt, Brace, and World, 1964), p. 16.
8. Ibid., p. 74.
9. Ibid., p. 207.
10. Richard Wolin, *Walter Benjamin: An Aesthetic of Redemption* (Berkeley, CA: University of California Press, 1994), p. 55.

11. Walter Benjamin, *The Origin of German Tragic Drama*, trans. John Osborne (London: Verso, 1998), p. 31.
12. Brophy, *Mozart the Dramatist*, p. 107.
13. Christine Buci-Glucksmann, *Baroque Reason: The Aesthetics of Modernity*, trans. Patrick Camiller (London: Sage, 1994), p. 139.
14. Brophy, *Mozart the Dramatist*, p. 88.
15. Benjamin, *The Origin of German Tragic Drama*, p. 37.
16. Brophy, *Mozart the Dramatist*, p. 89.
17. Ibid., p. 20.
18. Benjamin, *The Origin of German Tragic Drama*, p. 43.
19. Ibid., p. 44.
20. Eve Kosofsky Sedgwick, *Touching Feeling: Affect, Pedagogy, Performativity* (Durham, NC: Duke University Press, 2003), p. 64.
21. Ibid., p. 126.
22. Ibid., p. 128.
23. Giorgio Agamben, *The Man Without Content*, trans. Georgia Albert (Stanford, CA: Stanford University Press, 1998), p. 7.
24. Jane Stevenson, *Baroque between the Wars: Alternative Style in the Arts, 1918–1939* (Oxford: Oxford University Press, 2018), p. 1.
25. Ken Ireland, *Cythera Regained? The Rococo Revival in European Literature and the Arts, 1830–1910* (Madison, WI: Fairleigh Dickinson University Press, 2006), p. 165.
26. Brigid Brophy, *The Snow Ball* (London: Secker and Warburg, 1964), p. 18.
27. Ibid., p. 20.
28. Ibid., p. 16.
29. Ibid., p. 100.
30. Ibid., pp. 138–9.
31. Jacques Lacan, *Anxiety: The Seminar of Jacques Lacan Book X*, trans. A. R. Price (Cambridge: Polity Press, 2014), p. 192.
32. Ibid., p. 192.
33. Brophy, *Mozart the Dramatist*, p. 74.
34. Ibid., p. 238.
35. Brophy, *Snow Ball*, p. 81.
36. Ibid., p. 81.
37. Ibid., p. 20.
38. Ibid., pp. 20–1.
39. Samuel Beckett, *Disjecta: Miscellaneous Writings and a Dramatic Fragment* (New York: Grove Press, 1983), p. 172.
40. Brophy, *Snow Ball*, p. 97.
41. Alenka Zupančič, *Ethics of the Real: Kant, Lacan* (London: Verso, 2000), p. 250.
42. Brigid Brophy, *Black and White: A Portrait of Aubrey Beardsley* (London: Jonathan Cape, 1968), p. 38.
43. Buci-Glucksmann, *Baroque Reason*, p. 134.

44. Brophy, *Black and White*, p. 46.
45. Brophy, *Snow Ball*, p. 120.
46. Ibid., p. 116.
47. Buci-Glucksmann, *Baroque Reason*, p. 130.
48. Brophy, *Snow Ball*, pp. 156–7.
49. Brophy, *Mozart the Dramatist*, p. 291.
50. Brophy, *Snow Ball*, p. 157.
51. Ibid., p. 157.
52. Ibid., p. 200.
53. Ibid., p. 201.
54. Ibid., p. 202.

Chapter 14

# 'A Felicitous Day for Fish'

## Kim Stallwood

I was a student in 1973 and worked during the summer in a chicken slaughterhouse. Three years later, I was a vegan campaigning at Compassion in World Farming to end factory farming. I was an evangelising vegan – a *vegelical* – who was in a hurry to change the world. Today, I am still a *vegelical* and my life is still dedicated to changing the world. But four decades of campaigning full-time for animal rights demands a price. I now view the world through the prism of cynicism and melancholy, which is why you can follow me on Twitter as the Grumpy Vegan.

In 1977 Compassion's co-founder, Peter Roberts, took me to the RSPCA's 'Rights of Animals' symposium at Trinity College, Cambridge. This is when I first saw Brigid Brophy. Every speaker I heard at the symposium was for the first time. I went on to work with some of them, in various capacities and on various projects, including the Labour peer Lord Houghton of Sowerby; the campaigner Clive Hollands; the philosopher Tom Regan; the veterinarian Michael W. Fox; the author Jon Wynne-Tyson; the anti-blood-sports campaigner John Bryant; and the psychologist and campaigner Richard Ryder, whose contribution to animal advocacy is outstanding. The RSPCA symposium was a two-day crash course in philosophy, applied ethics, religious values, campaign strategy and political organising. I left Trinity College inspired with ideas and eager to learn more.

Foremost at the symposium was Lord Houghton's exhortation 'To Parliament we must go', which resonated with me as much then nearly forty years ago as it still does today. 'This is where laws are made', he said, 'and where the penalties for disobedience and the measures for enforcement are laid down.' His wise advice for the animal rights movement to go to Parliament and pass laws for animals is sadly still a challenge for some in the animal rights movement to understand. The single greatest challenge confronting animal rights is making the moral and legal status of animals a mainstream political issue, as animal rights is more than just a moral crusade and an optional personal lifestyle choice. This is something that I explore in my book, *Growl*, which is an animal rights memoir and manifesto.[1]

But what of Brigid Brophy at the RSPCA symposium?

I recall her presence as something rare and unusual. There was the dry humour, the deadpan delivery and the black nail varnish. Along with other speakers, Brophy spoke for me as my young self struggled to find ways to articulate in a meaningful way the passion and compassion I felt about animal cruelty and exploitation. My nascent cynicism and melancholy resonated particularly with Brophy's mordant humour and unrelenting analysis. I became a fan immediately. I never spoke with her but I must have sat near her at meal times. We few vegans and vegetarians at the RSPCA symposium – Peter Roberts, Tom Regan and his wife, Nancy, and presumably Brophy, but the memory is dim here – were relegated to separate tables away from the corpse-eating delegates in Trinity College's dining hall, dining on meagre rations of bland 1970s-style veggie food. The rest of the symposium's attendees ate venison that was once flesh that belonged to deer that once grazed the lawns in the college grounds.

I want to focus on the impact that Brophy made in animal rights, particularly emphasising the time when she was the inaugural speaker at a meeting of the Council for the Prevention of Cruelty by Angling (CPCA) on 11 April 1981 at Friends' Meeting Place on the Euston Road in central London. She was its national patron. I was its vice-president. I draw from documents in my animal rights archive, including the text of her presentation. I am also most appreciative of Kate Levey, who made it possible for me to have photographic access to Brophy's original manuscript for a speech, 'Is there a need for animal welfare legislation?', which she made at the Universities Federation for Animal Welfare symposium, 'Animals and the Law', in 1974.

First, I should say something about what it was like at the time of the RSPCA symposium, when the contemporary animal rights movement was forming. In 1977 James Callaghan was the British Labour prime minister and *Never Mind The Bollocks, Here's The Sex Pistols* was in the charts. Jimmy Carter was president of the USA and Apple Computers was first incorporated. And, two days before the RSPCA symposium, Elvis Presley died at his home, Graceland, in Memphis, Tennessee.

The Band of Mercy and its successor the Animal Liberation Front, along with the Hunt Saboteurs Association and another group called Animal Activists, laid the foundations for an emerging activist movement for animals in the 1960s and 1970s. Older organisations such as the National Anti-Vivisection Society and the British Union for the Abolition of Vivisection were led by sincere and dedicated people; however, as they aged so did the organisations under their leadership. The RSPCA Reform Group worked to modernise the society and free it from its domination from the 'shires', which included foxhunting supporters on the national council and in its membership. In the 1980s I was elected on a progressive platform to the RSPCA's national council. But after I spoke out publicly against the society holding shares in companies that experimented on animals, I was expelled by the council's ruling conservative majority not only from the council but also the society. Apparently, I acted inimically to the society's interests. This ignoble position of being an expelled member of the RSPCA I share along with red-coated wild animal killers. The struggle for the RSPCA and its ideology continues to play itself out today. Conservatives like nothing better than to bear a grudge against the RSPCA, which successfully prosecuted the Heythrop Hunt in 2012 for breaking the Hunting Act. The Heythrop Hunt is associated with David Cameron's former parliamentary constituency of Witney. Tory MP Neil Parish, chair of the Environment, Food and Rural Affairs Select Committee, referring to the committee's 2016 report on animal welfare, said that the RSPCA 'should step back from making prosecutions itself'.[2]

From the 1970s, opinion polls regularly showed the public to be overwhelmingly opposed to blood sports. This was a time when increasing numbers of 'sabs' (hunt saboteurs) intervened between hunters and the wild animals they sought to kill. Also, the League Against Cruel Sports, under the leadership of Lord Houghton, became more politically sophisticated. Thus, the campaign against blood sports increasingly attracted attention, and particularly when the League made donations to the Labour Party. For the first time, the Labour Party included in its manifesto in 1979 a commitment to legislate against hare coursing and stag hunting. Consequently, the League made two donations to the Labour Party. The first was for £50,000, which was for Labour's general election fund, and the second was for £30,000 and was restricted to publicising its commitment to animal welfare. These developments were the turning point in understanding the anti-blood-sports campaign, not only as a moral crusade but also as a mainstream political issue, paving the way for the Hunting Act in 2004. Hunt opponents learned that a legal ban on hunting could only be achieved when a political party is elected to form a government with a manifesto commitment to introduce and pass anti-blood-sport legislation. The campaign to protect Britain's wildlife continues with the Conservative government's attempts to repeal the Hunting Act and neuter the RSPCA.

But what of fishing and angling? Are they not blood sports?

Well, yes, they are; but there were reasons why neither the RSPCA nor the League would address fishing and angling as part of their anti-blood-sports campaign. Most people ate fish. Many people believe fish do not feel pain. Or, if they do, their pain is unimportant when human preferences dominate. Fishing and angling are popular pastimes, and particularly viewed as a hobby for the working class, which meant that no Labour government would ever address it. By the way, fishing is the general way to describe any method to catch fish and angling is generally a method of fishing that uses a hook attached to a fishing line and rod.

As part of my research for this essay, I searched angling and fishing on the League's and RSPCA's websites. The League makes no policy statement about angling and fishing on its website.[3] Angling and fishing are on the RSPCA website in the context of how discarded fishing litter (hooks and lines) causes harm to wildlife and birds. Further, in section 5.11 of its animal welfare policy document, the RSPCA states that it 'believes current practices in angling involve the infliction of pain and suffering on fish'.[4]

In 1980 the RSPCA published the *Report of the Panel of Enquiry into Shooting and Angling* chaired by the distinguished zoologist, Lord Medway, the 5th Earl of Cranbrook, which concluded that 'vertebrate animals (i.e. mammals, birds, reptiles, amphibians and fish) should be regarded as equally capable of suffering to some degree or another, without distinction between "warm-blooded" and "cold blooded" members'.[5] The RSPCA animal welfare policy document refers to the Medway Report as proving to its satisfaction that fish are capable of experiencing pain and suffering. Nonetheless, neither the League nor the RSPCA have campaigned on fishing and angling as part of their anti-blood-sports strategy from the 1970s to the present.

This is why the Council for the Prevention of Cruelty by Angling was founded in London in 1981, and why Brophy's inaugural address is interesting and important. Most people then, as now, do not care much about fish other than how to cook them. Fishing and angling are hugely popular hobbies. And any effort to highlight the plight of fish by such leading anti-blood-sports organisations as the RSPCA or the League Against Cruel Sports would be used by pro-blood-sports proponents in the public arena and political debate to make the thin end of the wedge argument: ban hunting now and fishing will be next.

How did Brophy respond to these issues in her speech, 'A Felicitous Day for Fish', at the inaugural CPCA meeting? From the outset, she seeks to frame the issue of fishing and angling as a 'fascist fantasy':

> Today a small group of human beings is setting itself formally and actively to dispel a specific corner of a fantasy to which our species is prone and which distorts our vision of the real world – the feudal, indeed the fascist, fantasy whereby we stamp around as the lords and bullies of everything and pretend that our most minor pleasures are so important in the scheme of things that they outweigh the entire life and outweigh the death agony of our fellow individual animals.[6]

She goes on to say that this inaugural meeting means that fishing rights, and she also includes shooting rights, will be seen as 'ludicrously and tragically out of touch with reality as the idea nowadays seems to us that a person could own and buy and sell another person as a slave'. But, she warns, 'angling poses as a sport', which 'disgracefully manages to get its hands on a certain amount of subsidy from public funds'. She further warns that as sport is 'one of the established religions of this country', angling becomes 'respectable': 'We shall be told that angling is the most popular participatory sport. We must point out that the participation of the fish is involuntary.' 'Oh, go on, be a sport' and 'Oh, don't be a spoil-sport', she advises, will be used against CPCA and its supporters. But she reminds us that it is the 'angler who is the spoiler': 'He despoils the fish of its health, happiness and life – of which it has only one; whereas if we succeed in spoiling the angler's sport, he has hundreds of alternative, non-injurious sports open to him.'[7]

Then there's the '*other* established religion of this country, namely Royalty', some of whom are 'frenzied in their passion for taking their fellow beings' lives':

> The British are given to confusing the Royal Family with the Holy Family, especially at Christmas time on television. No doubt some simple minded people will accuse us of blasphemy as well as lèse-majesté

[offending the dignity of a reigning sovereign or a state] when we remark that a trout does not feel deeply privileged to suffer torment and death at the hands of the Prince of Wales.[8]

Drawing together her thoughts about hostile reactions to the anti-angling message in the first section of her speech, Brophy concludes by making a statement that summarises well the fundamental opposition to all calls for ending animal cruelty and exploitation:

> In fact, angling is an activity, an atrocity, that depends on the most monstrous of all class barriers, the class barrier our species has fantasised between us, on the one side, and on the other all the other animal species on the face of the earth, all of whom are, remotely or closely, our kin; and we pretend that this class barrier gives us absolute rights, rights of an absoluteness never claimed by the most arrogant feudal lord or the most grinding capitalist boss, while the rights of all the other animals are absolutely forfeit.[9]

But, as she says, 'I am myself a Lefty, but I am in a sense an impartial Lefty':

> I do not feel very deep respect for my fellow Lefties' demands for social justice so long as they effectively ignore the colossal injustice of the class barrier we have put up between us and our fellow animals of other species. And equally and impartially, I do not feel much respect for the Right Wing's concern for the freedom of the individual so long as it is not prepared to defend the freedom of an individual fish to pursue his fishy life without wanton and bloody interference from humans.[10]

We must expect, she says, 'facetiousness and dismissive put-downs from Left, Right and, no doubt, Centre'. 'We shall be called extremists', she goes on to say, 'by, I presume, people who are in favour of maiming and killing moderately.' We shall be treated as 'eccentrics'. But she consoled us with knowing that 'People with the right idea always are until it becomes the general idea.' And with typical dry wit, Brophy concludes this section of her talk by saying:

> Indeed, there is only one stock reproach I can think of that probably won't be brought against us, and that is the one that says that people who care about the welfare of animals care only about the animals that are cuddly. Whatever our opponents may say about fish, I don't think they can call them cuddly.[11]

So, why fish, Brophy asks. She refutes the oft-put riposte along the lines of 'Don't you think that factory farming or bull-fighting is just as bad as, or even worse than, angling?' by saying

> The question is not designed to be answered. It is designed to provoke an interesting and cosy intellectual discussion, in the course of which the questioner can stifle the promptings he feels from his own conscience towards doing something about any of the atrocities he names; and it is designed to divide the now quite large and certainly growing pro animals-in-general movement.[12]

Brophy goes on to make a key point about strategy for the – as she calls it – growing pro animals-in-general movement:

> We need, the animals need, all the organisations that champion animals of any kind. In real life, there is no either/or. A man can, as indeed my father did, give up angling because he has come to realise that it is immoral without being obliged by some law of nature to become a factory farmer or a toreador the next day. And conversely, we can join the CPCA without forgoing our freedom to insist on free range eggs or to be, as I am and I expect many of us are, vegetarian.[13]

So, Brophy warns that those of us who stand up for fish will be accused of being spoil-sports, eccentrics, not caring about more important others, and worse not only by those who kill fish for fun but also those who profit from fishing:

> And we shall be attacked also, probably more viciously, by the groups that are parasites on the popularity of angling: the makers and sellers of the instruments of torture and execution; the people who run artificial lakes and stock them with fish to serve as sitting targets for anglers; the publishers of angling magazines and books – who would have to work so much harder are they to try to sell a real book, an actual work of literature, to everyone who likes to spend a day sitting on a folding chair at the waterside; and the television programmers, to whom angling presents an opportunity to fill up air time without having to pay actors at Equity rates or screenwriters at Writers' Guild rates.[14]

Rational and defiant in her views, Brophy calls upon those present at the meeting in her conclusion to know that

The opposition will probably hurt us, a bit at least, and, more dan-
gerously I am sure it will from time to time tempt us to despair by
making us think that our efforts are achieving nothing. Yet on we
must, and on I do not doubt we shall go – until we or our children
achieve a civilised country for humans and fish to live in on terms
of reciprocal non-aggression, a country in which the only form of
angling that is legal, and the only form anyone will <u>want</u> to participate in, is that highly skilled and vehemently competitive form where
the line ends in a magnet and the fish consists of a metal attachment
on a cardboard cut-out.[15]

In the June 1981 issue of *Hookup*, the CPCA's newsletter, Brophy's
speech was reported as having

held her audience spellbound [as] she put the case against angling.
But it was done in her own inimitable style, with wit, imagination,
intellectual brilliance that had her hearers laughing and sniffing in
turn. It tugged at the heartstrings; it was in fact vintage Brophy – a
speech to be savoured and returned to again and again.[16]

Earlier I wrote that CPCA's inaugural meeting with Brophy was
interesting and important. This is because she

- unequivocally opposed fishing and angling, situating them alongside slavery as examples of a 'fascist fantasy';
- placed fishing and angling into a historical context, in that in years
  to come we will look back on them – as we now do slavery – with
  disbelief and embarrassment;
- explained how fishing and angling were given legitimacy as a
  sport, including with royal patronage;
- rejected, as an 'impartial Lefty', left-wing demands for social justice and right-wing concerns for individual freedom while they
  exclude fish from the political arena;
- stressed that those who make a profit from fishing and angling
  will be among their most strident supporters, which reminds me
  of Brophy's celebrated quotation: 'Whenever people say, "We
  mustn't be sentimental", you can take it that they are about to
  do something cruel. And if they add, "We must be realistic," they
  mean they are going to make money from it';[17]
- and, finally, said that to oppose fishing and angling does not require
  opposition to all other forms of animal exploitation although, as
  a vegan, she intimated that it was preferable.

Two questions remain. First, what happened to the CPCA? And did Brophy's inaugural address in 1981 make a difference? CPCA continued to campaign until 1985, when at its AGM it dissolved and reformed as the Campaign for the Abolition of Angling (CAA), with similar objectives. I resigned as CPCA's vice-president in July 1981, as I needed to focus on my work as the campaigns organiser at the British Union for the Abolition of Vivisection. This was a more than full-time position and I had to prioritise my animal rights advocacy. The CAA launched an annual National Anti-Angling Week and released a campaign video called 'Angling – The Neglected Blood Sport'. In 2003 CAA stopped campaigning, although some local groups continued. It was later revived as the Fish Protection League and in 2012 merged with The Black Fish, a European-based conservation organisation whose mission is to 'end the industrial overfishing of the oceans'.[18]

There are other pro-fish organisations in addition to The Black Fish, including those that campaign against marine mammal displays. The anti-Sea World campaign waged by a number of organisations is a notable example. Generally, there is, I believe, more public awareness about fish and their sentience, which is partly due to an increasing number of scientists whose research shows this, but the estimated global number of fish captured, killed and used for various human activities is staggering. The US-based advocacy organisation, Fish Feel, estimates that worldwide

> one to three trillion wild-caught fishes and 37–120 billion farmed fishes are killed commercially for food each year. Hundreds of millions more are killed for 'sport' each year in the U.S. alone. Fishes are also increasingly replacing other animals for scientific experimentation. Approximately one-quarter of all the animals used for research and education in North America are fish. Additionally, some 1.5 billion are used for aquariums.[19]

Never have Brophy's words been more appropriate than when she says fishing and angling is a fascist fantasy. Actually it is not a fantasy. It is a reality, a fascist reality.

Nonetheless, 11 April 1981 was 'a felicitous day for fish' and a key date in the long animal liberation calendar. For as Brophy said on CPCA's inauguration:

> This is a felicitous day for fish. It is also, by a happy side effect, a felicitous day for birds, so many of whom are mutilated or poisoned by the lethal litter that anglers often leave behind them as though they were not content with the harm they do deliberately and knowingly. And as a matter of fact, it is also a felicitous day for humans.[20]

## Notes

1. Kim Stallwood, *Growl: Life Lessons, Hard Truths, and Bold Strategies from an Animal Advocate* (Herndon, VA: Lantern Books, 2013).

2. DEFRA Committee news, <https://www.parliament.uk/business/committees/committees-a-z/commons-select/environment-food-and-rural-affairs-committee/news-parliament-2015/animal-welfare-report-published-16-17/> (accessed 17 June 2019).

3. League Against Cruel Sports, <https://www.league.org.uk> (accessed 17 June 2019).

4. RSPCA Policies on Animal Welfare (revised 2014), <https://www.rspca.org.uk/documents/1494939/7712578/RspcaPolicies.pdf/abaa8964-9d49-6d85-c4e3-4e8dccf0af08?t=1559058681637> (accessed 17 June 2019).

5. *Report of the Panel of Enquiry into Shooting & Angling (1976–1979)*, Lord Medway, chairman (Horsham, West Sussex: RSPCA, 1981). See *Hookup*, Newsletter of the Council for the Prevention of Cruelty by Angling, June 1981. See also <http://www.fishpain.com/papers/medway_report.pdf> (accessed 4 October 2019); Richard D. Ryder, *Animal Revolution* (Oxford: Basil Blackwell, 1989), p. 197.

6. Brigid Brophy, 'A Felicitous Day for Fish', in *Hookup*, Newsletter of the Council for the Prevention of Cruelty by Angling, June 1981, pp. 9–12.

7. Ibid., p. 10.

8. Ibid., p. 10.

9. Ibid., p. 10.

10. Ibid., p. 11.

11. Ibid., p. 11.

12. Ibid., p. 11.

13. Ibid., p. 11.

14. Ibid., p. 11.

15. Ibid., p. 12.

16. Ibid., pp. 9–10.

17. Quoted in Jon Wynne-Tyson (ed.), *The Extended Circle* (Fontwell, Sussex: Centaur Press, 1985), pp. 28–30.

18. <https://en.wikipedia.org/wiki/The_Black_Fish> (accessed 17 June 2019).

19. <http://fishfeel.org> (accessed 17 June 2019).

20. Brophy, 'A Felicitous Day for Fish', p. 10.

# Chapter 15

# The Dissenting Feminist

## Carole Sweeney

Throughout the mid to late 1960s, women's groups began forming across Britain. Meetings chiefly took the form of small, informal gatherings in kitchens and church halls, but as the idea of 'women's liberation' as a collective politics gained momentum, increasingly larger venues were needed to accommodate rapidly growing numbers. On 27 February 1970 these groups congregated together for the first time at the inaugural National Women's Liberation Movement (WLM) conference at Ruskin College, Oxford. With upwards of 500 women attending, the conference marked a significant moment for British feminism in Britain, heralding a growing activism that consolidated around campaigns for free contraception, abortion rights, equal pay and access to education and equal employment opportunities.[1] A well-known, even notorious writer, regarded by detractors and devotees alike as the embodiment of the progressive spirit of the Swinging Sixties, Brigid Brophy was not among their number. Despite her almost indefatigable work on behalf of animal rights and the Public Lending Right (PLR), Brophy's social activism did not extend, as might have been expected, into any formal commitment to the burgeoning feminist movement.

While Brophy was not easily persuaded by the doctrine of the wider WLM, she did consider herself to be a 'natural' feminist insofar as she was convinced of the innate equality between women and men, particularly concerning questions regarding the sovereignty of biology in the production and regulation of the nuclear family. She was publicly outspoken on the restrictions of monogamous marriage, declaring that matrimony was only one of an 'infinitely flexible' number of ways in which human sexual and kinship relation might be arranged.[2] I suggest here, then, that although Brophy was broadly in agreement with some of feminism's aims, she was sceptical towards feminism as a homogeneous doctrine, especially when it involved questions of cultural and aesthetic authority; however, such scepticism did not hinder her from writing insightfully, if controversially, about what she called the 'sex war'. Not so much an anti-feminist as a non-conformist one, Brophy's innate intellectual scepticism and commitment to what she regarded as rigorous logical inquiry habitually won out over any unreserved commitment to ideology.

In distinctively contrarian style, Brophy seemed to suggest that she was and yet was *not* a feminist. On the one hand, she was not committed to any systematic ideological project of feminism, and in some of her non-fiction writing her ideas might, in fact, be regarded as conspicuously, even startlingly, anti-feminist. On the other hand, elsewhere in her work Brophy expresses a distinctly feminist awareness, one demonstrated rather circuitously in her fiction but far more explicitly in some of her journalism. Looking at both these dispositions in her writing, I suggest that Brophy was less an anti-feminist than a maverick or dissident feminist who, while agreeing with sexual equality, was nevertheless not easily corralled into the involuntary extension of ideology into artistic and intellectual domains. Thus, we get two sides of 'Brophyism'; someone who wrote that society ought to ask 'whether it is natural for women to be kept in the kitchen' and that the 'normal and natural thing for human beings to do is [. . .] to reform society and to circumvent or supplement nature',[3] but who also wrote that '[f]eminism may lack allure for individual bookbuyers, but the posse of jackboot feminists can no doubt be counted on to bully institutions'.[4]

Despite Brophy's ambivalence towards feminism, especially in the 1970s and 1980s when its effects began to take a more discernible hold on culture and politics, it has become commonplace to read that Brophy was not only an animal rights activist, which she most emphatically was, and a campaigner for PLR, which she also was, but also a devoted feminist. Accompanying the Faber and Faber reissues of *Flesh* and *The Finishing Touch*, Richard T. Kelly describes her thus: 'In hindsight Brophy still cuts a singular figure as novelist, critic, feminist, pacifist, campaigner for the rights of authors and of animals and connoisseur of art and opera.'[5] Similarly, in the anthology *Modern British Women Writers*, she is described as a 'vociferous' supporter of feminism.[6] Elsewhere, Cambridge University Press's Orlando project observes that Brophy became 'notorious for her politics' in the 1960s, no mean feat in an era renowned for its cultural iconoclasm.[7] Brophy is described here as 'a vegetarian, a sexual liberationist, an animal rights activist, a feminist, a writers' rights activist, a pro-pornography activist'.[8] In an obituary in *The Independent* we learn of Brophy's deep 'commitment to causes that were worth fighting for', namely, 'feminism, pacifism, vegetarianism, Public Lending Rights, pornography, and the Vietnam War'; such causes, it is claimed 'rarely found a better spokesperson'.[9]

More recently, in what might be legitimately called a critical revival of Brophy's work, critics seemed to have retained this unchallenged assertion of her feminism. Jennifer Hodgson writes that among her 'myriad political commitments', Brophy was 'pro-human, animal, women's, gay and writer's rights'.[10] In *British Fiction of the Sixties: The Making of the Swinging Decade*, Sebastian Groes describes Brophy as a writer of 'minor literature' whose sexual politics represented a radical challenge to the 'masculine, humanist "majoritarian" tradition'.[11] A more tempered approach, however, is to be found in *The Encyclopedia of British Writers*, where we read that although 'Brophy wrote much that could be described as feminist', she 'never fell into any particular school of feminism'.[12] A renowned literary agent and close friend of Brophy, Giles Gordon (1940–2003), also contributed to this myth of Brophy's feminism but added an important caveat concerning her intellectual practice. While Brophy was, he says, a 'feminist; lover of men and women', she was 'ever the Aristotelian logician', and 'above all' she was an 'intellectual'.[13]

In distinct contrast to the above, Janet Todd notes that Brophy was, in fact, well known for her 'acerbic anti-feminism'.[14] In addition to Brophy's reference to 'jackbooted' feminists, Todd may be referring here to her critical demolition of *The Handbook of Non-Sexist Writing*, edited by Casey Miller and Kate Swift, in the *London Review of Books* in February 1982, reprinted as 'He/She/Hesh' in her last collection of non-fiction, *Baroque-'n'-Roll* (1987).[15] At the time Brophy wrote this review, feminist debates around the politics of language and representation were at their height, but this did not deter Brophy's scathing assessment. She disagrees with the feminist assertion at the centre of Miller and Swift's project – one now widely acknowledged – that is, that language has a direct effect on the ways in which we understand the world, and that it has a disproportionately powerful effect on the interpellation of the subjectivity of girls and women: 'Every language reflects the prejudices of the society in which it evolved.'[16] In this they are engaging with a contemporary feminist debate on the politics of language and representation that had begun with *The Second Sex* (1949), and continued with Betty Friedan's *The Feminine Mystique* (1963) and Dale Spender's *Man Made Language* (1980).[17] Spender's work was significant to the feminist debate regarding the ways in which language conducted ideology even when it seemed apparently neutral and denotative. Language was, argued Spender, 'a symbolic system constructed by men', and as such worked to maintain the subordinate status of women.[18]

The argument that everyday language enforces gender stereotypes was fundamental to the feminist claim that the personal is the political and, further, that the idea of what constitutes the political needed to be extended to encompass, as Kate Millett said in *Sexual Politics* in 1968, 'powerstructured relationships, the entire arrangement whereby one group of people is governed by another, one group is dominant and the other subordinate'.[19] In the context of this feminist work on the relationship between language and wider networks of oppression and inequality, it may seem contrary, to say the least, to read Brophy's *précis* of Miller and Swift's arguments:

> They remark that people often resist linguistic change but that changes do happen [. . .] These truisms are not enough to establish whether language can and, if so, should be nagged into changing in a programmatic direction [. . .] Even if you accept the assertion, it does not follow that by changing the language you can change the prejudices.[20]

A rather curious assertion, surely, by a writer whose gender-fluid protagonist Pat/Patricia O'Rooley in *In Transit* experiments with gender roles and examines the function of language to influence subjectivity.[21] In her review, however, Brophy unreservedly rejects the notion that language use has any real or lasting effect on the ways in which we perceive and represent gender:

> There is not the smallest reason to expect that Britons and residents of the USA will turn non-sexist overnight should Ms Miller and Ms Swift succeed in persuading the 'writers, editors and speakers' for whom their book is confusedly designed (why do speakers need a handbook of writing?) to scrap the 'he' in sentences like 'Anyone who converses with *émigré* Hungarians will soon find that he is bewildered by their pronouns' and replace it by 'he or she' or one of the other formulae that carry Miller-Swift approval.[22]

Miller and Swift argue that the 'vocabulary and grammar' of English asserts a world view that upholds a 'white, Anglo-Saxon, patriarchal society' given to 'excluding or belittling women', a claim, Brophy assures us, that must be taken 'with a pinch of salt'.[23] But in the very next sentence, she adopts a quite contrary position on linguistic sexism insofar as it pertains to her own experience. She does not at all mind 'craftsmanship' or 'chairman' as do the authors, but was once 'driven to public expostulation' when introduced as an 'authoress'.[24] In a concluding remark that is commensurate with the idea that feminism equals humourlessness, comparable to Sara Ahmed's concept of the 'feminist killjoy', Brophy reproaches the two authors for trying to 'denature' anything in the English language that 'might pass for a joke'.[25] A lifelong advocate of the dextrous pun, Brophy seems here to privilege the right of language to be humorous over any political responsibility, observing that the authors' solutions have the 'depressive effect of sucking the imaginative content out of material that can ill spare it'.[26]

Brophy's ambivalence towards the cultural politics of feminism is also evident in her review of Germaine Greer's *The Obstacle Race: The Fortunes of Women Painters and their Work* (1979). An overtly feminist recuperation of female painters in history, Greer's project salvages women painters who have been lost or overlooked in cultural history for reasons of lack of education and training and patriarchal prohibitions on women's labour outside of the domestic sphere. Describing her feminist methodology as a 'singularly squinting vision of our culture', Brophy complains that Greer's one 'shut eye excludes painters who were men, except where they impinge, as teachers, lovers or parents, on painters who were women'.[27] By pointing up the fact that men are missing from Greer's account, Brophy misses or, more likely, refuses the point that Greer's is a study of the various obstacles that *women* painters have encountered, and that these hindrances have historically included men, or rather patriarchy, not unlike the ways in which Virginia Woolf talks of the absence of women writers from the canon in *A Room of One's Own* (1929).[28] To complain that Woolf neglects to talk at length about William rather than Judith Shakespeare parallels Brophy's quibbling critique of Greer's scholarly undertaking.

Brophy demonstrably repudiates the fundamental feminist premise of Greer's work:

> If you had nothing to go on except her chronicle of women painters whose works were later attributed to better-known (masc.) names, sometimes to the point where the woman's whole oeuvre was lost, and no guide but her saga of daughters apprenticed to painter fathers by whom they were exploited as assistants and prevented

from developing artistic individualities of their own, then you might
swallow her claim that women painters suffered these fates because
a society run by men dominated them either directly or by training
them to think self-sacrifice a virtue.[29]

Greer's project, she insists, should be a wider act of recovery: 'If lost
oeuvres are worth rescuing, whether for justice's sake or aesthetics',
surely the duty to rescue them must fall on men and women by the
tens of thousand – and apply, of course, to the oeuvres of men as
well as women painters?'[30] Greer's point is, of course, not about lost
oeuvres *tout court* but points to a more comprehensive silencing and
loss of women's talents. Undaunted by the justifiably piqued readers'
letters regarding her review, Brophy responds by describing Greer's
book as 'equivalent to a book that documents all the women in
London who have had 'flu this autumn and then argues that 'flu is
an illness to which only women are susceptible'.[31] While the Aristo-
telian/Brophyan logic here is technically unimpeachable, it mulishly
misses the point about women's intellectual exclusion and subsequent invisibility as cultural producers.

In much the same vein, Brophy ventures into feminist-baiting
territory in an excoriating review of Colin MacCabe's now seminal
critical study, *James Joyce and the Revolution of the Word* (1979).[32]
Referring to his chapter on *Finnegans Wake* and what he calls the
'impact' of 'feminine narcissism' on 'phallocentric male discourse',
Brophy is withering:

> 'Can we categorise the text as a feminine discourse despite its articu-
> lation by a male pen or must that pen be accounted for?' Alas, Mr
> MacCabe doesn't go on to say what a female pen is like and whether
> it manages to assume a non-phallic shape. Perhaps he has misunder-
> stood 'la plume de ma tante'.[33]

In a letter to the *London Review of Books*, a reader responds, perhaps unsurprisingly, by pointing up the narrowness of Brophy's
definition of what constitutes the political: 'Ms Brophy's concept of
politics and the political role of writers revolves around them being
or doing no more than nagging to death Arts Ministers over PLR.'[34]

Brophy's unconstructive attitudes towards feminism in these critical
reviews of scholarly work are, however, frequently undermined, even
contradicted, elsewhere in her non-fiction writing. Witness a newspaper article for the *Saturday Evening Post* from 1963, entitled quite

simply 'Women', in which Brophy discusses the coercive power of the 'confidence trick' of biology that has been perpetrated on women:

> Women are free. At least, they look free. They even feel free. But in reality women in the western, industrialised world today are like the animals in a modern zoo. There are no bars. It appears that cages have been abolished. Yet in practice woman are still kept in their place just as firmly as the animals are kept in their enclosures. The barriers which keep them in now are invisible.[35]

Presciently locating a problematic that would form the foundation of much feminist theory in the next three decades, Brophy identifies, in her habitually succinct, provocative style, the ways in which nature, imperceptibly doing the work of culture, is used to keep women in invisibly barred cages, and, further, persuades them to acquiesce to the idea that they 'are by nature unfit for life outside the cage', thus maintaining, she says, one of the 'most insidious and ingenious confidence tricks ever perpetrated'.[36] The invisibility of the bars is distressing for a woman, she argues, as she is 'unable to perceive what is holding her back' and thus may accuse her 'whole sex' of 'craven timidity' as they seem have not 'jumped at the appearance of an offer of freedom'.[37] Women are comforted by reassurances that there is 'nothing shameful in not wanting a career, to be intellectually unadventurous is no sin, that taking care of the home and family may be personally "fulfilling" and socially valuable'; all of which would be perfectly valid, Brophy says, were it not for the fact that such arguments are 'addressed exclusively to women' and as such constitute 'anti-woman prejudice revamped'.[38]

Three years later, in 'Women: The Longest Revolution', Juliet Mitchell writes:

> Like woman herself, the family appears as a natural object, but it is actually a cultural creation. There is nothing inevitable about the form or role of the family any more than there is about the character or role of women. It is the function of ideology to present these given social types as aspects of Nature itself. Both can be exalted paradoxically, as ideals.[39]

Here, Mitchell and Brophy share a strikingly similar position on the ways in which biology has been used as the tool of patriarchal ideology, whereby women have been kept subordinate to men. Brophy concludes in 'Women' that society has contrived to terrorise women with the idea 'that certain attitudes and behaviours' are 'unwomanly' and 'unnatural'.[40] Again, her words resonate with those of prominent feminist thinkers, such as Kate Millett, who argued at length in *Sexual Politics* that

> patriarchy's greatest psychological weapon is simply its universality and longevity [. . .] While the same might be said of class, patriarchy has a still more tenacious or powerful hold through its successful habit of passing itself off as nature [. . .] When a system of power is thoroughly in command, it has scarcely need to speak itself aloud.[41]

And yet, despite this clear affinity with feminist principles, Brophy continued to prevaricate over any identification of herself as a feminist: 'What is a feminist?', she asks Leslie Dock. 'I mean there are many women writers that I admire and I certainly admire any woman who gets on with the job as though she were not a woman. I may have a very slight dislike for, and contempt for, women who make a profession out of being women.'[42] In this interview she compares feminists to Frenchmen who live in England and 'make a profession out of being Frenchmen'.[43] Whether Brophy is being intentionally antagonistic here in her suggestion that nationality is comparable to biological sex is not entirely clear, but the possibility that this is indeed the case is reinforced by her next statement in which she complains about feminists who insist on talking about women: 'Perhaps I have the feeling that, if one has no subject matter except feminism, then one is trading on nothing, as though one were to make a career out of proclaiming that grass is green.'[44]

Brophy wrote these words in the mid-1980s, a time when second-wave feminism was at its peak, reaping the intellectual and academic benefits of the previous decade of feminist theory and increased political activism. Considering this context then, for Brophy to talk of feminists as 'trading on nothing' might sound, to our contemporary sensibilities, markedly un-feminist; the position becomes more complicated still when she later states in the same interview that she does, in fact, consider herself to be a feminist, but one of her own definition. She believed, she said, in women leading by example rather than by any kind of consciousness raising or, worse, didacticism: 'I basically think that the point of Women's Lib is better made by having more Jane Austens and George Eliots, and high-powered civil servants and so on, than by constantly reiterating a truism when you have nothing else to say.'[45] Political movements such as 'Women's Lib' and 'Gay Lib' are most successful when they facilitate rather than dictate: change happens, she argues, 'by people simply living their lives and being talented'.[46] While this is accurate to a certain extent, it might be argued that 'people simply living their lives' does not necessarily produce legislative change, nor does it account for those women who do not happen to be 'natural' feminists like Eliot and Austen, and whose quotidian lives are blighted by economic discrimination, sexual violence and political invisibility.[47]

Brophy's dissident attitudes towards feminism might valuably be compared to Angela Carter's maverick libertarian take on sexual politics as demonstrated in *The Sadeian Woman and the Ideology of Pornography* (1978).[48] Both Brophy and Carter reacted against the Anglo-American feminist aversion to both psychoanalysis and pornography; the latter an important register of broader ideas of social liberty for Brophy. In response to the Longford Report on Britain's obscenity laws in 1972,[49] Brophy wrote a lengthy, intellectually compelling essay, 'The Longford Threat to Freedom', in which she replies to the committee's findings on the morally corrosive nature of pornography and the problem of addiction; for most people, she argued, 'pornography does them no large harm and no large good either, [they] move on to types of books or films that are less repetitive and predictable'.[50]

Carter viewed pornography as useful for women in so far as it allowed them to examine femininity as a set of mythologies equally reviled and revered, and to explore 'their own complicity with the fictional representations of themselves as mythic archetypes'.[51] Like Carter, Brophy was in 'the demythologizing business',[52] and her creative work articulates this: 'I feel that mythology is a denial of imagination which I think one has to counter.'[53] Her novels abound with strikingly independent and sexually unconventional women who refuse the sexual morality of their times, in particular the myth of the faithful wife and mother. Actively desiring subjects, Brophy's women are educated, sardonic and witty in their approach to sex, adultery and marriage – Susan in *The King of a Rainy Country* (1956); Nancy's female Pygmalion shaping of her husband in *Flesh*; the queerly erotic repartee of middle-aged Anna and young Ruth Blumenbaum in *The Snow Ball*; and the gender-indeterminate Evelyn Hilary (Pat) O'Rooley of *In Transit* (1969).[54] The latter work gleefully unpicks the founding myths of masculinity and femininity, poking fun at them both, and suggests a keen feminist perspective at work, one preoccupied with the limitations of gender and how these are enacted within language.

There were other reasons, perhaps, for Brophy's resistance to feminism. An avid devotee of Freudian thought, she wrote a substantial (five hundred densely footnoted pages) study, *Black Ship to Hell* (1962),[55] pointing up Freud's enduring relevance for the mid-century. But Freudian psychoanalysis, in particular the concept of penis envy and Oedipal dynamics, was denounced by Anglo-American feminism in the 1970s, which regarded it as fundamentally misogynist, beginning from the premise that women represented a psychic and physiological lack.[56] While French feminism was inclined towards a sustained engagement with psychoanalysis, Brophy seems not to have registered its effects in her writing, perhaps evidence of its narrow dissemination, remaining, as Jane Gallop noted, as a network of 'stubborn polemic' that circulated between 'various exclusive little circles'.[57]

Despite Brophy's own vacillating attitudes to feminism, she was nonetheless regarded by the more reactionary sections of the British media as explicitly influenced by 'women's lib'. Consider, for example, the ways in which *The Spectator*'s Simon Raven discusses her work. Conceding that on the whole Brophy's journalism in *Don't Never Forget* is 'scrupulously and seriously written round a point which is of serious import', Raven nonetheless goes on to mockingly identify what he sees as two distinct aspects to her writing; one is the rational masculine voice of Brophy – 'tough, incisive and direct' – which dissects its themes with a masterful aplomb; the other, the feminine, 'faddy and finniking prig' that is Brigid.[58] Unsurprisingly, the latter, what he terms the 'asinine interruptions of the deplorable Brigid', is the ethical advocate, he mockingly suggests, of animals', women's and writers' rights:

> It's not as if the fussing ends with animals: Brigid is also much exercised about women's rights, about the selfishness of people who actually want to keep some of their own property, about the crudity of Kingsley Amis's jokes, and about the waste of domestic abilities in the male – why don't more men stay at home and help with the nappies, Brigid wants to know, instead of rushing off to make money?[59]

Raven refers here to Brophy's 1965 article in the *Sunday Times*, 'The Immorality of Marriage', in which she elaborated on ideas of sexual equality from the 'Women' article, arguing that 'traditionally marriage has been regarded as the price men had to pay for sexual intercourse, and sexual intercourse was the price women had to pay for marriage'.[60] Brophy upbraids reactionaries who only cite 'nature as an ideal' when they are arguing against sexual equality: 'They are to be heard nowadays complaining that our psychological and technological advances have produced an "unnatural" state where it is increasingly hard to distinguish men from women.'[61] Curious, then, to read these words from a writer who objected to the idea of non-sexist language and to a project that might recover lost female artists.

Brophy's relationship to the burgeoning second wave of feminism in the 1960s was marked by an intellectual scepticism that regarded the world, as A. S. Byatt noted, 'quite in her original way'.[62] Regarding feminism less as a political undertaking than a sensibility, one that was, for her, wholly instinctive and therefore in no need of doctrinal proclamation, Brophy did not take at all kindly to what she regarded as ideological imperatives and was resistant towards feminism as an organised political movement. At its most intense, this resistance was a defiance of creed and dogma, even when these involved ideas that she herself put into practice in much of her writing. Such recalcitrant attitudes to the feminist movement of her day do not, however, invalidate Brophy as a notable, even important, figure in the history of British women's writing. As Patricia Waugh has noted, not all women writers who experiment with concepts of gender and sexuality in their work have aligned themselves explicitly with contemporary feminism; indeed, some of them 'have refused to confine themselves to a narrow feminist agenda and have often taken up positions that are antithetical to those of the dominant feminist politics of their time'.[63] Brophy might best be viewed, then, not as an adversary of feminism but as a dissident or non-conformist feminist thinker whose provocative challenges to its doctrines have not always been endorsed by history, yet exist as a valuable reminder of the diverse intellectual landscape of her times.

## Notes

1. On this early history of feminism, see Sheila Rowbotham, *Promise of a Dream: Remembering the Sixties* (London: Allen Lane, 2000); Juliet Mitchell, 'Women: The Longest Revolution', *New Left Review*, 40 (November–December 1966), pp. 11–37; Beatrice Campbell and Anna Coote, *Sweet Freedom: The Struggle for Women's Liberation* (Oxford: Blackwell, 1982); Sara Maitland (ed.), *Very Heaven: Looking Back at the 1960s* (London: Virago, 1988).

2.  Brigid Brophy, 'A Woman's Place', *Enquiry*, BBC 2, 27 January 1965, <http://www.bbc.co.uk/archive/marriage/10510.shtml> (accessed 20 April 2019).

3.  Brigid Brophy, 'Women', in *Don't Never Forget: Collected Views and Reviews* (New York: Holt, Rinehart and Winston, 1966), pp. 38–45 (p. 43).

4.  Janet Todd, *Feminist Literary History* (Cambridge: Polity, 1988), p. 12.

5.  Richard T. Kelly, 'The Exquisite Sentences of "Flesh" and "The Finishing Touch" by Brigid Brophy', 29 August 2013, <https://www.faber.co.uk/blog/out-now-the-exquisite-sentences-of-flesh-and-the-finishing-touch-by-brigid-brophy/> (accessed 20 April 2019).

6.  Vicki J. Janik, Del Ivan Janik and Emmanuel S. Nelson (eds), *Modern British Women Writers: An A–Z Guide* (London: Greenwood Press, 2002), p. 47.

7.  Orlando: Women's Writing in the British Isles from the Beginnings to the Present, <http://orlando.cambridge.org> (accessed 18 January 2018).

8.  Orlando [online].

9.  Christopher Fowler, 'Invisible Ink No. 245: Brigid Brophy', *The Independent on Sunday*, 12 October 2014, <https://www.independent.co.uk/arts-entertainment/books/reviews/invisible-ink-no-245-brigid-brophy> (accessed 20 April 2019).

10. Jennifer Hodgson, 'Afterword', in Brigid Brophy, *The King of a Rainy Country* (London: Coelacanth Press, 2012), pp. 269–73 (p. 269).

11. Sebastian Groes, *British Fiction of the Sixties: The Making of the Swinging Decade* (London: Bloomsbury, 2016), p. 68.

12. Karen Karbiener and George Stade (eds), *Encyclopedia of British Writers: 1800 to the Present*, 2 vols (London: Eurospan, 2nd edn, 2005–09), vol. I, p. 78.

13. Giles Gordon. 'Obituary: Brigid Brophy', *The Independent*, 8 August 1995, <http://www.independent.co.uk/news/people/obituary-brigid-brophy-1595286.html> (accessed 20 April 2019).

14. Todd, *Feminist Literary History*, p. 11.

15. Brigid Brophy, 'He/She/Hesh', in *Baroque-'n'-Roll and Other Essays* (London: Hamish Hamilton, 1987), pp. 61–7. Originally published as 'Small Boys and Girls', review of Casey Miller and Kate Swift (eds), *The Handbook of Non-Sexist Writing for Writers, Editors and Speakers*, *London Review of Books*, 4.2, 4 February 1982, p. 17.

16. Casey Miller and Kate Swift (eds), *The Handbook of Non-Sexist Writing for Writers, Editors and Speakers* (London: Women's Press, 1989), p. 4.

17. Simone de Beauvoir, *The Second Sex*, trans. H. M. Parshley (London: Cape, 1953); Betty Friedan, *The Feminine Mystique* (New York: W. W. Norton, 1963); Dale Spender, *Man Made Language* (London: Routledge and Kegan Paul, 1980).

18. Spender, *Man Made Language*, p. 224.

19. Kate Millett, *Sexual Politics* (New York: Columbia University Press, 1970), p. 23.
20. Brophy, 'He/She/Hesh', p. 65.
21. Brigid Brophy, *In Transit: An Heroi-Cyclic Novel* (London: Macdonald, 1969).
22. Brophy, 'He/She/Hesh', pp. 61–7.
23. Miller and Swift, (eds), *The Handbook of Non-Sexist Writing*, p. 4; Brophy, 'He/She/Hesh', p. 63. Many of Swift and Miller's suggestions are now uncontroversial; for example, their suggestion that the term 'chairman' be replaced by 'chair' or that the pronoun 'he' should not stand for the universal subject have been widely adopted.
24. Brophy, 'He/She/Hesh', p. 63.
25. Ibid., p. 64. See also Sara Ahmed, *The Promise of Happiness* (Durham, NC: Duke University Press, 2010).
26. Brophy, 'He/She/Hesh', p. 62.
27. Brigid Brophy, 'The One-Eyed World of Germaine Greer', review of Germaine Greer, *The Obstacle Race: The Fortunes of Women Painters and their Work*, *London Review of Books*, 1.3, 22 November 1979, pp. 1–3, <https://www.lrb.co.uk/v01/n03/brigid-brophy/the-one-eyed-world-of-germaine-greer> (accessed 20 April 2019).
28. Virginia Woolf, *A Room of One's Own* (London: Penguin, 2004).
29. Brophy, 'The One-Eyed World of Germaine Greer', p. 3.
30. Ibid., p. 3.
31. Brigid Brophy, 'Letters: Women Painters', *London Review of Books*, 1.5, 20 December 1979, <https://www.lrb.co.uk/v01/n05/letters> (accessed 20 April 2019).
32. Brigid Brophy, 'James Joyce and the Reader's Understanding', review of Colin MacCabe, *James Joyce and the Revolution of the Word*, *London Review of Books*, 2.3, 21 February 1980, pp. 8–9, <http://www.lrb.co.uk/v02/n03/brigid-brophy/james-joyce-and-the-readers-understanding> (accessed 20 April 2019).
33. Brigid Brophy, 'Letters', *London Review of Books*, 2.7, 17 April 1980, <https://www.lrb.co.uk/v02/n03/brigid-brophy/james-joyce-and-the-readers-understanding> (accessed 20 April 2019).
34. J. D. MacShane, 'Letters', *London Review of Books*, 2.7, 17 April 1980, <https://www.lrb.co.uk/v02/n03/brigid-brophy/james-joyce-and-the-readers-understanding> (accessed 20 April 2019).
35. Brophy, 'Women', p. 38.
36. Ibid., p. 38.
37. Ibid., p. 39.
38. Ibid., pp. 39–40.
39. Mitchell, 'Women: The Longest Revolution', p. 11.
40. Brophy, 'Women', p. 43.
41. Millett, *Sexual Politics*, p. 58.

42. Brigid Brophy, 'An Interview with Brigid Brophy', interview by Leslie Dock, *Contemporary Literature*, 17.2 (1976), pp. 151–70 (p. 164).
43. Ibid., p. 164.
44. Ibid., p. 164.
45. Ibid., p. 164.
46. Ibid., p. 165.
47. The Married Women's Property Act was only revised in 1964 to allow women to keep the money they earned as well as the right to inherit property. Prior to this, everything a woman owned or earned became her husband's property once she was married. This revision allowed married women to keep half of any savings from housekeeping money that they received from their husbands.
48. Angela Carter, *The Sadeian Woman and the Ideology of Pornography* (London: Virago, 1979).
49. Frank Pakenham, Earl of Longford, *Pornography: The Longford Report* (London: Coronet Press, 1972).
50. Brigid Brophy, 'The Longford Threat to Freedom', speech to the National Secular Society, 3 October 1972, Conway Hall, London.
51. Sally Keenan, 'Angela Carter's *The Sadeian Woman*: Feminism as Treason', in Joseph Bristow and Trey Lynn Broughton (eds), *The Infernal Desires of Angela Carter: Fiction, Femininity, Feminism* (London: Longman, 1997), pp. 132–48 (p. 138).
52. Angela Carter, 'Notes from the Frontline', in Michelene Wandor (ed.), *On Gender and Writing* (London: Pandora Press, 1983), pp. 66–77 (p. 71).
53. Brophy, 'An Interview with Brigid Brophy', p. 159.
54. Brigid Brophy, *The King of a Rainy Country* (London: Secker and Warburg, 1956); *Flesh* (London: Secker and Warburg, 1962); *The Snow Ball* (London: Secker and Warburg, 1964); *In Transit: An Heroi-Cyclic Novel* (London: Macdonald, 1969).
55. Brigid Brophy, *Black Ship to Hell* (London: Secker and Warburg, 1962).
56. See, for example, Friedan's 'The Sexual Solipsism of Sigmund Freud', in *The Feminine Mystique*; Millett's 'The Reaction in Ideology', in *Sexual Politics*; and Germaine Greer's 'The Psychological Sell', in *The Female Eunuch* (London: MacGibbon and Kee, 1970).
57. Jane Gallop, *Feminism and Psychoanalysis: The Daughter's Seduction* (London: Macmillan, 1982), p. xi.
58. Simon Raven, 'Brophy and Brigid', *Spectator*, 25 November 1966, p. 25.
59. Ibid.
60. Brigid Brophy, 'The Immorality of Marriage', in *Don't Never Forget: Collected Views and Reviews* (New York: Holt, Reinhart and Winston, 1966), pp. 22–8 (p. 22); originally published in *The Sunday Times Magazine*, 1965.

61. Ibid., p. 23.
62. A. S. Byatt, 'An Explosive Embrace', *Times Literary Supplement*, 13 January 1987, p. 269.
63. Patricia Waugh, 'The Woman Writer and the Continuities of Feminism', in James F. English (ed.), *A Concise Companion to Contemporary British Fiction* (Oxford: Blackwell, 2006), pp. 188–209 (pp. 192–3).

# Chapter 16

# A Certain Detachment?

## *Kate Levey*

[Y]esterday reached a new low, when I had to cancel going out in the evening as Mama declared, hysterically, that it was 'inconvenient': she hadn't finished her *Mozart* piece for *The Sunday Times*.[1]

Brigid Brophy, the person I knew as 'Mama', was a figure of some prominence in the middle portion of the twentieth century. And yet she remains, broadly speaking, obscure. After my mother's death in 1995, my father, Michael Levey, would on occasion lament the lack of renewed interest in Brigid's novels. Now in my daughterly turn, although I am not in the literary sphere, I note that Brophy has eluded the type of revival enjoyed by some of her contemporaries. This, the first volume to focus solely on her, therefore forms a most welcome marker. Tribute is due the small bunch of acolytes who have sought by their sterling proselytising to rectify Brophy-blindness. And while I hope exploration of Brophy's reputational neglect does not develop into a branch of study in its own right, I am glad that the causes of her exclusion, thus far, from the strong beam of the spotlight of retrospection have also been examined.

A multitude of factors may militate against Brophy: antipathy towards intelligent, strong-minded women might be still be potent; certainly, sophistication is viewed with suspicion. It's true that her oeuvre is of a formidable scope. And there is the sheer laziness factor: Brophy is not an easy read, nor can she be safely be summed up in a pithy phrase – she demands more concentration than that. In a culture so fixated on artists who ended their lives by suicide, I have wondered whether that last chunk of Brigid Brophy's life, the twelve or so sequestered years when she was crippled by multiple sclerosis, when she faded from view, has skewed later perceptions of her adversely. I don't really discern it, nor can I imagine why it should be the case. But I note that, whether people have been delicate or dilatory, they have not asked me about my mother's last years. I aim to offer here a snapshot of that period about which outsiders know so little.

I have reread the letters my father sent when I lived some distance from London, when his distress was not so much about her physical deterioration as about the alteration in Brigid's personality as it fell under the yoke of incurable illness. Michael Levey, who as director of London's National Gallery could easily have done so, never considered publicising his wife's true state, let alone the burden it placed upon him. (He was disgusted by John Bayley's public portrayal of Iris Murdoch's pitiable condition while she was alive but uncomprehending.) Only a small number of people knew the extent of his profound despair: he genuinely feared that his life would be extinguished by the tyranny exerted on him by Brigid's ill-health.

Since this is not a case study, and the straight biographical facts of their lives can be readily found, I want to stress that an appreciation of my parents' private relationship and prior mode of life is key to what befell them. Through their thirty years of marriage Brigid and Michael were remarkably self-contained; only intimate friends were truly welcome visitors. (In the 1960s Brigid wrote to one couple, with her tongue only just in her cheek, 'We are much more misanthropic at heart than either you or the Carlyles.')[2] My parents had been a stable, loving duo, amorously unconventional within their partnership but bound together by affection, candour and deep mutual understanding. However, after the incursion into their lives of Brigid's multiple sclerosis, they slipped, over the course of a decade or so, into destructive and intractable opposition.

In February 1988 Michael succinctly expressed the bleak fact that he and Brigid were trapped 'in a strange and horrible battle of wills, of sickness *against* health, which may be typical of chronic invalids, and which, alas, disturbs the balance of love'.[3] In our tight, triangular family, the shock of Brigid's diagnosis had been ameliorated by relief that the prognosis was not worse, together with the consolation that her hospitalisation for tests, through which she had been stoical, had ceased.

Once home, and with characteristic clarity, Brigid told me that she would not fight her illness, having 'fought all my life for one thing or another'. At the time I saw in this statement nothing more than a thoroughly understandable affirmation of her right. Having enjoyed exceptionally robust health, Brigid had become an invalid. We thought that with adjustments, her tragic condition could be accommodated. It did not immediately strike us, I think, that my mother's new status conferred upon my father a new and equally unsought role: that of her carer.

I had long been regarded as the 'practical one' in our trio – it was my parents' euphemism for *non-intellectual*; now it was revealed to me how little equipped was each of my intelligent, erudite parents, with their refined sensibilities, to cope with the practicalities of my mother's debilitation. Neither Michael nor Brigid had experience of long-term illness, nor were they temperamentally suited to discussing or dealing with the stark physical aspects of disability.

When I inherited his private journal, I found that my father had recorded that

> [t]he closer you are emotionally to someone the more you are dis-qualified to be the carer 'in attendance' night and day, at the bedside and in the bathroom. You, in turn, grow disabled under the combination of empathy with the multiplicity of daily demands and pressures [. . .] Two people have now become the sufferers.[4]

Brigid had announced her multiple sclerosis by publishing a courageous article, which was sympathetically received.[5] Though unable to walk unaided, she could (until much later on) still manage to work; this was the only consolation in a terrible scenario, as friends and colleagues freely and sensibly commented. Largely confining herself to bed, she continued to write, and was notably brave in seeking to master, first, a walking frame, and then, when it became necessary, an electric wheelchair. Her bodily strength diminished gradually so that after a time she relied heavily on my father to supply in person all her fundamental physical needs; this dependence seemed to bring out in her a kind of angry inarticulacy which was quite new to me, and which I witnessed, to my great upset, on more than a few occasions. Brigid's huge power of will could not prevail on her actual condition, but seemed at times to be bent towards the destruction of harmonious relations. The flat in Old Brompton Road, previously permeated by an aura of shared creative tranquillity, was now a brutal arena, pierced by alarming groans or shrieks which my mother might issue at any point, as she tried to get to the bathroom or reach for an item that had dropped. I had never imagined I would see the simmering hysteria that now gripped her. I had no doubt of the veracity of my father's account of the night he cancelled his evening arrangements to allow Brigid to work, although it was not devoid of grim humour: 'yesterday reached a new low, when I had to cancel going out in the evening as Mama declared, hysterically, that it was "inconvenient": she hadn't finished her *Mozart* piece for *The Sunday Times*'.

What had developed by degrees over a period of years was quite terrifying – in fact, hellish: Brigid's almost pathological gentleness was ripped to shreds as illness incrementally stripped her of all that vital softness of consideration, of appreciation, of empathy, leaving in the end only a reduced, schematic persona, hostile towards my father particularly, and dissociated even from me. My father described Brigid as suffering from 'emotional Thatcherism'.[6] My self-deprecating Mama, ever ready to be teased, socially vulnerable, nimble-witted and charmingly sardonic, gradually collapsed into a bloody-minded version of her true self, as my father confirmed to me:

> What you wrote of Mama's state of mind is sadly apropos. There is just no continuity most of the time, and I think the detachment from any awareness (which is what it is, basically) of other people and their feelings, reactions, etc, is genuine, though also highly convenient.[7]

In their heyday, Michael used jokily to observe that Brigid's idea of heaven was to live full-time in a hotel, with unseen, preferably robotic minions attending to meals, laundry and so on. This mild jibe now took on a sinister cast, for Michael was subjugated to performing those functions without respite. For some years he continued work full-time at the National Gallery, notwithstanding broken nights and curtailed freedom. Brigid seemed deluded in thinking the care she required negligible. His resentment gathered, and a palpable sense of mutual mutilation set in: 'Is it too ridiculous to detect a profound psychological fury, leading to a refusal (unconsciously) to walk anymore? Every aspect of the illness, as now manifested, is connected with <u>refusal</u>, to have a bath, to eat this or that, and so on.'[8] Not many weeks later he wrote the following:

> I found myself reading old reviews of several of Mama's books [. . .] the reviewers were often obtuse, and even grudging in attitude [. . .] They felt, though not well able to express it, a certain detachment, 'coldness', indifference, which made them uneasy; even those who admired, I now suspect, detected a strange vein of detachment. It was most peculiar reading their comments and thinking of the personality today.[9]

This penetrating remark illustrates a facet of Brigid that I recognise: I never found her distant, but she was an introvert who functioned on an abstract level. I adored her for it, while knowing how marmoreal she could appear to those outside her circle of loved or venerated people. (My father noticed from their earliest days how impassive she was when awful, large-scale human events were in the news.) Yet until she was ill this detachment never intruded into our family unit. Brigid was unconditionally loving and loyal – sometimes in the face of behaviour she might otherwise call 'unforgiveable'. She was never inhumane, but in her mildly autistic way she could wound by insisting on her creed of unblenching honesty. Those who loved her found pure beauty in her truthfulness; however, not everyone could take it. I always assumed Brigid's detachment, that steely inner core, was self-protective: the necessary concomitant to that most essential Brophy trait of unremitting, critical lucidity. It was the price, so to speak, of her genius.

I found comforting, not horrifying, this passage from her will, drawn up in 1986:

> I am a declared and indeed proselytising atheist. I do not wish to impose on anyone who loves or esteems me so much as a veneer of social hypocrisy [. . .] I should like my dead body to be cremated and its ashes disposed of by someone who did not know me, without permanent memorial of when and where that was done [. . .] I request both [my husband and daughter] not to be present at my cremation. They have done everything for me while I can and do benefit.[10]

*

Might Brophy be too cool to handle? Her style grates against the current neo-fey climate where there is no death but people 'pass away', in a euphemism so ubiquitous that it is scarcely remarked. Brophy is an astringent in an era awash with feelings. In this affective world in which an individual's emotions are *the* validating force (and not only in the arts), Brophy's cerebral mode might well jar. Her strong-mindedness, assisted by her trenchant wit, is perceived as aggressive. Who wants transcendent observations when mid-century period detail can be relished? Something more sinister than mere nostalgia lurks under the fig-leaf of so much that is in vogue: we are in the stranglehold of a huge retreat from progress.

Brophy stands in the centre of an almost perfect ring of her fellow authors who have been exhumed and fashionably repackaged for posthumous exposure, merited or not. If the ebb and flow of changing tastes makes her fiction untrendy, Brigid Brophy's legacy as a campaigner is demonstrable: she instigated the modern animal rights movement, she wrote persuasively against nonsensical attitudes to sexuality, and most concrete of all, as co-architect of the scheme, she bequeathed to writers the Public Lending Right.

Against that backdrop of enduring relevance, I suggest that Brophy's is not a case of plain omission: a quarter of a century after her death she is still being treated badly by an establishment she antagonised, and which consequently still views her as too far removed from the compass of acceptability. Brophy has not, as it were, slipped down the back of the bookcase – she has not been overlooked or neglected – she has been, for the moment at least, *rejected*.

A poignant example of the continuing resistance to Brophy occurred when, in 2015, I applied for her achievements to be acknowledged by a 'blue plaque'. English Heritage wrote to say, after conceding her success with Public Lending Right, that the Panel did not feel Brophy's 'historical significance was on a par with that required by the scheme'.[11] (In English Heritage's system, superlative hypocrisy at least has not 'passed away': I noted the proportion of Panel members who were authors very probably eligible themselves to receive Public Lending Right.)

I imagine Brigid would eschew any such thing, but in honour of her subversive legacy I would like a tablet projected by laser onto 185 Old Brompton Road, where the stucco would exhibit it nicely. In deference to Brigid's classicism and correctness I had better include *mutatis mutandis*, and with a nod to her gender-playfulness I would quote her observation about her hero, G. B. Shaw: 'we have let him be posthumously assassinated by his own genius for personal publicity'.[12] Brigid Brophy well understood that anyone with a claim to a unique, wide-ranging and non-frivolous position in British culture is a dangerous dissident.

## Notes

1. Michael Levey to Kate Levey, 1 August 1990. KL private collection.
2. Exact date not known. KL private collection.
3. Michael Levey to Kate Levey, 9 February 1988. KL private collection.
4. Michael Levey, private journal, undated. KL private collection.
5. Brigid Brophy, 'A Case-Historical Fragment of Autobiography', in *Baroque-'n'-Roll and Other Essays* (London: Hamish Hamilton, 1987).

6.  Michael Levey to Kate Levey, 15 March 1988. KL private collection.
7.  Michael Levey to Kate Levey, 3 November 1989. KL private collection.
8.  Michael Levey to Kate Levey, 30 December 1989. KL private collection.
9.  Michael Levey to Kate Levey, 27 February 1990. KL private collection.
10. Brigid Brophy's will, 18 October 1986. KL private collection.
11. Letter to Kate Levey from English Heritage: Anna Eavis, Curatorial Director, Blue Plaques Secretary, 26 November 2015.
12. Brigid Brophy, *Black Ship to Hell* (London: Secker and Warburg, 1962), p. 132.

# Notes on Contributors

**Phoebe Blatton** is a writer from London. She regularly writes for international magazines, including *Art Monthly*, *Art Review* and *Frieze*. In 2012 she republished Brigid Brophy's 1956 novel *The King of a Rainy Country* (Coelacanth Press) with an afterword by Jennifer Hodgson and cover art by Bonnie Camplin.

**Michael Bronski** is an independent scholar, journalist and writer who has been active in gay liberation as a political organiser, writer, publisher and theorist since 1969. He is the author of numerous books including *A Queer History of the United States for Young People* (2019). He is Professor of the Practice in Activism and Media in the Studies of Women, Gender and Sexuality at Harvard University.

**Richard Canning** is the author or editor of ten books, including brief biographies of E. M. Forster and Oscar Wilde, and two volumes of interviews with gay novelists for Columbia University Press, *Gay Fiction Speaks* and *Hear Us Out*. His critical biography of Ronald Firbank is forthcoming from Harvard University Press. He is currently Visiting Professor at the University of Buckingham.

**John Dixon** is a writer and former librarian. He edited *Fiction in Libraries* for the Library Association. He has produced one collection of poetry and one of short stories. He has edited several anthologies. His novel *Push Harder, Mummy, I Want to Come Out* is due for publication shortly.

**Gary L. Francione** is Board of Governors Distinguished Professor of Law at Rutgers University, Visiting Professor of Philosophy at the University of Lincoln, and Honorary Professor of Philosophy, University of East Anglia. His primary area of research is animal rights from both philosophical and legal perspectives. He cannot understand why everyone who thinks that animals matter morally or is terrified of climate change is not vegan.

**Jonathan Gibbs** is a novelist, critic and academic. He is Programme Director on the undergraduate and postgraduate Creative Writing courses at St Mary's University, Twickenham. His published novels are *Randall* (Galley Beggar, 2014) and *The Large Door* (Boiler House, 2019), the latter explicitly inspired by Brophy's *The Snow Ball*.

**Rodney Hill** has had a career in local government working in leisure and cultural services at a senior level. He left local government in 2011 and is in advanced clinical training to be an accredited Gestalt psychotherapist. He works in private practice and volunteers for MIND, the mental health charity.

**Gerri Kimber**, Visiting Professor at the University of Northampton, is the deviser and Series Editor of the four-volume Edinburgh Edition of the *Collected Works of Katherine Mansfield* (2012–16). She is the author of *Katherine Mansfield: The Early Years* (2016), *Katherine Mansfield and the Art of the Short Story* (2015) and *Katherine Mansfield: The View from France* (2008), in addition to twenty further edited collections of essays.

**Miles Leeson** is the Director of the Iris Murdoch Research Centre at the University of Chichester. He is the author of *Iris Murdoch: Philosophical Novelist* (Continuum, 2010), the editor of *Incest in Contemporary Literature* (Manchester University Press, 2018) and *Iris Murdoch: A Centenary Celebration* (Sabrestorm, 2019), and is Lead Editor of the *Iris Murdoch Review*.

**Kate Levey**, M.Ed., is a retired primary school teacher who until recently has been reluctant to write about her prominent parents, Brigid Brophy and Michael Levey. She lives in Lincolnshire with her husband and a cat.

**Jill Longmate** studied modern history at Oxford, then worked in sixth form college education. She now writes full time and is researching the life and work of Maureen Duffy. Her most recent publication is 'Brigid Brophy's Role in the Struggle for Public Lending Right 1972–1979', *Contemporary Women's Writing*, 12.2 (2018), pp. 186–206.

**Peter Parker** has written two books about the First World War, *The Old Lie* (1987) and *The Last Veteran* (2009), biographies of J. R. Ackerley (1989) and Christopher Isherwood (2004), *Housman Country* (2016) and *A Little Book of Latin for Gardeners* (2018). He is an advisory editor of the *Oxford Dictionary of National Biography*.

**Allan Pero** is Associate Professor of English and Director of the Centre for the Study of Theory and Criticism at the University of Western Ontario. He is co-editor of *The Many Facades of Edith Sitwell* (University Press of Florida, 2017), and is currently working on a book-length project on camp.

**Kim Stallwood** is an animal rights advocate and theorist, who is an author, independent scholar, consultant and speaker. He has more than forty years of personal commitment as a vegan and professional experience in leadership positions with some of the world's foremost animal advocacy organisations. His website is www.kimstallwood.com.

**Carole Sweeney** is Reader in Modern Literature in the Department of English and Comparative Literature, Goldsmiths, University of London. She has published journal articles in *Textual Practice*, *Women: A Cultural Review* and *Contemporary Women's Writing* on Brigid Brophy, Christine Brooke-Rose and Anna Kavan. Her books include *From Fetish to Subject: 'Race', Empire and Modernism 1919–1935* (2004), *Michel Houellebecq and the Literature of Despair* (2013) and *Gender and Experiment in British Women's Writing 1945–1970* (2020).

# Index